The Informational Logic of Human Rights

The Informational Logic of Human Rights

Network Imaginaries in the Cybernetic Age

Josh Bowsher

EDINBURGH
University Press

Edinburgh University Press is one of the leading university presses in the UK. We publish academic books and journals in our selected subject areas across the humanities and social sciences, combining cutting-edge scholarship with high editorial and production values to produce academic works of lasting importance. For more information visit our website: edinburghuniversitypress.com

Edinburgh University Press Ltd
The Tun – Holyrood Road
12(2f) Jackson's Entry
Edinburgh EH8 8PJ

Typeset in 11/13 Adobe Sabon by
IDSUK (DataConnection) Ltd, and
printed and bound in Great Britain.

A CIP record for this book is available from the British Library

ISBN 978 1 3995 0990 9 (hardback)
ISBN 978 1 3995 0992 3 (webready PDF)
ISBN 978 1 3995 0993 0 (epub)

The research and writing of this book was completed thanks to an Early Career Fellowship from the Leverhulme Trust

Contents

List of Illustrations

Series Editors' Preface

Technological transformation has profound and frequently unforeseen influences on art, design and media. At times technology emancipates art and enriches the quality of design. Occasionally it causes acute individual and collective problems of mediated perception. Time after time technological change accomplishes both simultaneously. This new book series explores and reflects philosophically on what new and emerging *technicities* do to our everyday lives and increasingly immaterial technocultural conditions. Moving beyond traditional conceptions of the philosophy of technology and of techne, the series presents new philosophical thinking on how technology constantly alters the essential conditions of beauty, invention and communication. From novel understandings of the world of technicity to new interpretations of aesthetic value, graphics and information, Technicities focuses on the relationships between critical theory and representation, the arts, broadcasting, print, technological genealogies/histories, material culture and digital technologies and our philosophical views of the world of art, design and media.

The series foregrounds contemporary work in art, design and media whilst remaining inclusive, in terms of both philosophical perspectives on technology and interdisciplinary contributions. For a philosophy of technicities is crucial to extant debates over the artistic, inventive and informational aspects of technology. The books in the Technicities series concentrate on present-day and evolving technological advances but visual, design-led and mass mediated questions are emphasised to further our knowledge of their often-combined means of digital transformation.

The editors of Technicities welcome proposals for monographs and well-considered edited collections that establish new paths of investigation.

Ryan Bishop and Jussi Parikka

Acknowledgements

The coronavirus pandemic has made this a strange time to write this book. Though the combination of social distancing and lockdowns has often made the crisis feel lonely and isolating, the pandemic has, in several different ways, also emphasised the deep interconnectedness of the social world and its reliance on social infrastructures: those assemblages of (often devalued) people and practices that subtend everyday living. Covid-19 has not only made visible the fragile sinews of invisible or underappreciated workers in logistics and health care, as well as those involved in providing food and other essentials, it has also required new infrastructures of mutual aid and support that have ensured the material and social sustenance of many, including me. Though it is undoubtedly insufficient recompense for all that has sustained me over the last few years, I nevertheless want to express my gratitude for these infrastructures and solidarity with the people who work – and struggle – within them.

Given that this book is partly concerned with infrastructure and the kinds of practices it stabilises and makes possible, the pandemic has also reinforced some of the principal lessons I have learned while reading, researching and writing the text. Perhaps most of all, that the act of writing a book is not only the work of me, the author whose name appears in print, but is also the result of an assemblage of social and academic infrastructures, interlocutors, fellow thinkers, friends and family whose ideas, support and invisible labour have congealed in the making of this text.

I am grateful to the Leverhulme Trust for funding the project that led to this book. I also want to offer my thanks to Brunel University and, in particular, Brunel Law School for hosting my research fellowship. Within the Law School, I am grateful to Arad Reisberg, Bimbo Olowofoyeku and Alexandra Xanthaki for their support at various points in the project. The friendship and intellectual engagement of Kathrin Hamenstaedt, Serena Natile, Isobel Renzuilli, Paula Westenberger and Ermioni Xanthopoulou has also been an important source of inspiration and support both personally and professionally.

It would be remiss not to acknowledge the often-invisible work within the institutional infrastructures that enabled me to conduct my archival research. The International Institute of Social History (IISH) in Amsterdam, where I explored the archives of Amnesty International's International Secretariat, provided the resources for some of the key arguments of this book. I particularly want to thank Mandy Kamper, Monique van der Pal, Rose Spijkerman, Tobias van der Knap and Nina van den Berg who helped organise a constant stream of materials during the several weeks I spent there. I am also grateful to Fiona Bolt and Gillian Boll at Amnesty International for being generous and accommodating in providing additional archival resources. Some of the archival material was also gathered from HURIDOCS and I would like to thank both Friedhelm Wienberg and Bert Verstappen for providing me with various documents, newsletters and manuals. Bethany Antos and Kanisha Greaves at the Rockefeller Archive Center, and Tara Craig and Vianca Vamos at Columbia's Rare Book and Manuscript Library organised reproductions of archival documents when the pandemic made it impossible to travel there in person – my thanks to you. My thanks are also due to the many staff at the British Library who provided me with a vast number of academic texts that were necessary to complete the project.

The editorial team at Edinburgh University Press, including Ryan Bishop, Jussi Parikka and Carol Macdonald, were both enthusiastic and supportive of this project and I thank them for their important comments and editing of the book. I also owe John Armitage a thank you for encouraging me to persist with this project as I envisaged it, advice that ultimately led me to Edinburgh University Press. Additional thanks must go to Nour Awada for kindly providing me with the cover image for the book. The image is taken from Awada's performance of her work, *Le Bruit et Le Signal*, co-produced by L'Association Françoise pour l'œuvre contemporaine and Ekimetrics, at the Fondation Lafayette Anticipations in Paris in November 2019.

Though this project began in September 2018, it is also indebted to the people and places who have shaped my thinking long before then. I would especially like to thank those at the Centre for Critical Theory at the University of Nottingham where I did my Master's degree and PhD for helping to shape not only my academic interests but also my socio-political orientation to the world, which is inextricable from this book. I am deeply indebted to my PhD supervisors Colin Wright and Tracey Potts, as well as Neal Curtis, Andy Goffey, James Mansell and Jen Birks for shaping much of that critical orientation by sharing their time, thinking and creativity with me. I am eternally grateful to Alex Baker, Tom Harding, Stefanie Petschick, Kathryn Telling, Teo Todorova and Joe Willis who shared different stages of my journey through the Centre and have been good friends, comrades and sources of support. I also would like to thank Cosmin Cercel for his engagement with, and enthusiasm for, my intellectual projects over the years. You have all shaped my thinking for the better.

I am not sure I would have ever made it this far in the academic world without the considerable emotional, intellectual and material support of both Eva Giraud and Greg Hollin – I owe you both so much. I am also thankful to Eva for reading several chapters of this book and for offering important critical feedback which has improved many of the book's arguments (though any and all errors remain my own). Other readers of this book include Ben Bowsher, David Eckersley, Theo Reeves-Evison and David Young, whose generous feedback has been invaluable in improving the manuscript. But more than that, each of them has been an important friend and confidant. The sharpness and creativity of their own thinking has helped me develop this project and, as such, is invisibly inscribed across the pages of this book. I am grateful that each of them is in my life.

I am enormously lucky that the family I was born into remains part of the family I choose. Thanks to my parents, Andii and Tracy, my siblings, Ben and Bekih, as well as their partners, Ami and Michael, and children, Tilly, William and Oli. Collectively, they have been a constant source of support, encouragement and friendship. Finally, I owe an unpayable debt of gratitude to my partner Georgie who has been there to talk through my ideas, my anxieties and my doubts and who has been unwavering in her support for me. For believing that I could write a book during the times I thought I could not: thank you.

Introduction: Beyond the Neoliberal Critique?

> The process of receiving and of using information is the process of adjusting to the contingencies of our environment [. . .] The needs and the complexity of modern life make greater demands on this process of information than ever before.
>
> – Norbert Wiener, *The Human Use of Human Beings*

On 9 June 1977, the *New York Times* published an editorial by Democratic Party senator and one-time presidential hopeful, George McGovern, titled simply 'The Information Age'.[1] Noting that there was a 'growing agreement' that we were now in a new era of information, McGovern's article considered the international implications of this new epoch, a task, he argued, few had come to terms with even in the United States. In many ways, the article was a public declaration of the anxieties that were occupying McGovern in the Senate. The day before its publication McGovern had begun chairing a series of hearings on the implications of 'International Communications and Information', in areas such as media, banking, business and labour.[2] Cognisant of the scope and scale of this new information order, McGovern was especially concerned that information could be 'a new economic weapon in the arsenals of both developing and developed nations'.[3] Both opportunity and threat, then, information seemed to engender a new socio-economic terrain but with consequences for international relations.

The article reflected mounting social concerns regarding 'information' in a decade marked by the rapid emergence of new technologies. In 1971, Intel released the first commercially available silicone 'microprocessor', which, in integrating a computer's central processing unit into a single chip, paved the way for digital computers to enter the mass market. By 1982, the personal computer had become *Time Magazine*'s 'person of the year', the first time the award was given to a non-human entity.[4] As the 'information revolution' took root in the 1970s, a popular literature on its consequences multiplied

1

not only through newspaper and magazine editorials but also through the futurological writings of Daniel Bell, Yoneji Masuda and Alvin Toffler as well as reports sponsored by various Western governments such as Marc Porat's *The Information Economy* and Simon Nora and Alain Minc's *The Computerization of Society*.[5] Like McGovern, these assorted 'prophets' of the information age were largely united in their predictions that the new computational machines would completely transform the social world, a prognosis that now – in the era of big data and the planetary infrastructure(s) of the internet – seems at least superficially accurate.

McGovern's editorial was a relatively minor contribution to the body of work assembled by the aforementioned 'prophets'. But crucially, it did catch the attention of Amnesty International (AI), just months before the organisation's acceptance of the Nobel Peace Prize would mark the definitive arrival of the contemporary human rights movement as a major force on the global stage. In July 1977, a clipping of the article was distributed for discussion at a meeting of Amnesty's executive body, the International Executive Committee (IEC). Its circulation was accompanied by a short memo written by Margo Picken, then newly appointed as AI's representative to the United Nations in New York, indicating its potential significance to the organisation: '[the article] addresses itself to a most important issue which will, and should be, of increasing concern'.[6]

Though the conversations that McGovern's editorial may have provoked within the meeting cannot be recovered, its distribution was indicative of a growing sense within Amnesty not only that theirs was primarily an informational project but perhaps also that in some way the informational qualities of their work tied them to the then burgeoning information age. For instance, also under discussion at the July IEC meeting was an internal report penned by senior Amnesty officials at a meeting in Cambridge the previous month, which outlined plans for the organisation's future direction. The report of the 'Cambridge Crash Committee' not only gave information a central place in the putative future it imagined for Amnesty but, in doing so, also seemed to carry the residue of the era's broader informational landscape. The report both argued that information was 'crucial for AI work at all levels', and, though only in passing, drew on the language of new information technologies to describe 'AI' itself as a 'data bank'.[7] One year later, and still undergoing rapid expansion, Amnesty International would publicly declare information to be 'the core work of our movement'.[8]

Leaving aside for now what it might mean to be a 'data bank' or to make information 'core work', this historical fragment neatly introduces the socio-historical knot that sits at the centre of this book. On the one hand, the vignette it provides serves as a reminder that information has always been a fundamental component of the now hegemonic human rights project since it began its meteoric rise to 'worldwide normativeness', with the growth, as has often been noted, of organisations like Amnesty International in the 1970s.[9] But more importantly, this fragment draws critical attention to the fact that this embrace of information cannot easily be disentangled from a broader set of shifts contemporaneous to it, often gathered both under and alongside terms like the 'information economy', the 'information society' or, as McGovern put it, the 'information age'. The wager of this book is that a critical reading of the human rights movement today relies on drawing out and analysing these connections between the informational modality of contemporary human rights practices and the broader socio-technical milieu within which they have emerged. In other words, grasping the politics of human rights requires a thorough reading of their contemporary and now hegemonic iteration as an informational project that is both of and for the information age.

Of course, there is nothing particularly ground-breaking about the suggestion that the fight for human rights has become an informational project. Over the last two decades, scholars have persistently argued that novel informational practices are a distinguishing feature not just of Amnesty International but of the wider human rights movement that emerged alongside it.[10] The contemporary movement, it is argued, congealed around a distinctive mode of activism: the creation of 'thick rivers of fact', a truly monumental flow of reports about human rights violations, designed to influence elites and shame states into changing their behaviour.[11] And today, as developments instigated by the information revolution have bled seamlessly into the digital age, information remains, as Joel Pruce and Alexandra Cosima Budabin put it, the 'currency' of human rights.[12] The movement's abiding relationship with information can be traced in both contemporary scholarly concerns with the informational modalities of rights activism today as well as cautious optimism that developments in big data, data analytics and machine learning can be harnessed for human rights.[13]

Across these discussions, however, the significance of the information age as the socio-historical context which has shaped this project is often either missed entirely or simply gestured to as a largely uninterrogated backdrop, a purely technical mise-en-scène, for the development of human rights practices. Appreciation of human rights as an informational project thus often leans, even if implicitly, on a kind of technological determinism that, historically at least, has afflicted much writing on the information age, particularly the popular literature that circles around Bell, Toffler and Masuda.[14] In this model, social change is simply determined by the ostensibly neutral and asocial development of new technologies such that the microelectronics revolution is figured as a technical change that (re)constitutes different social milieus and practices (human rights being among them). As a result, critical questions of how this 'technological' revolution might have been shaped by, or intertwined with, a set of related socio-political shifts and, moreover, the possibility that this might have inflected the cultural politics of human rights itself are, rather unhelpfully, cast to one side.

In contrast, this book argues that understanding the contemporary human rights movement requires facing up to these questions; and, moreover, that a set of important political stakes are raised in answering them. With this in mind, the book insists precisely on a socio-cultural and, ultimately, political interpretation of the so-called information revolution which sees the far-reaching technical changes it has instigated – from computational machines, factory automation and the internet to more recent developments in data analytics and artificial intelligence – as intimately connected to a broader set of socio-economic reconfigurations that also began to emerge in the 1970s. Conceptualising the information age in this way, I suggest, does not just pose critical questions about human rights as an informational project that was articulated within the closing decades of the twentieth century. Perhaps more crucially, it raises pressing concerns about human rights in the present as the embrace of new digital technologies imposes an increasing datafication of its already informational sensibility. At a time when advanced statistical modelling, data visualisation, satellite imaging and curating large corpuses of social media content have become increasingly vital to the practice of human rights, the book is thus designed to develop an analysis that critically connects the embrace of these technologies to the social, historical and political context(s) in which they have been articulated. Indeed, through an investigation that tracks the emergence of human rights practices in relation to this knot of socio-economic and technological shifts from the latter decades of the twentieth century to the present, the book aims to shed important light not only on the limitations of human rights today but also on how we might overcome them.

But how should this broader socio-political context, which has so far only been obliquely referred to, be conceptualised? Some readers will already recognise both the periodisation I have been emphasising as well as the call for a more critical and politically oriented reading of human rights as central to an already existing and highly influential body of scholarship, the 'neoliberal critique' of human rights.[15] Noting that the 1970s was a crucial decade not only for human rights but also for neoliberal globalisation, proponents of the neoliberal critique have argued that their parallel rise to becoming the twin doxas of contemporary global governance is not a coincidence but points to the fact that they are deeply intertwined projects. Consequently, by the beginning of the twenty-first century the politically and culturally hegemonic articulation of human rights, it is argued, had become a 'neoliberal version of human rights'.[16]

Certainly, these arguments provide an important, if not vital, point of departure for this book. The deep and widespread socio-economic transformations that, within those debates, are conceptualised as neoliberalism provide a framework that is valuable for reading together the emergence of the information age and the informatisation of human rights. Nevertheless, my own intervention contends that if 'information' is a crucial term for understanding both human rights and the broader social context in which their contemporary iteration emerged, then the conceptual parameters offered by the neoliberal lens also need to be complicated. The book proposes that the neoliberal counterrevolution taking shape since the 1970s be reconceived as both structuring and structured by the articulation of a new informatic mode of capitalism for which the 'information age' provides only one depoliticising euphemism. The conceptual shifts inaugurated by this change of emphasis, I suggest, call for a rethinking of neoliberalism as but one, admittedly crucial, part of a socio-economic conjuncture that is better understood as cybernetic capitalism. However, to understand what might be gained from turning to this new theoretical landscape, particularly how it can be utilised in an analysis of contemporary human rights, it pays to first take a closer look at the neoliberal critique to which it responds.

Neoliberal Human Rights?

Ongoing questions regarding the political valences of human rights have given birth to a lively set of critical debates over the last few decades. A more optimistic strand of thought has insisted on the potential of human rights as a resource for an emancipatory politics. In the political philosophy of Jacques Rancière, for example, rights are understood to harbour an egalitarian logic which has been, and could still be, utilised by exploited groups to stake a claim for equal inclusion within the socio-economic orders that have marginalised them.[17] And, though in different ways, the emancipatory potential of human rights as an engine for substantive equality and even radical democracy is increasingly being taken up in contemporary debates through the valuable work of scholars such as Paul O'Connell, Kathryn McNeilly and Boaventura de Sousa Santos.[18]

But even within these optimistic readings there is an acknowledgement that the dominant version of human rights, the one which has been integrated into global governance since the end of the Cold War and thus circulates not only through the UN but also through the World Bank and the IMF, has fallen short of this radical promise.[19] There is a growing consensus that the relatively harmonious cohabitation of human rights and the muscular global capitalism of the twenty-first century has coincided with an attenuation of their emancipatory potential in the contemporary world. By the late 1990s, Upendra Baxi already saw that human rights had predominantly become 'market-friendly' rights remade 'in the image of markets that produce, exchange, and service production/reproduction of symbolic goods'.[20] Only a few years later, Wendy Brown voiced concerns that as human rights were increasingly being articulated as 'negative' and individualised freedoms, they might now have become a barrier to a more emancipatory politics, rendering 'other political possibilities more faint'.[21]

This critical suspicion of human rights has been reinforced over the last decade by the arrival of the historicising framework offered by the neoliberal critique of rights. For its proponents, the limits of human rights today can be contextualised, as I have hinted earlier, with reference to developments taking shape within the crisis era of the 1970s. Undoubtedly, the crises of that decade were truly legion: the terminal crisis of Fordist capitalism, for which the oil shocks and 'stagflation' are only two of the most obvious signifiers, as worker militancy brought capital to a standstill in the Global North and the radicalism of non-aligned postcolonial states put pressure on the global economy;[22] the subsequent crisis of social democracy and the reformist left that the 'Keynesian' compromises of post-war capitalism had made possible;[23] and the arrival of Soviet dissidents such as Aleksandr Solzhenitsyn in Europe and North America, which accelerated a growing disenchantment with the revolutionary left.[24] These overlapping crises, the neoliberal critique demonstrates, provided the protean conditions not only for neoliberal orthodoxies to begin their deleterious sweep across the globe but also for human rights to emerge as their correlate.

As neoliberalism 'resolved' the crisis of capitalism through privatisations, trade liberalisations, and processes of financialisation that disassembled the twin threats posed by the industrial working class and the Third World, human rights, it is argued, also began its meteoric rise as a new mode of activism that seemed to neatly align with the emerging 'realism' of the post-Fordist economy.[25] With an inherent minimalism that sought simply to protect individuals from state violence, the human rights movement represented a very different kind of activist practice to the worker and anticolonial struggles that, over the course of the 1970s and 80s, it also seemed to supersede. For unlike the latter, the new human rights activists transgressed neither the individualising logic underpinning neoliberalism's competitive market order nor its aversion to economic redistribution and equality.

This line of critique is taken up by Susan Marks, who follows Naomi Klein in arguing that the human rights movement, through organisations like AI and Human Rights Watch, emerged as a kind of political narrowing whose effect was to reduce activism to the denunciation of violent abuses of civil and political rights at the expense of a socio-economic analysis of injustice.[26] If the politics of both class struggle and decolonisation were premised on collective questions of socio-economic justice and the distribution of resources, then human rights, by comparison, offered a distinctly anti-political model of activism whose individualism enabled neoliberalism by shifting attentions away from precisely these redistributive questions. Other scholars such as Jessica Whyte argue that the movement was more proactively integrated within the neoliberal counterrevolution; its individualistic model of rights mobilised to delegitimise not only state communism but also the increasingly powerful postcolonial states as well as to develop a moral defence of the market as a guarantor of rights.[27]

Joseph Slaughter follows this trajectory when he brings together an impressive cast of Southern scholars including Antony Anghie, Walden Bello and Paul Zeleza to provide a timely reminder that this human rights project was constructed in opposition to other struggles also operating under the banner of human rights.[28] Though often forgotten or marginalised, the decolonial struggles of the mid-twentieth century were also human rights movements that saw the right to self-determination enshrined in the UN International Covenant on Economic, Social and Cultural Rights (ICESCR) as central to their redistributive projects of 'worldmaking'.[29] For Slaughter, it is particularly noteworthy that across the 1970s, the same decade in which the now hegemonic human rights movement was articulated, this more radical version of human rights was at the heart of postcolonial demands for a New International Economic Order (NIEO) designed to reorganise the global economy on more equitable terms. From the perspective of the Third World, as Slaughter argues, the rise of civil and political rights activism appears less as an 'emergence' and more as a neoliberal 'retrenchment and repossession' – a 'roll back' – of human rights that was mobilised against these more expansive struggles for self-determination and socio-economic redistribution.[30]

Slaughter argues that as the new 'common sense' of neoliberal structural adjustment both dissipated the NIEO and remade much of the globe, human rights served as a 'sentimental adjustment program' that also confronted more redistributive articulations of rights by reframing their cause as both violent and authoritarian. At the same time, by 'reducing rights to the suffering of individuals and promoting personal sympathy', this new model of rights succeeded in realigning the global ethical imaginary on neoliberal terms, that is, as a personal relation with victims rather than the 'collective problem of politics and the redistribution of resources'.[31] Slaughter's crucial intervention thus not only demonstrates that radical articulations of rights have been part of a very recent history but also traces the ways in which this emancipatory potential has been drastically attenuated by a neoliberalisation of rights over the last forty years.

Or Cybernetic Human Rights?

It is worth reiterating that the periodising gesture at the heart of the neoliberal critique is particularly valuable because it decisively situates a political account of the rather attenuated human rights project which enjoys hegemonic status today in its socio-historical context. The starting point for my own intervention is the contention that, on its own, the analytic aperture provided by 'neoliberalism' simply provides too narrow a lens through which to conceptualise the capitalist offensive that took shape in the 1970s, and, consequently, for developing a critique of human rights. To be clear, I am not suggesting that privatisations, trade liberalisations, deleterious welfare reforms or any other processes usually described as 'neoliberal' be ignored, nor do I seek to downplay their salience as a set of principles and processes that have now become an economic and socio-cultural common sense. Indeed, my own work has previously been nourished by the neoliberal critique of human rights and the insights it can provide.[32] But it is my contention that developing an analysis of human rights which can account for their peculiar relationship to information requires a different approach. I suggest that what have hitherto been understood as the 'neoliberal' configurations of capital need to be reconceived through the critical perspectives made available by the term cybernetic capitalism.

To take up this vantage point, the book is oriented by a different set of theoretical tools than those usually reserved for discussions of human rights. Principally, I draw together critical and cultural theories of information society and digital culture, particularly those that are in dialogue with autonomist Marxist tradition, which have often found themselves more at home in critical media studies and digital sociology. These tools are important because they take as axiomatic a socially embedded view of technology. They share a conviction, as Raymond Williams might put it, that new technologies are always articulated within specific socio-economic formations and are thus inscribed by, whilst also reinscribing, the relations of power in which they are embedded.[33] Accordingly, the theoretical perspectives I assemble do not treat the information revolution as a purely technical and strangely autonomous development independent of the broader political and socio-economic shifts outlined above. Instead, they demonstrate that the informational technologies, practices and logics that swept through the 1970s were central to the strategies by which capital reconfigured itself and disassembled the threats of both labour and decolonisation. From this perspective, the socio-economic conjuncture articulated through the closing decades of the twentieth century becomes legible not so much as neoliberalism but as an increasingly informatised mode of capitalism.

As I argue in Chapter 1, where I develop the overarching framework of the book, the term cybernetic capitalism is used to describe this conjuncture because it brings together and clarifies what might otherwise seem to be disparate informational strategies. Taken principally from the work of Nick Dyer-Witheford and the anarchist collective Tiqqun, cybernetic capitalism foregrounds that the reconfigurations of capital in the 1970s are in fact heavily indebted to the development of cybernetics by military-sponsored researchers in the 1940s, largely in the United States.[34] Most obviously, the discoveries of cybernetics directly underpinned the invention of new information technologies and the computational machines that defined the 'information revolution'. By drawing together a range of theoretical and historical resources, I demonstrate that these technologies were mobilised by capital to extricate itself from the Fordist crisis, by both routing around and decomposing the industrial working class that capitalism had previously relied upon.[35] The effect of this process has been the gradual integration of information technologies into the technical-economic substrates of capital as an increasingly planetary infrastructure for global capitalism.

But the crucial insight I take from the theoretical accounts of Seb Franklin, Philip Mirowski and others is that the influence of cybernetics goes well beyond the creation of computational machines.[36] Drawing on their work, I argue that the cybernetic conviction that principles of information control could be used for modelling human behaviour and complex social systems has led to the permeation of its logics into all kinds of theories and practices of social and economic management that are central to the functioning of late capitalism. In particular, the cybernetic sciences have had a profound influence upon both neoliberal intellectuals and neoclassical economists, shaping a conceptualisation of markets as communication machines or information processors which remains central to both academic and popular discourses of contemporary economics. Hence, neoliberalism has, in some ways, always been a cybernetic project with a distinctly informational conception of the social world and, moreover, the market as the best way to organise it. In this respect, cybernetic capitalism provides a framework that helpfully bridges the social and economic processes that are associated with neoliberalism and the rise of computational machines as two loosely intertwined legacies of cybernetics, which nevertheless appear to have (re)converged as a multi-layered and interlocking social and economic formation that now governs the current epoch.

The critical lens afforded by this approach shifts my own analytic framework onto a rather different terrain than the neoliberal critique of human rights, which tends to centralise the individualising processes of neoliberalism as the fulcrum for its analysis.[37] What cybernetic capitalism draws attention to instead is the emergence of information as an important socio-cultural concept, largely as a consequence of the rise of informational commodities and 'immaterial' work across the emerging post-industrial societies of the Global North.[38] However, what is at stake in contemporary capitalism is not simply the diffusion of cybernetic information either as concept or as commodified object which circulates ubiquitously through society. Rather, as scholars such as Tiziana Terranova have argued, cybernetic capitalism has resulted in the 'informatisation' of culture so that cultural, social and economic processes are progressively modelled as information systems.[39] The bind of configuring social processes as systems is the inherent limits that lie in their vision of the social. For information systems are largely premised on the communication of unambiguous codes and signals between a sender and a receiver, which requires both stability and predictability from the system.

The result, I suggest, is that cybernetic capitalism unfolds a socio-cultural logic that operates through the reification of standardised, quantifiable, or apparently objective facts, which can move smoothly – and predictably – through social, cultural and economic systems as 'information'. Often it is only that which can pass as simply 'given', an auto-effectively produced object that seems to emerge from an unmediated real, which is endowed with the quality of being informational. Critical and socially marginalised knowledges, on the other hand, are excluded as illegible and politically dangerous 'noise'. Information thus gives shape to socio-cultural practices as systems that are designed to bracket out communicational forms and contents that put these systems into question and thus limit the possibilities of their transformation. It is precisely this informational logic of contemporary capitalism, I contend, that sketches out the contours for a critique of human rights which grasps the crucial role that the movement's embrace of information has played in the attenuation of their radical potential.

The Informational Logic of Human Rights

The central argument of this book is that as the contemporary human rights movement emerged, rather self-consciously, within the information age it embraced the dominant informatic modalities of cybernetic capitalism sketched above. In doing so, the contemporary human rights movement has developed its own informational logic, configuring much of its work as the production and subsequent shuttling of information through a system. Key aspects of this information system are easily traced, even if only crudely, in something as straightforward as the description, noted at the start of this chapter, of human rights work as 'combining thick rivers of fact to influence elites'.[40] In this admittedly cursory schema, human rights facts circulate or, as the metaphor of rivers suggests, 'flow' as information between a sender (a human rights organisation) and a receiver ('elites' – government officials, media professionals, and so on). The aim, from the perspective of the sender, is to produce and disseminate information that is both systemically stable, in that it can be recognised or 'read' by the receiver, and predictable in its effects, likely influencing a change in elite behaviour.

For many, the model crudely sketched above is used to describe, and even to celebrate, the very basic structure of human rights as a unique form of 'information politics'.[41] In contrast, the book argues that this model touches upon key aspects of the informational logic embraced by the human rights movement which has in fact provided the strategy by which human rights have been depoliticised. The book contends that as the contemporary human rights movement emerged in the 1970s, it developed informational practices that emphasised operational functionality and, accordingly, interventions that led to predictable informational effects. These dual requirements have meant that a hostility to politics, particularly political knowledge claims grounded in conceptions of social exploitation and the political economy of violence, has become deeply embedded within the informational logic of human rights. From the perspective of human rights as information system such political claims are so replete with contestation, they threaten to destabilise the transparency of information and the predictability of its operative effects. Consequently, operational information has come to mean the utilisation of radically positivistic and empiricist epistemologies to constitute and compile facts that seem so self-evident they appear to simply 'speak for themselves'. This illusion of auto-effectivity, I suggest, has become a means of securing the 'objectivity' of human rights information and thus its systemic recognition and efficacy against the potentially deleterious interference of politics.

Reproducing the broader logic of cybernetic capitalism, then, human rights information has become a matter of reifying empirical facts, apparently objective snapshots of the real, as 'signal' that must be separated and distanced from the threatening 'noise' of politics. Consequently, the embrace and development of an informational logic has led to the paradoxical creation of a depoliticising information 'politics' formatted according to the limited imaginary of capitalism's informational modalities. For it renders the knowledge claims and practices that put the deleterious structures and effects of contemporary capitalism into question as so much noise. The possibility of radical transformation through the language of human rights is thus foreclosed by the informational logic that dominates its practice. This poses very thorny problems if one considers, as Kiran Kaur Grewal has recently noted, that 'human rights have become the hegemonic language for social and political struggle'.[42] At a time when contemporary capitalism has greatly exacerbated inequality and, moreover, threatens the future survival of the planet, it does not bode well that the language of rights, in its hegemonic figurations at least, has been rendered an ineffective tool of resistance, a point I return to at the end of this Introduction.

Both the theoretical and historical contours of this informational logic are traced in Chapter 1. Where the first half of the chapter sets out an account of cybernetic capitalism as the crucial context in which the now hegemonic human rights project was articulated, the second half traces the emergence of the informational logic of human rights in the work of the largely Western human rights organisations that rose to prominence in the 1970s. To do so, the book draws on extensive archival work that brings together a 'grey' literature of publications, reports, memos and other documents generated by organisations such as Amnesty International, Human Rights Watch and HURIDOCS (Human Rights Information and Documentation Systems), an NGO network specialising in human rights information systems, across the crucial decades of the 1970s–80s. This archival work is supplemented with a range of secondary literature designed to develop an introductory sketch of the informational logic I am interested in, identifying its key components as they are embedded in discourses that are mobilised within and around the human rights practices that emerged in the latter part of the twentieth century.

But if Chapter 1 only outlines the crucial aspects of the informatisation of human rights, it also poses a number of questions. How might we follow the ways in which the informational logic works in practice? How can we understand the informational logic of human rights not simply as a historical problem emerging in the 1970s but also as a critical issue that animates human rights today? And moreover, insofar as this informational logic continues to attenuate the radical, emancipatory potential of human rights, what prospect is there for overcoming these difficulties in the present conjuncture? These questions articulate a set of crucial points that occupy the rest of the book. What remains of this introductory chapter addresses how I respond to these questions, whilst also outlining the book's general trajectory.

Informational Logic: From the Microelectronics Revolution to the Digital Age

A conviction that leads my investigation is that comprehending the stakes of the informational logic of human rights requires going beyond the surface of informational discourses and paying closer attention to the various informational technics that underpin human rights work. Information, after all, is bound up in systems, and a precondition of its production is the infrastructural configurations through which it is made and travels. If, as research across many fields now demonstrates, socio-technical devices constitute rather than simply reflect the objects, discourses and social worlds they support, then investigating the technical tools that are used in making, storing and transmitting information offers critical insights into how this informational logic works in practice.[43] Consequently, much of the book focuses on specific technologies by which human rights information is produced. It explores the processes and techniques human rights organisations and practitioners have used to construct information and develops a critical account of the socio-political effects of these technical devices.

To develop this analysis, I draw from yet more tools that are largely unfamiliar in critical human rights scholarship by bringing together theoretical insights from science and technology studies (STS), software studies and digital sociology. Like the Marxian approach that inspires the overarching framework of the book, the theoretical perspectives I assemble emphasise the reciprocity between society and technology and thus the ways technologies shape, and are shaped, by the social relations in which they are situated. But what these approaches add to my analysis is a much sharper and more granular set of tools with which to investigate the now ubiquitous technologies of the information age. They share a capacity to locate and unravel the potentially profound social and cultural assumptions and effects that are rendered operational in something as seemingly banal as, for example, the model underpinning a database. Accordingly, the theoretical perspectives I deploy are well equipped to avoid the fairly common temptation to see technical devices simply 'as a question of realised instrumentality [. . .] a tool, something that you do something with'.[44] Instead, it becomes possible to trace the inner workings of human rights technologies, drawing out the socio-political implications embedded within them in order to demonstrate how they are imbricated in a much broader social reality.

I use this theoretical assemblage to trace the informational logic of human rights as it is deployed in three key sets of socio-technical devices or practices, which serve as case studies for the book. For reasons that will become clear, I insist that each of these practices corresponds to a key moment in the development of the contemporary human rights movement which has been articulated since the late 1970s. Each represents, in other words, a distinctive informational paradigm or strategy which, in its own way, has contributed to the formation of a depoliticised vision of rights that seems to fit comfortably within the cybernetic imaginaries of late capitalism. Tracking these different paradigms has relied on a wide range of materials. Each case brings together a grey literature of software, manuals, newsletters and conference proceedings with secondary literature(s) and, occasionally, ethnographic insights glimpsed during time spent with various human rights organisation that make or rely on information technologies in order to develop a close reading of these practices. To understand what is at stake in each of these examples, and particularly why they represent distinct informational strategies, what follows provides a cursory outline of each of the cases I have chosen.

In Chapter 2, I focus on HURIDOCS in the 1980s–90s, an NGO network concerned with developing information tools for human rights organisations, and their creation of a standardised data model, the Events Standard Formats, for recording information about (largely civil and political) violations, which remains a standard for the field and continues to be widely used today. Developed alongside and thus reflecting the interests of many international NGOs, UN agencies and other international bodies, the Events Model emerged from concerns about the clarity and effectiveness of human rights information, particularly in the Global South. As a result, efforts to standardise the recording of violations as 'events' came to be justified using the utopian language of the information age and the possibilities of mobilising a standardised – if depoliticising – approach to human rights.

After outlining the history and key stakes involved in the creation of the Events Standard Formats, the chapter focuses on a critical analysis of the data model itself. Noting the gap between the complexity of the social world and any attempt to model it as data, the analysis explores how the events approach constructs human rights information through a process of 'cutting' it away from, and thus excluding, issues of structural violence, social exploitation and the political economy of violence. This process of 'cutting', I suggest, is an instantiation of cybernetic practices that, as Seb Franklin identifies, capture and construct social realities through exclusionary processes of discretisation, filtration and optimisation.[45] Its effect is to produce information about violations as a seemingly 'unmediated' snapshot of the real, precisely by cleaving the events from the 'noise' of politics.

Chapter 3 follows parallel, if much more discontinuous, efforts to measure social and economic rights through indicators, of which the Human Development Index (HDI) is but one, highly contested example, from the 1980s until their ascendency in the noughties. The chapter argues that this turn to indicators reflects a strategy to depoliticise social rights by turning them into information. Indeed, from the middle decades of the twentieth century until the late 1970s, the quest for social and economic rights was pursued through a very different set of means. Across the post-war period, social and economic rights were synonymous with the expressly political project for postcolonial justice pursued by what would eventually become the non-aligned movement. Their efforts were, I argue, part of a necessarily speculative project: a 'worldmaking' programme, as Adom Getachew describes it, which confronted Fordist capitalism with a critique of the global economy and demands to reconstruct it from the perspective of the Global South.[46]

Juxtaposing indicators with this earlier project for postcolonial justice, the chapter demonstrates that indicators arose as a response precisely to anxieties about the political nature of social rights with seemingly objective forms of measure systemised around very narrow interpretations of their legal inscription in international law. The result, the chapter argues, is an informatised practice of 'doing' rights work that reconfigures and reduces social and economic rights to a process of finding and measuring information. To ground these arguments the chapter develops a critical analysis of various indicator projects, including, but not limited to, the HDI, and the Social and Economic Rights Fulfilment (SERF) index. Doing so demonstrates that the technical instruments embedded within indicators are imbued with a neoliberal ambition to depoliticise the economy by transforming it into a purely technical object. Moreover, because indicators foreground an incremental approach to realising social rights, they align neatly to the model of market-based development through economic growth. In this sense, indicators reflect an effort to 'do' social rights in a way that embraces not only the technologies and techniques but also the logics of cybernetic capitalism.

In addressing the example of indicators, the book demonstrates what its conceptual framework can add to the neoliberal critique of human rights. Because the neoliberal critique has tended to focus on the individualising tendencies of civil and political rights, it often sidesteps questions about the much less explored fate of social and economic rights in the era of late capitalism.[47] Undoubtedly, this reflects the fact that civil and political rights have often been the main point of focus for human rights organisations. But as my analysis of indicators reveals, from as early as the 1980s there have indeed been attempts to integrate and mainstream socio-economic rights within the contemporary movement. As the example of indicators demonstrates, by placing the informational modalities of human rights at the fulcrum of my critique it becomes possible to develop an analysis that accounts for how the full gamut of rights have been made more amenable to the logics of contemporary capitalism. Moreover, in doing so, this book also complicates simplistic claims that greater visibility for social and economic rights could, in and of itself, adequately address the so-called neoliberalisation of rights. For it demonstrates that the contemporary movement's previous engagements with socio-economic issues have not led to a recuperation of the emancipatory potential of human rights.

Having charted these two key moments in the (admittedly recent) history of the contemporary human rights movement, the book moves to the present in Chapter 4 to address the informational logic of human rights as it operates today. It poses the question of what is happening to human rights practices as the era of big data and its attendant technologies – algorithms, machine learning and the availability of ever greater corpuses of data – increasingly shapes contemporary rights activism. The chapter argues that while the vernacular of 'data' has altered some of the epistemic coordinates that define what counts as 'information', the imaginaries this new discourse unfolds nevertheless retain an informational logic that, while transformed by the material processes and technical syntax of data, continues to operate within human rights practice. If the informational logic traced in earlier chapters relies on the idea that information is a kind of self-evident 'substance', the imaginary of data reinforces this principle with a similar premise. As Lisa Gitelman has recently suggested, data imaginaries often assume 'that data are transparent [. . .] the fundamental truth of stuff itself'.[48]

To explore how this data imaginary shapes the movement's informational logic today, Chapter 4 draws together three practices now emerging within contemporary human rights activism: the use of machine learning in statistical estimations of human rights violations; algorithmic processes for marshalling large corpuses of video evidence; and the practice of scraping Twitter for early warnings of human rights violations. I suggest that each of these informational processes harbours a faith in the idea that, through various forms of capture, fitting and enumeration, good data can better reveal positive facts about violence and violations. Consequently, the greater quantities of information and the supposedly deeper insights offered by new technological practices become an end in themselves. This growing 'datafication' of human rights, I conclude, underpins a new iteration of the movement's informational logic that suspends socially and politically inflected conceptions of human rights with the promise of 'cleaner' and better data.

In opting to focus on these three informational 'moments' in contemporary human rights practice, the analysis developed throughout the book is not intended as an exhaustive or encyclopaedic list of informational techniques mobilised by the movement in the course of its work. Such a task would be well beyond the constraints of time and space afforded by this book. It is, nevertheless, my modest hope that my approach might provide a useful lens for others wishing to develop a critique of human rights practices. At the same time, the depoliticising informational logic I foreground in my analysis is not designed to be so totalising a concept as to deny the possibility of contradictions, of examples that may not neatly align to my analysis, or even go beyond it. In fact, though I argue that the informational

valence of human rights has become its dominant tendency in contemporary practice, the final part of the book affirms the prospect of
moving beyond the present conjuncture in order to reclaim some of
the more radical possibilities embedded within human rights. I introduce some of these considerations in the section below.

Radicalising Rights/Radicalising Information

The sketch outlined above is already indicative of some of the ways
that informational logic poses new and very particular challenges for
thinking about how human rights might recuperate their emancipatory
potential. As I have already suggested, the danger with concerns about
the 'narrowing' of the human rights project around an individualised
civil and political rights is that it can end up figuring any embrace of
social and economic rights as signifying the end of 'neoliberal human
rights'. My own intervention, however, not only demonstrates the ways
socio-economic rights claims have been moulded to the logic of capital but, in doing so, foregrounds that such claims are not necessarily
enough in and of themselves because they encounter another, rather
different problem: the limits placed on what is sayable and doable once
any kind of rights claim is rendered informational.

Above all, the book suggests that the informatised version of
human rights that predominates today provides a difficult terrain
upon which to mobilise and cultivate a more radical vision of rights.
For what is reified as 'informational' is shaped by a totalising gesture,
an epistemological closure, that emphasises stability and coherence.
Signal, after all, is that which is already recognisable to the system.
Conversely, the array of critical, radical and speculative knowledges
necessary to problematise, imagine and construct a world transformed (rather than simply describe it as it is) tend to be forced outside this informational realm. Politics, to reiterate, becomes noise.
As I trace throughout the course of the book, the result is either the
exclusion of political claims that put social structures and systems
into question altogether or their recuperation through the processes
of 'cutting' and 'cleaning' that typify the kinds of discretisation and
formatting characteristic of cybernetic capitalism. This leads the
analysis to a critical question, namely: how to address the attenuation of human rights as an emancipatory resource in the face of
a logic designed precisely to strip out the transgressive and noisy
radicalism, leaving only that which can be rendered informational?

Rather than shying away from this problem, the final chapter of
the book is designed to explore how a more radical vision of human

rights might be cultivated in opposition to the deleterious effects of informational logic. Throughout these considerations I am careful to avoid the temptation of imagining an escape from the vernacular of information altogether. Perhaps such an escape is possible, but the spaces within which to do so, I would suggest, have been progressively reduced to a set of crevices and cracks that are vanishingly small. As Terranova has suggested (and Tiqqun would no doubt agree), what is at stake in the development of cybernetic capitalism is not simply the proliferation of computational machines as its new technics but, more radically, the formatting of social, cultural and economic processes so that they become an information system.[49] That such a totalising tendency has now become a reality is recognised by the software studies scholar Andrew Goffey, who suggests that contemporary information infrastructures now subtend 'a determinate configuration of a social field that is increasingly planetary in scope [. . .] a form of governmentality that formats populations at a problematically planetary scale'.[50]

Given, then, that information has become the largely inescapable fabric of the digital age, I propose that a strategy of working 'within and against' the problem of information might bear more fruit. I argue, in other words, that the human rights project needs to rethink its conception of, and relationship to, information if human rights are to regain their radical potential as a vehicle for transformative social change. My determination to do so rests on a couple of astute observations made by cultural theorists of information over the years. In his critical analysis of information capitalism at the turn of the millennium, Shunya Yoshimi problematised the way the much narrower, shallower concept of information had superseded knowledge 'to occupy a central position in the world of human consciousness'.[51] Nevertheless, for Yoshimi, information could also be a potentially productive site for political engagement. For information is itself 'a field of struggle in which different definitions confront each other leading to the creation of new practices and alternative concepts'.[52] And while Terranova is equally aware of information's deleterious social consequences, she has also called for a cultural politics of information that destabilises the closure and limitation of alternatives which inheres in information systems by developing 'radically other codes and channels' that 'stab at the fabric of possibility'.[53]

Taking these calls as inspiration, Chapter 5 argues that developing a more emancipatory vision of human rights requires precisely a 'struggle' over the concept of information. Such a struggle, I suggest, is predicated on the construction of informational discourses and practices that explicitly reject the hegemonic configuration of information as an auto-effective and transparent substance that simply 'speaks for itself', as well as the positivistic and empiricist epistemologies that underpin it. Importantly, the approach I take should not be confused with arguing that information, its logic, its practices and technologies, can imminently and immediately be turned against themselves. Instead, my contention is that a more substantive engagement with what information can and should mean, one that rethinks its logic, practices and technologies, is an important prerequisite for new and emancipatory practices to emerge. Consequently, the chapter explores the possibilities of creating an alternative, perspectival approach to human rights information that establishes connections between theoretical concepts of exploitation that take aim at the structural conditions of violence with the experiences of the exploited. Such a perspectival approach, I argue, requires not only an accountability to the perspectives it mobilises but also a capacity to transgress the dominant codings valorised by the dominant informational logic.

To explore these ideas, I put Donna Haraway's now famous work on 'situated knowledges' into dialogue with the radical epistemology at the heart of Maurizio Lazzarato's recently translated work *Experimental Politics*.[54] On the one hand, the value of Haraway's work is that it both rejects the epistemological appeals to objectivity and positivism that underpin much human rights information as a 'god trick', while laying the groundwork for a feminist perspectival epistemology that foregrounds the concept of accountability. On the other hand, Lazzarato is both allied to the perspectival approach taken by Haraway while also adding to it a transgressive sensibility that demonstrates how 'radically other codes', as Terranova puts it, can impose themselves upon and transform a socio-political situation. Taken together, these epistemic coordinates, I suggest, can sketch out the contours of an informational model able to 'stab at the fabric of possibility'.[55]

Crucially, I bring these insights into dialogue with a number of more critically minded approaches to creating human rights information, notably insights gathered from Third World approaches to human rights outlined by scholars like Pooja Parmar and the Forensic Architecture project run by Eyal Weizman.[56] What emerges from these critical discussions is a series of reflections on how other epistemological frames might underpin a more radical approach to information politics, which, for reasons that will become clear, I term in(-)formation politics. It then considers what this new vision of in(-)formation might mean for the practices, technologies and organisation of the contemporary human rights movement. In doing so, the chapter not only develops an alternative conception of human rights information but also attempts to think through its material consequences for the informational practices that have defined the contemporary movement since its emergence in the late 1970s. This set of ideas is offered as one possible starting point for those whose own informational experiments are, in the end, where the real possibilities for alternatives are located.

Coda: Rights after Shame

Of course, I understand that my calls for a radically different informational strategy based on a perspectival approach are bound to rankle with some. My conclusions will no doubt be particularly difficult not only for those who insist on a doggedly universalistic approach to human rights but also for those concerned that abandoning the movement's informational logic risks losing the fragile gains it has made over the last forty or so years. However, there are increasingly compelling reasons for thinking that now, more than any other, is a good time to consider a vastly different informational approach. The intertwined crises of capitalism and climate today promise not only to intensify and proliferate human suffering through ongoing structural adjustments, forced migrations and authoritarian borders, drought, famine, growing inequalities, and more. They also represent an existential threat to both human and non-human life on this planet. The current articulation of the human rights movement has shown little sign of arresting, let alone reversing, these crises. In fact, the present conjuncture might even usher in an era of waning effectiveness for the informational project that presently defines the movement.

As the famous expression 'naming and shaming' implies, one of the predictable informational effects that human rights organisations have been able to count on is shame. But what happens now, in a time when shame has become less and less operative? The imbrications between the avatars of silicone valley – of whom the tech financier and alt-right sympathiser Peter Thiel is just one of the most pronounced examples – and the rise of the new far right suggests that the latest transmutations of cybernetic capitalism represent a break from the liberal cosmopolitanisms whose hegemony in the post-Cold War era enabled human rights to flourish. The shifting sands of the present moment appear as a melding of the governmental possibilities of cybernetic surveillance, control and regulation with what Max Haiven has recently described as a structure of racist, sexist and homophobic revenge.[57] Consequently, as former UN High Commissioner for Human Rights Zeid Ra'ad Al-Hussein suggested in 2018, 'Shame is also in retreat. Xenophobes and racists [. . .] are casting off any sense of embarrassment.'[58] What unites Bolsonaro, Orbán, Modi, Erdoğan, Duterte and the rest is a revanchist mode of governing which appears entirely without shame. The gleeful turn to 'Fortress Europe', the detention of migrant children, and border walls are all the signs of a kind of shamelessness – a boastful cruelty – that seems largely impervious to the revelatory power of information qua information.

Is this an existential challenge to human rights? The answer I present in this book is that the present conjuncture does not necessarily signal the 'endtimes of human rights' that Stephen Hopgood evoked nearly a decade ago.[59] Nevertheless, if human rights are to have a future, what it may in fact signal is the endtimes for a certain way of doing human rights. In the face of these existential challenges, perhaps there is less to lose in pursuing a more transgressive and explicitly political strategy than the defenders of the 'fragile gains' of the last forty years might like to admit. Perhaps now more than ever, it is time to construct a transformative human rights project rather than persist with one that simply tries to protect us from the sharper edges of a social structure whose gross deficiencies it implicitly accepts. Given that it has never been clearer that the technological and economic configurations of cybernetic capitalism are driving the potentially apocalyptic combination of climate crisis and human insecurity, then addressing the multitude of human rights issues, not least migration, land use and indigenous rights, bound up with these crises demands no less than the full-blooded embrace of a transformative strategy.[60] Insofar as this might be the case, I hope the kinds of informational strategies I modestly sketch out towards the end of this book are useful contributions to such a project.

Notes

1. George McGovern, 'The Information Age', *New York Times*, 9 June 1977.
2. *International Communications and Information*: Hearings Before the Subcommittee on International Operations of the Committee on Foreign Relations, United States Senate, 95th Congress, 1 (Washington DC: US Government Printing Office, 1977).
3. McGovern, 'The Information Age'.
4. 'The Computer, Machine of the Year', *Time Magazine* 121, no. 1 (3 January 1983).
5. Daniel Bell, *The Coming of Post-Industrial Society: A Venture in Social Forecasting* (Harmondsworth: Penguin, Peregrine Books, 1973); Yoneji Masuda, *Information Society as Post-Industrial Society* (Washington

DC: World Future Society, 1981); Alvin Toffler, *Future Shock* (New York: Random House, 1970); Marc Porat, *The Information Economy: Definition and Measurement* (Washington DC: US Department of Commerce, Office of Telecommunications, 1977); Simon Nora and Alain Minc, *The Computerization of Society* (Cambridge, MA: MIT Press, 1981).

6. Memo from Margo Picken to IEC members, 20 June 1977. Folder 118, Amnesty International. International Secretariat Archive. International Institute of Social History, Amsterdam.

7. 'Report of the "Crash Committee" on the Growth and Development of Amnesty International'. ICM/14/01/77 June 1977. Folder 458, Amnesty International. International Secretariat Archive. International Institute of Social History, Amsterdam.

8. Amnesty International, *Amnesty International Annual Report 1978*, POL 10/0001/1978 (London: Amnesty International, 1978), 7, <https://www.amnesty.org/download/Documents/POL100011978ENGLISH.PDF> (last accessed 24 February 2022).

9. Joseph R. Slaughter, *Human Rights, Inc.: The World Novel, Narrative Form, and International Law* (New York: Fordham University Press, 2007), 2. On the historical origins of human rights in the 1970s, see Jan Eckel and Samuel Moyn (eds), *The Breakthrough: Human Rights in the 1970s* (Philadelphia: University of Pennsylvania Press, 2015); Samuel Moyn, *The Last Utopia: Human Rights in History* (Cambridge, MA and London: Harvard University Press, 2010).

10. Kenneth Cmiel, 'The Emergence of Human Rights Politics in the United States', *Journal of American History* 86, no. 3 (1999): 1231–50; James Ron, Howard Ramos and Kathleen Rodgers, 'Transnational Information Politics: NGO Human Rights Reporting, 1986–2000', *International Studies Quarterly* 49, no. 3 (2005): 557–88; Margaret E. Keck and Kathryn Sikkink, *Activists beyond Borders: Advocacy Networks in International Politics* (Ithaca, NY: Cornell University Press, 1998); Margaret E. Keck and Kathryn Sikkink, 'Transnational Advocacy Networks in International and Regional Politics', *International Social Sciences Journal* 51, no. 159 (1999): 89–101; Samuel Moyn, *Not Enough: Human Rights in an Unequal World* (Cambridge, MA and London: Harvard University Press, 2018).

11. Cmiel, 'The Emergence of Human Rights Politics', 1246.

12. Joel R. Pruce and Alexandra Cosima Budabin, 'Beyond Naming and Shaming: New Modalities of Information Politics in Human Rights', *Journal of Human Rights* 15, no. 3 (2016): 408–25.

13. See, for example, A. Trevor Thrall, Dominik Stecula and Diana Sweet, 'May We Have Your Attention Please? Human-Rights NGOs and the Problem of Global Communication', *International Journal of Press/Politics* 19, no. 2 (2014): 135–59; Mahmood Monshipouri (ed.), *Information Politics, Protests, and Human Rights in the Digital Age* (Cambridge: Cambridge University Press, 2016); Molly K. Land and Jay D. Aronson (eds), *New Technologies for Human Rights Law and Practice* (Cambridge: Cambridge University Press, 2018); Ben Miller,

'Attacks with Knives and Sharp Instruments: Quantitative Coding and the Witness to Atrocity', *Leonardo* 45, no. 1 (2012): 86–7; Katharina Rall, Margaret L. Satterthwaite, Anshul Vikram Pandey, John Emerson, Jeremy Boy, Oded Nov and Enrico Bertini, 'Data Visualization for Human Rights Advocacy', *Journal of Human Rights Practice* 8, no. 2 (2016): 171–97.

14. For more on technological determinism as a dominant tendency not only in academia but in contemporary culture, see Nick Dyer-Witheford, *Cyber-Marx: Cycles and Circuits of Struggle in High-Technology Capitalism* (Chicago: Illinois University Press, 1999); Frank Webster, 'Making Sense of the Information Age', *Information Communication and Society* 8, no. 4 (2005): 439–58.

15. See Naomi Klein, *The Shock Doctrine: The Rise of Disaster Capitalism* (London: Allen Lane, 2007); Susan Marks, 'Four Human Rights Myths', in *Human Rights: New Problems, Old Possibilities*, ed. D. Kinley, W. Sadurski and K. Walton (Cheltenham: Edward Elgar, 2013), 217–35; Anna Selmeczi, 'Who is the Subject of Neoliberal Rights? Governmentality, Subjectification and the Letter of the Law', *Third World Quarterly* 36, no. 6 (2015): 1076–91; Joseph R. Slaughter, 'Hijacking Human Rights: Neoliberalism, the New Historiography, and the End of the Third World', *Human Rights Quarterly* 40, no. 4 (2018): 735–75; Jessica Whyte, 'Powerless Companions or Fellow Travellers? Human Rights and the Neoliberal Assault on Post-Colonial Economic Justice', *Radical Philosophy* 2, no. 2 (2018): 13–29.

16. Slaughter, 'Hijacking Human Rights', 768.

17. Jacques Rancière, *Dis-Agreement: Politics and Philosophy* (Minneapolis and London: University of Minnesota Press, 1999); Jacques Rancière, *Dissensus: Politics and Aesthetics* (London and New York: Bloomsbury, 2015).

18. Paul O'Connell, 'On the Human Rights Question', *Human Rights Quarterly* 40 (2018): 962–88; Kathryn McNeilly, 'After the Critique of Rights: For a Radical Democratic Theory and Practice of Human Rights', *Law and Critique* 27, no. 3 (2016): 269–88; Boaventura de Sousa Santos, 'Toward a New Universal Declaration of Human Rights (I)', Critical Legal Thinking, 25 January 2020, <https:// criticallegalthinking.com/2020/01/25/toward-a-new-universal-declaration-of-human-rights-i/> (last accessed 23 February 2022).

19. The integration of human rights into World Bank policy was made clear in 1998 when it published a report that claimed human rights were central to its policy goals vis-à-vis sustainable development. See World Bank, *Human Rights and Development: The Role of the World Bank* (Washington DC: World Bank, 1998).

20. Upendra Baxi, *The Future of Human Rights* (Oxford: Oxford University Press, 2008), 216.

21. Wendy Brown, '"The Most We Can Hope For . . .": Human Rights and the Politics of Fatalism', *South Atlantic Quarterly* 103, no. 2–3 (2004): 462.

22. On the capital–labour struggles central to the Fordist crisis, see Pierre Dardot and Christian Laval, *The New Way of the World: On Neoliberal Society* (London and New York: Verso, 2013). For more on how Third Worldism was part of the crisis, see G. Garavini, 'Completing Decolonization: The "Oil Shock" and the Struggle for Economic Rights', *The International History Review* 33, no. 3 (2011): 473–87; Timothy Mitchell, *Carbon Democracy: Political Power in the Age of Oil* (London and New York: Verso, 2011).

23. As Pierre Dardot and Christian Laval make clear, the framing of the crisis of capitalism as a crisis of governability and social democracy was part of an elite strategy that eventually laid the ground for neoliberal reform developed by agencies such as the Trilateral Commission made up of industrialists from Europe, the US and Japan. See Dardot and Laval, *The New Way of the World*.

24. Moyn, *The Last Utopia*, 121.

25. Jessica Whyte, 'Human Rights: Confronting Governments?', in *New Critical Legal Thinking: Law and the Political*, ed. Costas Douzinas and Illan Rua Wall (Abingdon and New York: Routledge, 2012), 11–31.

26. Klein, *The Shock Doctrine*; Marks, 'Four Human Rights Myths'.

27. Whyte, 'Powerless Companions or Fellow Travellers?'; Whyte, 'Human Rights'.

28. Slaughter, 'Hijacking Human Rights'.

29. Adom Getachew, *Worldmaking after Empire: The Rise and Fall of Self-Determination* (Princeton, NJ: Princeton University Press, 2019); Bradley R. Simpson, 'Self-Determination, Human Rights, and the End of Empire in the 1970s', *Humanity: An International Journal of Human Rights, Humanitarianism, and Development* 4, no. 2 (2013): 239–60.

30. Slaughter, 'Hijacking Human Rights', 737.

31. Slaughter, 'Hijacking Human Rights', 768.

32. Josh Bowsher, '"Omnus et Singulatim": Establishing the Relationship Between Transitional Justice and Neoliberalism', *Law and Critique* 29, no. 1 (2018): 83–106; Josh Bowsher, 'The South African TRC as Neoliberal Reconciliation: Victim Subjectivities and the Synchronization of Affects', *Social and Legal Studies* 29, no. 1 (2020): 41–64.

33. Raymond Williams, *Towards 2000* (New York and Harmondsworth: Pelican Books, 1985), 128–52.

34. Nick Dyer-Witheford, *Cyber-Proletariat: Global Labour in the Digital Vortex* (London: Pluto Press, 2015); Tiqqun, *The Cybernetic Hypothesis* (Los Angeles, CA: Semiotext(e), 2020).

35. Dyer-Witheford, *Cyber-Proletariat*; Nick Dyer-Witheford, 'Cybernetics and the Making of a Global Proletariat', *The Political Economy of Communication* 4, no. 1 (2016): 35–65; McKenzie Wark, *Capital Is Dead: Is This Something Worse?* (London and New York: Verso, 2019).

36. Seb Franklin, *Control: Digitality as Cultural Logic* (Cambridge, MA: MIT Press, 2015); Philip Mirowski, *Machine Dreams: Economics*

Becomes a Cyborg Science (Cambridge and New York: Cambridge University Press, 2002), Table.

37. A particularly strong theoretical engagement with the individualising tendency shared by neoliberalism and human rights is given in Louiza Odysseos, 'Human Rights, Liberal Ontogenesis and Freedom', *Millennium: Journal of International Studies* 38, no. 3 (2010): 747–72.

38. Maurizio Lazzarato, 'Immaterial Labour', in *Radical Thought in Italy: A Potentional Politics*, ed. Michael Hardt and Paolo Virno (Minneapolis and London: University of Minnesota Press, 2006), 133–47.

39. Tiziana Terranova, *Network Culture: Politics for the Information Age* (London: Pluto Press, 2004).

40. Cmiel, 'The Emergence of Human Rights Politics', 1246.

41. 'Information politics' has been invoked not only by Cmiel but by several other authors. See Winifred Tate, *Counting the Dead: The Culture and Politics of Human Rights Activism in Colombia* (Berkeley: University of California Press, 2007), 118–21; Ron et al., 'Transnational Information Politics'; Håkan Johansson and Gabriella Scaramuzzino, 'The Logics of Digital Advocacy: Between Acts of Political Influence and Presence', *New Media & Society* 21, no. 7 (2019): 1528–45; Pruce and Budabin, 'Beyond Naming and Shaming'.

42. Kiran Kaur Grewal, *The Socio-Political Practice of Human Rights: Between the Universal and the Particular* (London and New York: Routledge, 2017), 3.

43. See, for example, Oriana Bernasconi, Elizabeth Lira and Marcela Ruiz, 'Political Technologies of Memory: Uses and Appropriations of Artefacts that Register and Denounce State Violence', *International Journal of Transitional Justice* 13, no. 1 (2019): 7–29; Evelyn Ruppert, 'The Governmental Topologies of Database Devices', *Theory, Culture & Society* 29, no. 5 (2012): 116–36; Geoffrey C. Bowker and Susan Leigh Star, *Sorting Things Out: Classification and Its Consequences* (Cambridge, MA: MIT Press, 2000); Paul Dourish and Melissa Mazmanian, 'Media as Material: Information Representations as Material Foundations for Organizational Practice', in *How Matter Matters: Objects, Artifacts, and Materiality in Organization Studies*, ed. Paul R. Carlile, Davide Nicolini, Ann Langley and Haridimos Tsoukas (Oxford: Oxford University Press, 2013), 92–118.

44. Matthew Fuller (ed.), *Software Studies: A Lexicon* (Cambridge, MA and London: MIT Press, 2008), 3.

45. Franklin, *Control*.

46. Getachew, *Worldmaking after Empire*.

47. In fact, Samuel Moyn has only recently written perhaps one of the only histories of social rights that engages with questions regarding their relationship to neoliberalism. For Moyn, the answer is negative: social rights are only a powerless companion and not a fellow traveller with neoliberalism. See Moyn, *Not Enough*.

48. Lisa Gitelman (ed.), *'Raw Data' Is an Oxymoron* (Cambridge, MA and London: MIT Press, 2013), 2.

49. Terranova, *Network Culture*.
50. Andrew Goffey, 'Automation Anxieties and Infrastructural Technologies', *New Formations* 98 (2019): 32.
51. Shunya Yoshimi, 'Information', *Theory, Culture & Society* 23, no. 2–3 (2006): 272.
52. Yoshimi, 'Information', 277.
53. Terranova, *Network Culture*, 26–7.
54. Donna Haraway, 'Situated Knowledges: The Science Question in Feminism and the Privilege of Partial Perspective', *Feminist Studies* 14, no. 3 (1988): 575; Maurizio Lazzarato, *Experimental Politics: Work, Welfare, and Creativity in the Neoliberal Age* (Cambridge, MA: MIT Press, 2017).
55. Terranova, *Network Culture*, 26–7.
56. Pooja Parmar, 'TWAIL: An Epistemological Inquiry', *International Community Law Review* 10, no. 4 (2008): 363–70; Eyal Weizman, *Forensic Architecture: Violence at the Threshold of Detectability* (Cambridge, MA: Zone Books, 2017).
57. Max Haiven, *Revenge Capitalism: The Ghosts of Empire, the Demons of Capital, and the Settling of Unpayable Debts* (London: Pluto Press, 2020).
58. Zeid Ra'ad Al Hussein, 'Opening statement by UN High Commissioner for Human Rights', 37th session of the Human Rights Council, 26 February 2018, Geneva, <https://www.ohchr.org/EN/HRBodies/HRC/Pages/NewsDetail.aspx?NewsID=22702&LangID=E> (last accessed 3 March 2022).
59. Stephen Hopgood, *The Endtimes of Human Rights* (Ithaca, NY: Cornell University Press, 2013).
60. See Sean Cubitt, *Finite Media: Environmental Implications of Digital Technologies* (Durham, NC and London: Duke University Press, 2017); Dyer-Witheford, *Cyber-Proletariat*; Jason W. Moore, 'The Capitalocene, Part I: On the Nature and Origins of Our Ecological Crisis', *Journal of Peasant Studies* 44, no. 3 (2017): 594–630.

Chapter 1

Cybernetic Capitalism/
Informational 'Politics'

The cybernetic hypothesis is a political hypothesis, a new fable that, beginning with the Second World War, has definitively supplanted the liberal hypothesis. [. . .] [I]t would have us think of biological, physical and social behaviours as being integrally programmed.
— Tiqqun, *The Cybernetic Hypothesis*

The suppression of noise is from the standpoint of communication theory a technical matter. Here we understand it as a matter of politics and economy. Noise suppression directly correlates to people's oppression.
— Jonathan Beller, *The World Computer*

In *The Inertia of Fear*, the Russian cyberneticist and Soviet dissident Valentin Turchin developed a critique of Marxism based on the cybernetic theories that shaped his scientific work.[1] Published in 1981 after Turchin fled from Soviet Russia, the book offers a distinctive critique of socialism directed not so much at the ethical aberration of the gulag as the deformations caused, in his opinion, by Marxism's unsound scientific basis. For Turchin, the error of Marxism resided in its attachment to the physics of the nineteenth century. A 'mechanistic picture of the world', rooted in thermodynamics, he argued, furnished Marxism with a worldview in which the 'state of the world is determined, in a unique way, by its preceding state'.[2] Seeing human societies as 'aggregates of particles' moving in preordained directions, Marxist determinism was totalitarian because it provided no room for human agency.[3]

Against historical materialism's thermodynamic model, Turchin developed his own 'historical idealism', based on theorising society as a 'multi-level cybernetic system', which 'affirms that it is precisely ideas which dominate society'.[4] For Turchin, cybernetic principles would be the basis of a new and anti-totalitarian model of the social world that would overcome the 'barbarous socialism' of Soviet Russia. Cybernetics, Turchin argued, provided a template for the full

28

integration of individuals into society as 'complex subsystems' which encouraged individual freedom and creativity to flourish. Cybernetic society would be a social 'metasystem' that '[would guarantee] the free exchange of information and ideas', continuously reshaping social life for the better.[5]

Turchin's hypothesis relies on the proposition, common in the mid-twentieth century, that cybernetics superseded thermodynamics as a new scientific paradigm and then maps this teleology onto forms of social organisation. The totalitarian present of Marxism is thus derided as antiquated while, conversely, hopes for a new utopian society rest on reconstructing the social world in novel cybernetic configurations. In making this opposition, Turchin's arguments bear a striking resemblance to theoretical and ideological arguments that uphold the superiority of capitalism over other 'totalitarian' forms of social organisation. As this chapter will later demonstrate, proponents of 'free' markets have argued that they represent a more effective social-cybernetic system than obsolete forms of socialist planning since the emergence of the cybernetic sciences in post-war America.[6]

For now, however, what is most fascinating about Turchin's work is his elevation of the human rights movement as central to his putative cybernetic utopia. As a founding member of Amnesty International's Moscow chapter, Turchin was well aware of the rapid expansion of the human rights movement in the 1970s. But his commitment to human rights, it seems, was intrinsically linked to his interest in cybernetics. For Turchin, the value of the new human rights movement was that it fought for the basic civil rights necessary for the informational exchanges that would make human societies successful cybernetic organisms. Even more importantly, Turchin argued that one of the deforming effects of Marxist influence on societies all across the world was the increasing politicisation of every aspect of societal life. 'What the world needs now', Turchin concluded, 'is the opposite – a depoliticization of the most important aspects of life.'[7] To Turchin, the new human rights movement, with its inscrutably impartial mode of activism, represented the best hope for just such a depoliticisation.

The arrival of dissidents like Turchin in the capitalist West is often emphasised not only in the neoliberal critique of human rights but in a broader critical historiography that explores the curious rise of the human rights movement in the 1970s. Usually, however, it is not Turchin but Aleksandr Solzhenitsyn and his *Gulag Archipelago* that acts as a metonym for the dissidents who, it is argued, contributed to growing disenchantment with left-wing utopianisms and the subsequent embrace of human rights as a 'minimalist, hardy utopia'.[8] But what if Solzhenitsyn is the wrong dissident? What if, in bringing together a denunciation of Marxism, cybernetic social organisation and human rights, it is Turchin who serves as a better figure for grasping the contemporary world? Turchin's writings, I would argue, provide a prophetic, if idealised, vision not only of the cybernetic world we now live in but also of the depoliticising role of human rights within it. The constellation of points he draws together offers up a tantalising decoupage of the key stakes of this book, affording glimpses of both the informational logic of human rights I seek to trace and the cybernetic socio-economic context that has shaped it.

The objective of this chapter is to critically (re)arrange and build upon Turchin's points in order to provide the overarching theoretical and socio-historical framework for the rest of the book. To do so, the first half of the chapter reconceptualises the 'neoliberal' reconfigurations of capital in the late 1970s as the emergence of a socio-economic conjuncture that – as I have already suggested – is better grasped as cybernetic capitalism. Seeing neoliberalism and the information revolution of that decade not as distinct entities but as entangled legacies of the cybernetic sciences that flourished in the Cold War, I foreground the intertwining of neoliberal political economy and new information technologies in the latter decades of the twentieth century as a key feature of late capitalism's informatic mode. A significant effect of this cybernetic conjuncture, I contend, has been the gradual reconfiguration of cultural, social and economic processes as information systems that are secured around stable, predictable forms of communication. Standardisable and positivistic forms of knowledge are reified as information, while politically contentious and thus destabilising forms of knowledge are excluded as noise.

In the second half of the chapter, I then explore how these issues fold into and configure the informational logic of human rights. Delving into the archives readily demonstrates that the informational qualities of human rights practices which emerged in the 1970s and the relevance of cybernetics to this work did not escape organisations which gave shape to the movement like Amnesty International. An understanding that the key work of human rights was to produce and transmit information drove a preoccupation with conceptualising and configuring the movement as networks, information systems and databanks. I show that these informational concerns have tended to reproduce the broader socio-cultural tendencies of cybernetic capitalism: producing effective information means constituting empirical and objective facts that appear able simply to 'speak for themselves', whilst political knowledges and epistemologies, particularly those which call the system into question, become noise. The movement's informational 'politics' thus somewhat ironically engenders a depoliticising activist modality amenable to cybernetic capital, which I conceptualise as the informational logic of human rights.

Cybernetic Capitalism: A History

The socio-economic transformations often conceptualised as 'neo-liberalism'; the technological advances of the so-called information revolution; the rise of human rights: the 1970s provides the crucial temporal juncture at which each of these developments appeared to catalyse. Consequently, there is a certain methodological temptation to jump straight to that decade so these phenomena might readily be bridged together as interlocking components of what I am calling cybernetic capitalism. But just as critics of both neoliberalism and human rights have recognised that understanding the late 1970s requires turning further back to the mid-twentieth century, a similar journey is also necessary here to rethink the dense historical interconnections between these developments through the framework of cybernetic capitalism.[9]

Scholars concerned with the emergence of cybernetic capitalism have often argued that the seeds of the informational revolution were already sown in the nineteenth century, particularly by Charles Babbage's 'analytical engine', first described in 1837.[10] The analytical engine was the first general-purpose computing machine and, even if it was never actually built, was driven by concerns for how to automate and deskill labour. As is clear from Babbage's broader writings, particularly his 1832 book *On the Economy of Machinery and Manufactures*, his desire to build computational machines was interwoven with concerns for reducing and eventually eliminating 'from production a human factor whose presence could appear [. . .] only as a source of constant indiscipline, error, and menace'.[11] For this reason, Babbage's machine is understood not only to prototype later developments in digital and informational technology; it also portends the ways that these technologies are intertwined within the logic of capitalism as 'a strategy of class war'.[12]

Nevertheless, as the term cybernetic capitalism suggests, the more pressing historical juncture lies just over a century later, with the emergence of cybernetics and a related set of interdisciplinary academic fields. Surfacing within UK and US efforts in the Second World War before seamlessly gliding into place as the knowledges through which the latter would wage the Cold War, cybernetics cohered alongside operations research and information theory to address military conundrums as varied as cryptography, radar, ballistics and atomic weapons. But it was through their passage from military to socio-economic applications over the course of the twentieth century that these cybernetic sciences also laid the foundations for the discursive, computational and network infrastructures of the post-industrial world.[13]

Through pioneers such as John von Neumann, Claude Shannon, Warren Weaver and Norbert Wiener, the innovation of cybernetics was its development of the concept of 'information control', which revolutionised our understanding of machines. Where machines of the nineteenth century were organised around thermodynamic concepts of energy and entropy, 'a glorified heat engine', as Weiner put it, cybernetics suggested that machines 'govern' through information exchange and control.[14] It is for this reason the name cybernetics is rooted in the Greek *kybernētēs* meaning 'steersman' or 'governor'. With 'information' given primacy, cybernetics concerned itself with 'self-governing' machines, automata that maintained their stability or homeostasis through feedback loops that allowed them to compute the effect of their action on the environment and adjust accordingly. In theorising machines as information processors, the cybernetic hypothesis radically collapsed the distinction between living organism and machine. Both were figured as information processors and, consequently, automata could exist either in 'in the metal or in the flesh'.[15] The fundamental proposition of cybernetics, then, was that 'organisms and machines [could] be considered formally interchangeable', and could also be integrated, opening up the cyborg possibility of man–machine interfaces.[16]

Understanding cybernetics as concerned with self-regulating infor-mation processors provides a framework to trace its contribution to the informatic reconfigurations of capitalism in the 1970s through two distinct but intertwining trajectories. First, the more materialist strand of our cybernetic heritage emerges directly from the 'rapid calculating machines' built by the cyberneticians in their quest for information control. Machines such as von Neumann's Mathemati-cal Analyzer, Numeric Integration and Computer (MANIAC), which famously contributed to atomic weapons research, are a precur-sor and prototype 'for all subsequent mainframes, minicomputers, PCs, laptops and tablets, that would become collectively known as cybernetic technologies'.[17] More than the machines themselves, however, it is the logic underpinning them that best explains why cybernetic technologies have been so readily integrated into capital-ism's technical substrates. In collapsing distinctions between human and computer, cybernetics already implies a project in which human behaviours might be optimised or entirely superseded by machines of sufficient complexity. Much like Babbage's analytical engine, cybernetic technologies furnished capitalism with new strategic possibilities for undermining labour.[18] It is this propensity for weaponisation, I will later argue, which is central to understanding the industrial applications of the cybernetic technologies that proliferated within the latter decades of the twentieth century.

Before doing so, however, it is necessary to unpack a second, 'discursive' legacy of cybernetics. As John Johnston contends, cybernetics posited the computational machine not only as a specific technical system but as an 'abstract machine', a conceptual tool able to deal with problems far beyond computer science and engineering.[19] In actuality, cybernetics was always a transdisciplinary project, a fact reflected in the now famous Macy Conferences held between 1946 and 1953, which were pivotal to the development of the field. Discussions there brought together computer scientists, psychologists, biologists and anthropologists, enabling cybernetics to evolve into a metatheory underpinning models, for example, of individual psychology and social community.[20] From its beginnings, then, cybernetics was imbued with a kind of 'mania', understood not only as a promiscuous tendency for diffusion but also as a propensity to fold outwards into ever grander applications. While the whole enterprise began with a limited set of military applications, as Peter Galison has noted, it would eventually claim to model 'the human mind, then life, then even the world system as a whole'.[21] The argument made by some scientists that the universe itself is essentially computable perhaps signals the logical conclusion of this mania, reinforcing the intuition that potentially everything is a cybernetic system.[22]

As it was founded in the early Cold War era, cybernetics thus provided a set of onto-epistemological principles able to ontologise all things as information systems. This enabled cybernetics to become a discourse that, drawing from and reinforced by related fields like information theory and operations research as well as the development and dispersal of new computational machines, readily interlaced with, and subsequently reconfigured, all manner of social, economic and cultural practices. Even as enthusiasm for the term cybernetics would eventually dissipate, its discourse would continue to leave a lasting influence in arenas as varied as organisational and industrial management, art and music, economics and finance, as well as health care and education.[23] Where this analysis is concerned, however, the influence of cybernetic discourse on neoliberal thought and practices constitutes one of its most consequential legacies.

Neoliberalism: A Cybernetic Project?

In 1947, just as Wiener et al. were bringing together the ideas that would eventually crystallise as the cybernetic sciences, neoliberal intellectuals including Friedrich Hayek, Frank Knight and Wilhelm Röpke convened the first meeting of the Mont Pelerin Society (MPS). Fighting against the rising tide of Keynesian and socialist state planning, their central task was to renovate and restore liberalism's ailing, if not entirely discredited, principle of market individualism. Though MPS was an independent entity, entirely separate from the military-backed RAND corporation and the other nodal points for cybernetic research, it is still intriguing that the think tank, as the seedbed for what would grow into neoliberalism, emerged in parallel with early cybernetic thought. In fact, the immediate post-war period provided occasion for cybernetic ideas, with their tendency for manic proliferation, to fertilise neoliberal thought. As the green shoots of MPS flowered into the neoliberal project, the slow drip-feeding of cybernetic concepts over the middle decades of the twentieth century would see information become a crucial concept that distinguished neoliberal doctrine from the classical liberalism that MPS sought to revive.

The staging for neoliberalism's first encounters with cybernetics, as Mirowski has shown, was the socialist calculation debate.[24] An epoch-defining tussle in economics that eventually pitted neoliberal economists against their socialist counterparts, the debate provided the context in which various informational ideas crossed over into neoliberal thought. The debate opposed the socialists' conviction that a central planner could rationally allocate resources to the arguments of neoclassical economists like Ludwig von Mises who claimed that only the price system of the market could effectively perform this task. By the early 1940s, however, Hayek's intervention into the debate introduced cybernetic themes, recasting it as an informational problem. The cybernetic dimensions of Hayek's arguments are particularly clear in 'The Use of Knowledge in Society', first published in 1945.[25] Hayek conceptualised society as a distributed information system which central planners could not hope to understand because they could not access all the relevant information. Only the market could properly compute the information distributed across society. In developing this argument, Hayek's approach reimagined the market as a giant computer, 'which passes on [. . .] the available information that each individual needs to act, and to act rationally'.[26]

It is important to tread carefully, however. Even though Hayek clearly traces the outlines of a cybernetic theory of markets, it was, as Mirowski notes, shaped by only brief encounters with the new thinkers of information control such as von Neumann and Weaver.[27] For this reason, it is perhaps best to understand Hayek 'as someone who filtered various cyborg themes into economics at second- and third-hand'. And yet, it is not for nothing that Hayek's work has retrospectively been hailed as a 'manifesto [. . .] of the Cyborg Revolution'.[28] Hayek's intervention led to the revision of the neoclassical conceptualisation of the market away from 'notions of exchange as brute allocation – that is, as physical motion in commodity space [. . .] and toward the image of the market as a conveyor and co-ordinator of "knowledge" or "information" between agents'.[29] In this respect, Hayek is one progenitor of a more thoroughgoing engagement with 'information' through which the neoclassical economics underpinning neoliberalism have been infused with cybernetic ideas. Diffusing through not only game theory and behavioural economics but the legal theory of Geneva School neoliberals like Jan Tumlir, an informational conception of the economy has become a central tenet of neoliberal doxa.[30]

Interestingly, the conceptualisation of the market as an information processor far superior to the central planner was not simply an ideological argument but furnished the neoliberal project with its epistemological grounding.[31] The neoliberal reworking of homo œconomicus, as the self-maximising suite of human capitals that many scholars situate at the heart of neoliberal thought, is a key artefact of this cybernetic epistemology. If neoliberal rationality expands markets across ever greater parts of social life so that all individual choices become market investments in human capital, then the human is figured as a 'decision unit', a self-regulating computer responding to market information. Or, to put it another way, the subject becomes 'both a communication system and a component in such a system'.[32] The implications are clear. Neoliberalism has in an important sense been defined by its engagements with cybernetic discourse.

The Cybernetic Offensive

Once neoliberalism's informational onto-epistemology is laid bare, the socio-economic transformations of the 1970s, fated by some as the 'neoliberal turn', already begin to look like a distinctly cybernetic project: the construction of the market as a global computer in which the human subject is a mere node. The centrality of this cybernetic vision can be detected in Quinn Slobodian's astute observation that structural adjustment policies deployed against the Global South were promoted by neoliberal thinkers as a way of disassembling forms of state-based economic planning to enable the 'homeostatic system', of market signals to flourish.[33] However, the global turn to neoliberalism, and the imposition of its cybernetic market order, need to be understood as just one, admittedly crucial, component of a broader informatic shift that characterised capitalism's post-Fordist reconfigurations. This more extensive social formation – which I call cybernetic capitalism – can be grasped by paying closer attention to some of the cybernetic progeny that came of age alongside neoliberalism, but which are often missed by those who centre neoliberal market order in their accounts of late capitalism.

Once can see, for example, the influence of cybernetic discourse in industrial and business organisation where a turn away from vertical structures of management towards flat and networked organisational structures was propagated and popularised by forecasters like John Naisbitt and management consultants like Peters and Waterman throughout the 1970s and early 1980s.[34] Developing alongside the emerging neoliberal orthodoxy, the figure of the network increasingly became a feature of corporate management in this period, with firms seeking to escape the stagnation of industrial capital by embracing the techno-future of the information economy. Luc Boltanski and Eve Chiapello contend that the reconfiguration of organisational structures according to the logic of the network is now a central aspect of what they call the 'new spirit of capitalism'.[35] Crucially, these networked forms of socio-economic management are strongly rooted in the industrial cybernetics developed by thinkers such as Jay Forrester and Anthony Stafford Beer in the 1950s and 60s, which, in conceiving of 'workers, machinery and capital as balanced systems of inputs and outputs', aimed at reconceptualising organisations as information systems.[36] The shift in which corporations are reconfigured by the 'langue' of networks and information processors, as Franklin suggests, is thus a 'telling endowment passed from cybernetics to late capitalism', even if the former has become a largely unmarked discourse ventriloquised by organisational gurus and management manuals.[37]

Even more crucial, however, is the central role of the information revolution, and its novel technologies, in capitalism's reconfigurations. As McKenzie Wark contends, grasping the profound socio-economic shifts in the final third of the twentieth century requires an appreciation of how the (already cybernetic) project of neoliberalism was enveloped and striated by new information technologies, which became the crucial 'information infrastructure to route around labour's power'.[38] Taken from this standpoint, neoliberal political economy might well be grasped as but one aspect of a broader 'cybernetic offensive', mobilised against the twin threats of the industrial working class and the increasingly organised nations of the Global South.[39] But how to track these developments? Dyer-Witheford has recently asserted that computerised automation, digital supply chains and electronic financialisation each describe a different site at which information technologies were integral to capitalism's strategic reconfigurations. In doing so, Dyer-Witheford provides a useful framework to trace cybernetic technologies as they have been strategically weaponised within the processes of retrenchment and dispossession often associated with the 'neoliberal turn'. A brief exploration of each site in turn readily demonstrates the information revolution's critical role in capitalism's post-Fordist transformation.

In a wonderfully detailed analysis, David Noble demonstrates that systems for automating factory work were one of the first points at which cybernetic technologies crossed over from military to industrial applications in the 1950s.[40] But the advent of microprocessors and the development of computer-aided design and manufacturing (CAD/CAM) in the 1970s marks a more critical juncture for factory automation. The acceleration of automation at this later period was not simply a consequence of asocial technical innovation ensuing from the microelectronics revolution, however. In actuality, the high fixed costs of cybernetic technologies meant adoption was initially slow.[41] Automation intensified only under growing competition, as part of the strategy to circumvent the rising labour and energy costs that were at the centre of capital's crisis.[42] New computer-automated tools emerged as a means of extricating capital from the crisis within 'a renewed cultural offensive', and were promoted in the name of 'competitiveness, productivity, and progress'.[43]

Concomitantly, market deregulation and trade liberalisation were slowly remaking the globe as a vast index of competitive territories for the movement of capital, enabling the construction of global networks of production and consumption. The more 'flighty' propensities of neoliberal capital could only be fully actualised, however, through new supply chain technologies which enabled the control of information flows and linked different spatial locations through 'detailed cybernetic tracking, inventory control and labour monitoring systems'.[44] Alongside the development of standardised shipping containers, which greatly streamlined the logistics of production, the creation of the barcode by IBM in the early 1970s followed by the gradual development of ever more sophisticated supply chain management systems from the early 1980s have allowed corporations to develop increasingly agile networks.[45] The informatic capacity to control logistical flows has facilitated processes such as outsourcing, making it easier to bypass organised labour by displacing production into less costly territories.

Finally, the steady expansion of finance since the 1970s has itself become a tool that, through the power asymmetries between creditors and debtors, has supported the reshaping of the world in neoliberal ways.[46] Finance compels: states to adopt neoliberal policies, including market deregulation and the rollback of social security; firms to reduce costs through ever more flexibilised and individualised labour; the deproletarianisation of people, by hook or by crook, as individualised entrepreneurs.[47] But finance is also fundamentally an informational project, operating through a complex informatics that is driven by advanced computer networks, trading algorithms and forecasting methods that are themselves part of the technological legacies of cybernetics.[48] For instance, Michael Castelle has recently demonstrated that technical advances in transaction processing and data management in the 1970s–80s were a prerequisite for organising the information circulating in extremely high volumes of financial trades.[49]

Crucially, while each of these 'sites' engenders forms of creative destruction, they also imply within them the construction of new post-industrial sectors and the forms of valorisation that define the contemporary information economy. As Dyer-Witheford points out, for example, even the cybernetic management of logistics 'has become a whole sub-sector of capital'.[50] Perhaps more crucially, as the information revolution has marched on through factory automation, the computerisation of workspaces, the development of planetary network infrastructures, and the advent of big data, information has become an increasingly dominant force of production. That is, cybernetic technologies have 'informatised' the economy, reaching both 'all the way into the production process' and 'all the way out to global networks of measurement, command and control'.[51]

In the Global North where the contemporary human rights movement was forged, what might now be more appropriately called the 'cybernetic turn' of the 1970s has resulted in the proliferation of new kinds of informational work that (post-)autonomist Marxists such as Maurizio Lazzarato conceptualise as 'immaterial labour'. Recognising not only the outgrowth of communicative technologies in all kinds of work but also their organisation around informational commodities in areas such as culture, software and biotechnologies, immaterial labour refers to the 'labor that produces the informational and cultural content of the commodity'.[52] Above all, informatisation envelops the tasks of labour so that the worker is 'subordinated to the "circulation of information"' and, in a description (not unco-incidentally) reminiscent of neoliberal homo œconomicus, becomes

a 'relayer of codification and decodification [. . .] within a communications context [. . .] normalized by management'.[53] This general
trajectory reaches its apex in the digital economy where the configuration of internet searches, clicks and likes within processes of
valorisation relies on the free 'labour' of 'users'.[54]

All of this, I would suggest, demonstrates that it is necessary to
move beyond the conceptual parameters offered by neoliberalism and
embrace new nomenclature. The alternative – continuing to rely on
the explanatory power of neoliberalism and simply subordinating
'information' to the role of its 'privileged technology', as someone like
David Harvey does – is clearly insufficient.[55] Such a diagnosis fails to
capture the cybernetic legacies that have shaped both the processes of
socio-technical change and the economic theories and practices which
intertwine in contemporary capitalism. As we have seen, 'neoliberal'
techniques of governance are indelibly shaped by informational concepts of social self-regulation and by the casting of markets and their
agents as programmable. And the proliferation of cybernetic discourses
and technologies has both supplemented and intertwined with the strategies and techniques of 'actually existing' neoliberalism. Better, then, to
conceptualise the weaponisation of information technologies and the
predilection for neoliberal governance as 'blended' components of a
single project.[56] Each represents intertwined but distinct strands of a
broader socio-economic configuration: cybernetic capitalism.[57]

The Cultural Hegemony of Information

Under cybernetic capitalism, 'information' is not only a commodity; it
has also become a central framework through which the social world
is both understood and configured. The growing articulation of all
social, cultural and economic practices as information systems, networks and other informational forms has become a key marker of the
digital age. As Terranova has demonstrated, there has been an 'informatisation' of contemporary culture through which social and cultural
processes have '[taken] on the attributes of information', and are thus
'increasingly grasped and conceived in terms of their informational
dynamics'.[58] Information, in this respect, has come to constitute 'the
essence of our "age"'.[59] But what should be understood by information and, more importantly, what are its socio-political effects as it has
become an operative concept across much of contemporary life?

A deeper engagement with information as it is conceptualised in
cybernetics provides a crucial starting point to answer these questions. With clear similarities to Wiener's own writings on information,

the model of information was nevertheless most clearly developed by Shannon and the subsequent exposition of the broader implications of his work by Weaver.[60] Interested in a technical theory of communication, Shannon took the approach of severing information from semantic problems regarding meaning, which he famously suggested were 'irrelevant to the engineering problem'.[61] Figuring information as probabilistic quanta instead, Shannon conceptualised communication as the selection of a message from a finite, calculable number of possible choices, which could then be encoded and sent as a signal to a receiver to be decoded. Within this framework, information refers to the measure or degree of choice in selecting a message such that the greater the number of choices, the more information a message contains. In practical terms, this is because as the number of possible messages increase, more binary digits are required to encode the message and send it through a channel. For example, where the result of a coin flip can be coded into one binary digit (heads = 0, tails = 1) so its transmission conveys just one bit of information, a single letter from the alphabet obviously implies a much greater degree of choice and requires more bits of information.

While Shannon's approach made a foundational contribution to the field of information theory, its emphasis on both probability and quantification also delineates the key contours of a broader cybernetic theory of information, which, as Katherine Hayles suggests, transforms information into something disembodied and abstract; a quantifiable 'entity' or substance that flows between points in a network or communication system.[62] For his part, Shannon was adamant that his information theory was a strictly technical innovation that unlocked new methods for encoding and decoding data as well as filtering out 'noise' – extraneous material that interferes with, and distorts, the desired signal.[63] But, for others, the possibility of broader social applications was already written into the venture. In his exposition of Shannon's theory in their joint publication *The Mathematical Theory of Communication*, Weaver suggested that information theory laid the foundation for a more general theory of communication, which encompassed 'all human behaviour'.[64] Similarly, cyberneticians like Wiener (though somewhat ambivalently), Karl Deutsch and Stafford Beer saw quantitative and probabilistic conceptions of information as having socio-political applications in areas such as law, politics, government and industrial management.[65] The probabilistic model became a valuable foundation for cybernetics because it provided 'information' with a stable form that could be applied to the multiple contexts cybernetics aimed to deal with, whether a robot, a man–machine interface or a social system.

It is unsurprising, then, that as a cybernetic onto-epistemology has pervaded social, cultural and economic processes, the traces left by information theory have also become an enduring feature of the socio-cultural and 'common-sense' meanings of information. The pervasive influence of cybernetic discourse in socio-cultural realms can be detected not only in contemporary concerns with how information became a thing or substance that flows or circulates.[66] Perhaps more crucially, it can also be traced in critical discussions about how 'shallow', quantitative informational forms have superseded deeper, qualitative forms of knowledge to assume 'a central position in the world of human consciousness'.[67] Conceptualisations of information as a 'compressed' and 'byte-like' entity that excludes the possibility of more reflective forms of knowledge provide another, particularly revealing, framing of this issue.[68] But while these debates already allude to some of the political stakes inherent in contemporary articulations of information, drawing out the informational logic I am concerned with requires a more thoroughgoing examination of the ways in which cybernetics has shaped 'how "information" is understood as an important cultural concept for us [. . .] as a so-called "global information" society'.[69]

My starting point for this investigation is to take note of a considerable irony embedded within the cybernetic model of information: while Shannon was explicit in formally severing information from semantics, the cybernetic concept of information nevertheless implies a structured system that imposes a certain fixity of meaning. As Ronald Day suggests, it assumes that all possible communications are predictable, that a message is constituted from a vocabulary that is 'controlled' and is thus one choice from many possible forms that are known in advance. For Day, this logic of information has folded into and now buttresses a utilitarian socio-cultural ideal of information as denoting clear communications capable of generating predictable effects. Information maintains a stable meaning between sender and receiver that exists only by demarcating, either implicitly or explicitly, '"safe" limits on meaning and expression'.[70] What tends to be reified as information, then, is that which appears to be empirically observable, factual and objective, and whose meaning is thus less open to contestation.

Consequently, the concept of information that is hegemonic today does not only valorise quantitative data as other critics of information society might suggest.[71] In contemporary information cultures, it also underpins 'the privilege that a certain "factual" and "clear" information is given in communication (in writing in general, in the media, in organizations, in education, and in politics) [. . .,] the demand that the arts represent reality rather than "distort" it', and an 'informational' history understood as simply 'the transmission of the past to receivers in subsequent generations'.[72] More broadly, then, insofar as information is always already that which can be imagined and described within a system, it is imbued with a kind of self-evidence, what Day calls an 'auto-effective presence', that lends itself to radically positivist and empiricist epistemologies – a tendency, as I will explore in more detail in the next chapter, no doubt reinforced by the cybernetic predilection for positively measurable behaviour rather than deeper, interpretive engagements with the world.[73] Information is thus conditioned by a belief in an objective reality whose image can be 'captured' so faithfully that it seems as if it can simply speak for itself.

However, as scholars from many different critical traditions have suggested, any claim to objectively observe reality cannot easily be disconnected from questions of power.[74] For example, Donna Haraway (whose work I engage with more substantially in the final chapter of this book) demonstrates that traditional notions of objectivity rely on a kind of epistemic 'god trick' in which the classed, raced and gendered perspectives embedded in Western epistemology are universalised and naturalised so that it appears as a god's-eye view 'of everything from nowhere'.[75] What has often been considered objective knowledge simply reflects broader relations of power and social authority rendered epistemically as the capacity to leave one's own position 'unmarked' and thus claim its transcendence. As Day insists, a similar process conditions what can be parsed as informational within the information age. The hegemonic logic of information under cybernetic capitalism rests on an intensive standardisation that renders informational only those 'formalised encodings' that are 'embedded so deeply in [dominant] institutions and practices of knowledge that those contexts or frames disappear, leaving the appearance of an auto-effectively produced, self-evident object of knowledge'.[76]

Accordingly, if a now socially dominant concept of information is aligned to capital it is because, in becoming synonymous with technical utility and operational efficacy, it perpetuates an epistemic enclosure, securing itself around hegemonic and thus socially stable forms of communication and representation. What becomes informational are those social forms and meanings that are embedded within, and thus maintain, capital's institutions, discourses and norms. Unfortunately, as Jonathan Beller has recently argued,

> such normative encodings render a world where what can be recognized as plot, as thought, as information by its 'conscious organs,' all but excludes as [. . .] noise, the possibility of interrogating, much less smashing, the structural and epistemic limits of the code's very mode.[77]

Transgressive utterances, especially political contestation and conflict over norms, values and ends, are reduced to, and dismissed as, potentially destabilising noise.

In his study of how cybernetics has transformed late capitalism, Franklin suggests that information theory, with its discrete binary coding and exclusion of noise, becomes one model for practices of discretisation, filtration and exclusion that are central to cybernetic capital's management of the social.[78] My own argument is that 'Information' as a concept is readily mobilised within similar discursive and ideological strategies designed to depoliticise the social through processes of standardisation and filtration where, as Terranova notes, 'the real is [all that] remains while all other competing possibilities are excluded'.[79] Of course, this is not to say that information is so conceptually determined that it is entirely closed off from contestation – the arguments made towards the end of this book rest on the assumption that the concept of information itself can be and, in fact, is an important terrain of struggle.[80] But it is to suggest that cybernetic capitalism harbours a distinctive informational logic that, as it formats socio-cultural institutions and practices, tends to suspend and nullify forms of political contestation, conflict and critique that bring the social system or structure into question. It does so by limiting legitimate knowledge to a reductive repertoire of seemingly auto-effective 'facts' and filtering out the rest as noise.

Human Rights as an Informational Project

It is precisely this informational logic that is also at stake in the practices and strategies embraced by the contemporary human rights movement as it emerged in the information age. My attempts to trace this logic not only provide a critical reading of the movement as an informational politics that materialised alongside cybernetic capitalism in the 1970s but emphasise the ways this project was shaped by a cybernetic imaginary. The analysis that follows largely focuses on Amnesty International and its articulation of its mission and its practices over the course of that decade. It does so not simply because Amnesty was at the forefront of the new human rights organisations that proliferated in that period but also because, insomuch as this is true, AI was also 'the prototypical human rights organization', pioneering many of the movement's modes of action.[81] Tracking the concerns that animated AI thus provides an important window into the broader movement.

That said, the movement's composition as a set of 'informational dynamics' can also be grasped from multiple points.[82] As my analysis develops, I introduce material from other organisations, primarily HURIDOCS (Human Rights Information and Documentation Systems), a self-described 'network' of NGOs particularly concerned with human rights information, and Helsinki Watch (HW, the forerunner to Human Rights Watch), to demonstrate how developments at Amnesty travelled outwards, or were paralleled across different parts of the movement. The effect is to underscore the ways in which a cybernetic onto-epistemology has moulded the movement's embrace of information politics, shaping an informational logic that has served to 'tame' human rights within the ideological and discursive limits of late capitalism.

Focusing on Amnesty International readily demonstrates that the movement's 'informatisation' cannot easily be extricated from the information revolution it paralleled in the 1970s. Though AI launched in 1961, utilising a small membership which 'adopted' prisoners of conscience and advocated for their release, it was only following the organisation's phenomenal growth in the 1970s that it began to conceptualise itself in informational terms.[83] An indicator of the rising fortunes of human rights, the rapid expansion of Amnesty and its swelling international membership prompted much reflection regarding AI's purpose, structure and techniques. The decentralisation of the organisation as well as the appearance of new departments and techniques all emerged from a long process of contemplation as the organisation developed over the decade.[84] Woven through all these transformations was a growing understanding that information was central to its work.[85]

The year 1975 marks a particularly important moment at which information became a key conceptual term for Amnesty, not so much by design but as the result of mounting institutional anxieties. A worrisome staff report submitted to the IEC in April of that year contended that 'though the IEC has never before discussed or even identified the information problem [. . .] it is now A MATTER OF URGENCY'.[86] The roots of this upper-cased panic lay a year earlier when Winston Riley, an information expert from the International Labour Organization, was invited to conduct a study of information handling within the International Secretariat (IS), the epicentre of Amnesty's day-to-day work. Riley's findings placed information firmly on Amnesty's agenda: 'the function of information handling is so fundamental to the purposes of the secretariat that immediate steps need to be taken to [address it]'.[87] The troubling staff report submitted in April 1975 expanded on Riley's initial findings. Emphasising that information was central to Amnesty's activities, it urged the organisation to radically rethink its structure to ensure the effectiveness of its information. The key recommendation was the transformation of the organisation's library into a documentation centre 'responsible for information handling and able to respond to internal and external needs'.[88] Amnesty's Documentation Centre was operational by 1976 and, teasing some of the cybernetic ideas shaping AI's interest in information, would later be described as 'the nucleus for the future information network structure of the whole movement'.[89]

By the late 1970s, the centrality of information to Amnesty's work was inescapable. '[Our] fundamental and basic working tool is information', AI declared; 'all work [. . .] all actions, campaigns etc., are based on information received, evaluated, processed, transformed into new information and disseminated.'[90] Above all, Amnesty had realised that its project was fundamentally one of producing information about violations and using it to effectuate changes in state behaviour. But this was a double-edged sword. The understanding that its project was an informational one could not be extricated from Amnesty's concerns with the snowballing 'paper avalanche' that it engendered.[91] Amnesty International's IEC convened a meeting in Cambridge in June 1977, the so-called Cambridge Crash Committee (CCC), specifically to discuss these issues alongside questions of the organisation's future direction. The meeting developed two organisational responses which are of immediate interest here.

First, the CCC argued that 'the absorbing of information cannot in the long run live without mechanised information handling – computerisation'.[92] Experiments with creating databases went hand in hand with the adoption of computerised systems. The publication of a computer-compiled list of 2,665 *desaparecidos* from Argentina in June 1979 is an important marker in this respect. The experiment successfully demonstrated the possibilities of a computerised system that could support the organisation's research.[93] By the mid-1980s, Amnesty International's informational project had fully embraced the emerging infrastructures of the information age. If 'information on human rights violations under our mandate is our "stock in trade"', as an information technology manual designed for AI's national sections argued, then 'new developments in the techniques and technology of information handling are of vital importance'.[94] Over the next decade, microcomputers and database software became standard infrastructures scaffolding not only the work of the Secretariat but also AI's national sections.

Second, acknowledgement of Amnesty's informational character was underlined by a worry that its membership lacked the necessary skills to fully realise the organisation's fast developing informational project. Training and professionalisation were key themes at the CCC. The Committee gave 'special attention to the importance of raising the level of qualification in the membership', and it was emphasised that training in 'the techniques applied and the reasons behind the strategies are a prerequisite for the effective work of each member'.[95] As AI headed into the 1980s, seminars and new guidelines on the 'responsible handling of information' were accompanied by new forms of training, handbooks and informational standards for both workers in the Secretariat and the organisation's broader membership.[96]

Much like other organisations – such as Helsinki Watch, whose work relied on a small team of researchers – Amnesty's core work required a skilled kind of labour for producing, formatting and controlling information.[97] But because AI's work was distributed across its members and workers, it saw training as a prerequisite for enabling 'members/workers to sit – so as to speak – at the other end of the line handling a decentralised information centre which in the same time could be developed into a pool for incoming information to the [International Secretariat]'.[98] From this perspective, the organisation's base of 'members/workers' (or should that be member-workers?) increasingly resembled communicational nodes in a system 'controlled' by the IEC and the Secretariat. Given these developments are coextensive with the rise of cybernetic capitalism, it is tempting to read Amnesty's work as strangely mirroring the kinds of immaterial labour that are now commonplace in the digital age. Echoing a post-Fordist corporation, the member-worker becomes a 'relayer of codification and decodification [. . .] within a communications context that has been completely normalized by management'.[99]

Informational and Network Imaginaries

The turn to novel information infrastructures and the configuration of activist practice as informational work both speak to the zeitgeist of the 1970s. The burgeoning information age and the ways new technologies would revolutionise work were tropes widely circulating, as we have already seen, through the writings of informational prophets like Bell and Toffler. But the appropriation of informational discourses and practices by Amnesty (and the broader human rights movement) went beyond a passing acquaintance with a mood hanging in the air. A fascination with cybernetics was rendered operational through a range of strategies and techniques that structured the informatisation of human rights.

Cybernetic ideas were central to AI's informational turn. Through-out the late 1970s, a series of seminars, executive discussions and background papers focused on developing 'a policy for information handling within AI', frequently turned to the question of how the organisation might itself be understood 'as an information system, databank or network'.[100] Technical and policy considerations regarding new information systems and forms of computerisation were, in other words, shaped by a revealing slippage between deliberations about concrete socio-technical devices and a more conceptual discussion where Amnesty was itself theorised as various informational devices.[101] This shift in register, whereby narrower discussions concerning technical and policy matters folded out to render the organisation itself indistinguishable from a cybernetic system, offers a telling glimpse of the expansionary logic or 'mania' inherent in cybernetics.

As it turns out, attempts to model the organisation as a cybernetic system run through the pages of various strategy and policy papers in areas such as documentation and press and communications. As I will demonstrate momentarily, not only were organisational structures and processes described as information flows, feedback systems and networks but, tellingly, an unmistakeably cybernetic mode of visual representation, 'black box' diagrams such as network and information flow diagrams, accompanied these linguistic descriptions and rendered them intelligible. As a method for interpreting the world, these 'system' diagrams occupy an important place in the toolbox that emerged from cybernetics, which it is worth giving some further explanation of here before tracing their mobilisation by Amnesty International (and beyond).

Modelling phenomena as systems of boxes or nodes connected by input and output lines (Figures 1.1–1.3), cybernetic diagrams, particularly in the form of the network diagram, have become a ubiquitous representational mode in capitalism's informatic episteme, as authors such as Alexander Galloway and Ulises Mejias lament.[102] With some earlier precedent in electrical engineering, these diagrammatic methods largely originate in the black box thinking developed by cyberneticists such as von Neumann and W. Ross Ashby.[103] For them, the black box was a valuable conceptual tool that enabled concerns with the inner functions of phenomena to be bracketed off (or 'black boxed') so that attention could be paid to how information inputs observably transformed their behaviour. Both information flow and network diagrams evolved as a common way of mapping phenomena as systems, which directly leans on the behaviourism implied by the black box. They 'diagram' and thus articulate any object or process they seek to model, from technical infrastructures to socio-cultural processes, as a 'flat ontology of black boxes' or a 'series of nodes connected only by communicative action'.[104] The deleterious effects of ontologising social processes through such diagrams are explored in the next chapter, where I argue that their conceptual power contributes to practical manifestations of the informational logic of human rights. For now, however, it is important to note that the uptake of these diagrams already presupposes a thoroughgoing attempt to model phenomena as information systems.

The influential role of informational discourses and system diagrams within Amnesty emerges most clearly in a working paper presented to participants at a seminar on information handling in March 1978 and the policy discussions that followed it. The paper, titled 'AI Seminar on Information Handling – Working Paper', deployed the language of networks to link the development of an 'AI information system' with ongoing plans to decentralise the organisation. Arguing that 'any information system for AI has to be [. . .] closely linked to the structure of the organisation', the paper described Amnesty as having 'a clear hierarchical network structure', which, though less desirable than a non-hierarchical network, was inevitable given the International Secretariat's central role within the organisation. Not all was lost, however. 'AI's unique structure as a network could be strengthened by the information system', the paper argued, so long as the latter's composition could 'allow for decentralization of parts of the system, [and] feedback and coordination [. . .] to be built into the system'.[105]

Tellingly, the proposed structure of this decentralised information system was largely defined through the information flow diagram supplied in the middle of the paper intended to clarify the discussion (Figure 1.1). The diagram sketches a feedback system in which informational responsibilities are shared between the International Secretariat and regional centres. By connecting various nodes that represent the stages of AI's information flow, the diagram describes a system for 'internal' and 'external users' that is divided between 'central' and 'regional' units and which operates through interconnected lines of input and output. Feedback lines from 'users' represent the way their reactions would reshape the content and form of AI information.

The framework outlined in the paper, and the diagram at its centre, became an influential blueprint for the organisation's decentralised structure, instigating a whole series of policy discussions in the language of systems and networks. Subsequent policies to strengthen national sections and 'deconcentrate' information flow in the Secretariat closely resembled the recommendations that came out of the

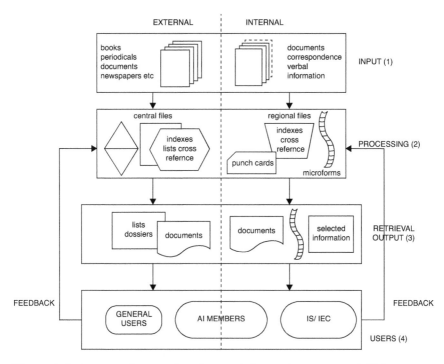

Figure 1.1 Amnesty International as an information system, 1977. Amnesty International. International Secretariat Archive. International Institute of Social History, Amsterdam.

information handling seminar, which were explicitly proposed to reconfigure Amnesty as 'a global information system'.[106] The network structure that defines AI today, in which the Secretariat shares responsibilities with national and regional sections, might thus be considered a distant relative of the informational framework articulated in the late 1970s.[107]

As Amnesty International adapted to its rapid development, its predilection for reticular forms went well beyond the organisation's structure. A more extensive figure of the network was taken up in the Press and Communications Strategy paper AI endorsed as policy in 1977.[108] One of its considerations was how the membership was being utilised to extend AI's reach, particularly in the Global South. These discussions leant heavily on two diagrams intended to illustrate the informational function of the membership in both liberal and non-liberal societies (Figure 1.2). In each of them, information flows as an output from the membership into society, which is figured as either an 'open' or 'closed' network depending on whether the society in question is 'liberal' or 'non-liberal'. The ideological

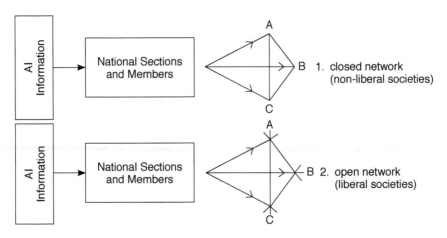

Figure 1.2 Communications in liberal and illiberal societies, 1977. Amnesty International. International Secretariat Archive. International Institute of Social History, Amsterdam.

trope at work in the opposition made between liberal (open) and non-liberal (closed) societies notwithstanding, what is particularly interesting here is the assumed interface between Amnesty International and a social world already unproblematically understood as a network. Reproducing the conceptual expansionism of cybernetic thought, it is indicative of a worldview in which Amnesty envisions itself as one network nested within a larger set of social 'systems'.

The examples above crystallise Amnesty's investment in the cybernetic figure of the network as an onto-epistemological model which could not only define what the organisation and the world are but also provide a way of knowing them that made it possible to intervene in their functioning. The multitude of theoretically consistent descriptions of the movement as a network which pop up in quite disparate arenas attests to the degree to which this cybernetic imaginary permeated the organisation. A 1977 report submitted to the United Nations, for instance, is a less obvious place to find an invocation of the network. But in its explanation of the informational support AI provided to the UN, the report argues that, by moving its information 'from the International Secretariat in London to the national sections [who] in turn transmit the information to groups and individual members', Amnesty International had 'devoted considerable resources' to disseminating UN information 'through this communication network that is its members'.[109]

The embrace of cybernetic forms at Amnesty International represents a microcosm of broader discussions that were percolating across the whole human rights movement. As the informational qualities of the broader movement rushed into view, there was a recognition that the fight for human rights relied on gathering 'reliable and extensive human rights data', and that this required new information infra-structures.[110] These sentiments were the focus of a working group that emerged out of a series of Ford Foundation conferences between 1978 and 1979, which brought together individuals 'from almost every major inter-governmental organisation actively concerned with human rights', as well as from international NGOs such as AI and the International Commission of Jurists.[111] Sharing a concern for 'the need to improve the reliability, comprehensiveness and accessibility of human rights information', the working group formed to explore the possibilities for an international documentation service.[112] The group formally became HURIDOCS in 1982 with former General Secretary of Amnesty International Martin Ennals as its president.

Though initial plans for HURIDOCS focused on a centralised information clearing house, the working group very quickly proposed that the documentation service should take the form of a decentral-ised network.[113] An early working paper presented by the famous Norwegian human rights expert Asbjørn Eide imagined the docu-mentation service as a 'Human Rights Network of organisations, centres for research and education and others', open to any number of 'contributors and users'.[114] Sketched out in a network diagram that displays a familiarity with methods and ideas that are rooted in cybernetics (Figure 1.3), the documentation service envisaged by Eide was made up of regional nodes that stored and transmit-ted information based on their specialisation. The regional centres were to be linked to a central node or 'nucleus', intended to 'ensure the information flow among the centres and other members of the work', partly by 'developing standards in information processing', and 'facilitating co-ordination'.[115]

As it grew over the course of the 1980s, the HURIDOCS network did not emerge exactly as Eide had predicted. But it did nevertheless model itself as a global network that included not only institutions such as UNESCO, the UN Commission for Refugees and the Council of Europe but also NGOs across Europe, Africa and Latin America. As its resident technologist, Bjørn Stormorken, would later argue at a UNESCO-organised conference, HURIDOCS was already an example of the kind of network, based on 'principles of decentralization and autonomy', that should be adopted by the broader movement.[116] In this respect, well before the late 1990s heralded an informational triumphalism that figured contemporary human rights activism as a networked movement, the network form had already long become part of the movement's established imaginary.[117] If, as Terranova

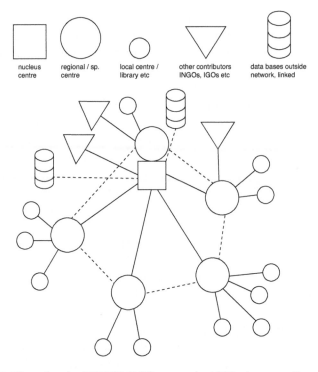

Figure 1.3 Plans for the HURIDOCS network, 1979. Amnesty International. International Secretariat Archive. International Institute of Social History, Amsterdam.

suggests, the reticulation of social, cultural and economic milieus is a key feature of life under cybernetic capitalism, then it is fascinating that the network form was being mobilised in quite sophisticated ways to conceptualise and construct the human rights movement just as capital was taking this informatic turn.[118]

Whose Network/What Information?

Though they were not often mentioned alongside the invocations of networks described above, it is nevertheless clear that governments and other state actors did not exist outside of, but were in fact part of, the very network structure that the human rights movement sought to construct. After all, the different techniques developed by AI and other human rights organisations – letter writing, published reports, media communications and utilising the elite channels of the international community, to name but some – describe different forms of 'shaming' governments to instigate changes in their behaviour.

But using information as 'the difference that makes the difference', to use the cyberneticist Gregory Bateson's maxim, already implies governmental recognition of signals and thus their inclusion in the system.[119] This has important consequence for our understanding of the brand of informational politics developed by the contemporary human rights movement.

In her analysis of network culture, Terranova demonstrates that the figure of the network always implies the necessity of 'establishing a bridge of contact between a sender or receiver'.[120] The network is de facto an act of collaboration. As Terranova, drawing on the philosophy of Michel Serres puts it, 'the two extremities of the channel "are on the same side, tied together by a mutual interest: they battle together against noise"'.[121] Where human rights are concerned the implications are clear. While the term naming and shaming might imply a confrontational configuration between two or more opposed parties, it depends instead on a channel of communication based on mutual recognition, on the possibility of signal.

This sense of mutual recognition is articulated no more clearly than in the preface to AI's 1978 annual report written by the then chairman of its Executive Committee, Thomas Hammarberg. 'Our basic approach to governments is always the same', wrote Hammarberg: 'we seek a dialogue [. . .] this means that we do not fight governments as such.'[122] Recognition, as the basis for informational politics, is also traceable in Jessica Whyte's recent and important contribution to the neoliberal critique of human rights. In her analysis of human rights activism in Pinochet's Chile, Whyte contends that even as the regime attempted to eliminate the Chilean left, 'it allowed overseas human rights organizations [. . .] to enter the country and gave them extensive freedom of movement'. The reason, Whyte suggests, is that the junta was 'anxious to present itself as a modern [. . .] "civilised" nation', and thus 'did not disavow the language of human rights, even at the height of the repression'.[123] The 'channel' Whyte observes between Pinochet's regime and the human rights movement, I would suggest, reflects the 'information system' – though fragile and fraught – in which both human rights organisations and the junta were placed.

Undeniably, the battle against noise often required more from human rights organisations than it did the governments they wished to persuade. For Amnesty International, keeping a channel open for constructive communications required an attentiveness to the form, content and quality of its communications. Above all, maintaining the signal relied on developing a disciplined membership that was meticulous in its informational work. Accordingly, in emphasising the important role of local letter-writing groups in pressuring governments to address human rights issues, Amnesty set out exacting standards for communications by members. As the organisation's 1978 *Handbook* implored, 'letters to government authorities should always be formal and courteous [. . .] remember that the correct form of address, the style of the letter, and even the language in which it is written may determine whether it is attended to or ignored'.[124]

At the same time, a key feature of Amnesty's informational efforts was its development of, and contribution to, a distinctive human rights epistemology that has cut right across the contemporary movement since its emergence in the late 1970s. AI's emphasis on the 'accurate reporting' of 'sober facts' about violations reflects a broader epistemological commitment to empirical, positively observable evidence that is central to contemporary human rights work.[125] It underpins efforts to produce an 'undeniable record of human rights violations', as Human Rights Watch put it, and drives ongoing investment in research, fact-finding and documentation.[126] But as the rhetorical invocation of an 'undeniable' record indicates, this empiricist epistemology was, and remains, inextricable from concerns with reception and recognition, signal and noise. Within AI, it was frequently noted that a condition of the organisation's effectiveness was the 'accuracy' and 'impartiality' of its information. Filtering out the noise of 'distortions, false information or misunderstandings' from its information was a prerequisite for a project that could 'command the confidence and respect [of its stakeholders]', particularly 'governments of all political persuasions'.[127] Those involved in the initial Ford Foundation conferences for what would become HURIDOCS similarly argued that 'judgemental conclusions should be eschewed; otherwise international credibility of the proposed endeavour would be flawed or impeded. The facts would speak for themselves.'[128]

The assumption that it is possible to find 'undistorted' facts presupposes a faith in knowledge as rendering reality so accurately it seems to 'speak for itself' and is placed beyond political contestation. Trust in the auto-effective quality of facts is indicative of the positivistic empiricism which, as Claire Moon has suggested, marks much of contemporary human rights activism. For Moon, the epistemological register of human rights is based on a tight representational correspondence between data and a (positively observable) reality, which basks in the 'virtue of its mimetic authority – "this is life"'.[129] Even where the testimony of victims and witnesses is added to the 'bare facts' of the case, Moon suggests, it is assumed that they can be 'meticulously pared down', stripped of social and political information so that they 'preserve and consolidate' the objective status of the empirical evidence. Human rights information thus claims to unveil a 'real', which can be assiduously separated from the thorny political issues that inhere within matters of social context and lived experience.

In her *History of the Modern Fact*, Mary Poovey traces the genealogy of the 'fact' as a product of liberal Enlightenment thought. Poovey's analysis is particularly astute in drawing attention to the peculiar status of the fact as a brute epistemological unit which, seemingly deracinated from systematic, interpretive or theoretical forms of knowledge, appears as an 'observed particular' that is 'preinterpretive or somehow noninterpretive'.[130] My own argument is that the human rights movement redeploys this liberal structure of fact as a definition not only of what its information is but, as a necessary corollary, of the epistemic line that regulates distinctions between signal and noise. Even if, as we saw earlier, there are good reasons to be suspicious of the claim to deal in objective facts, for the human rights movement facts hold open the channel by dispelling the potentially distorting effects of the political. Moon's description of an epistemological process in which social and political information can simply be 'stripped out' to leave only 'preinterpretive' or 'noninterpretive' facts is, in this sense, one example of a filtration system that ensures the clarity of information by similarly deracinating signal from political noise.

The Informational Qualities of Law

Leaving a more thoroughgoing discussion of what might be understood by the concepts of politics and the political to one side for the moment, it is important to first understand the critical functions human rights law performs in the interpretation and further legitimisation of human rights facts as they circulate across the system. These functions stem from a distinctly 'informational' quality of law that becomes particularly acute as the human rights movement mobilises these legal discourses. Law's informational properties can be grasped by first turning briefly back to the cybernetic thinking that emerged in the Cold War era.

Interestingly, cybernetic theories of the social have often given a special role to law. In his popular treatise on social cybernetics, for example, Wiener argued that law 'could be defined as the ethical control applied to communication', and '[t]hus the problem of law may be considered communicative and cybernetic – that is, they are problems of orderly and repeatable control of critical situations'.[131] The law provides a normative structure that frames the possibilities of human communication and action. But, for Wiener, the structuring properties of law rest on its transparency and reproducibility. Law must 'see that the obligations and rights given to an individual in a certain stated situation are unambiguous' and, in this way, 'make clear and unambiguous statements, which [. . .] the common man of the times will interpret in one way and in one way only'.[132]

Law is informational because it provides the grounds for clarity, consensus and, subsequently, the ethical control of human action. Law both is and defines what constitutes signal (and does so very precisely) and is opposed to the 'noisy' ambiguity that marks, say, political contestation over values, means and ends. Even if the absoluteness of law's clarity within cybernetic thought has troubled legal scholars insofar as it effaces the 'plurality of interpretations' underpinning legal judgment, it was vital for a 'cybernetic' proponent of human rights like Turchin.[133] Indeed, it is law's transparency that underwrote Turchin's faith in human rights as depoliticisation. Against the 'anti-cybernetic' and unethical forms of control shaped by the will and whims of politics, Turchin argued that law provided a form of control 'determined not by the will but by rights and duties', which laid out the best foundation for 'combining freedom and integration'.[134] Law thus set out common standards, a consensus on human action, separate from will or interest and the pitfalls of politics.

This cybernetic idealisation of law undoubtedly reflects the influence of a liberal legal tradition that sees law as a disinterested arbiter of interests, which, it should be noted, has been vehemently critiqued by Marxist and critical legal scholars as inattentive to power relations.[135] But it is precisely this informational ideal that is often assumed to be embodied in the inscription of human rights in international law. The normative proposition of the International Bill of Human Rights – composed of the 1948 Universal Declaration and the two International Covenants on Civil and Political Rights, and Economic, Social and Cultural Rights ratified in 1976 – is a consensus regarding international standards and norms that are beyond contestation. As UN Secretary-General Kurt Waldheim would argue on the occasion of the twenty-fifth anniversary of the Universal Declaration in 1972, the Declaration 'was an expression in simple and clear language of the principles that should govern human relations [. . .] [I]t created standards by which all must be judged.'[136]

In emphasising the clarity and universality of the Declaration, Waldheim celebrated human rights in a language of which both Wiener and Turchin would undoubtedly approve. It should be remembered, however, that such claims also tend to obfuscate not only the diverse political and ideological positions that were contested in the formal inscription of human rights in the post-war period but also the contestations of their meaning by the anticolonial movements after the adoption of the Universal Declaration in 1948.[137] In this sense, the appeal and purpose of human rights law as an informational form is the additional sheen of objectivity bequeathed by consensus, even if this is merely a consequence, as Day might predict, of its construction as a set of 'formalised encodings' that are 'embedded so deeply in [dominant] institutions and practices of knowledge that those contexts or frames disappear'.[138]

Despite these obvious tensions, it is this informational sense of law which is taken up and utilised by the human rights movement. For AI, the claim that its 'impartial approach [. . .] is based upon the provisions of the Universal Declaration of Human Rights', which 'the peoples of the United Nations have pledged themselves to uphold and observe', ran along much of its literature.[139] But it was in AI's work alongside the United Nations where the practical advantages of law as information were articulated most clearly. In her 1978 strategy paper for future AI–UN relations, Margo Picken claimed it was 'axiomatic that when making recommendations or criticisms to governments it is better to be able to quote accepted international standards endorsed by the governments concerned'.[140] For this reason, supporting the UN in the development of standards was an important part of AI because 'once endorsed such standards provide a permanent basis for comparison in letters from AI groups, national sections, campaign leaflets, mission reports, and high level missions'.[141] Picken's subsequent conclusion that reference to agreed 'universal or regional standards' protected AI from accusations of bias should thus be read in an informational sense: universal standards provided a legitimising function that prevented the organisation's signals from being confused as political noise.

A similar logic was also at work in the formation of Helsinki Watch. For HW, the signing of the Helsinki Final Act by the US, USSR and many European countries of both socialist and capitalist persuasion in 1975 provided an informational foundation for its work following its formation in 1979. While the Helsinki conferences were really an attempt to cool an already cold war into a period of détente, they are now more famous for the human rights obligations to which the Final Act bound its signatories.[142] Echoing Amnesty's own turn to law, the human rights provisions within the Final Act helpfully underpinned HW's premise that human rights represented universal ethical norms, even if the Act was not itself legally binding. This principle clearly underpins the organisation's 1982 decision to make and distribute a facsimile copy of a 1975 edition of *Pravda* that contained the entire text of the Helsinki Final Act. The copy of *Pravda* was circulated within the USSR and beyond to emphasise the Soviet regime's recognition of universal norms 'that it has subsequently violated over and over again'.[143] Such practices demonstrate a foundational commitment to informational law that, well after the fall of communism, has continued to bolster the 'presumption of shared values' that Peter Slezkine argues has become key to Human Rights Watch's image of impartiality.[144]

It is impossible to know whether, as Amnesty has sometimes claimed, 'human rights would exist without the Universal Declaration'.[145] But the Final Act and the ratification of the International Covenants portended a massive growth of recognised international legal standards from the 1970s onwards, which has helpfully reinforced the 'institutional framework' or 'metalanguage' that, recalling Day's work, structures communication and, concomitantly, demarcates between signal and noise. On the one hand, law could increasingly specify which observed behaviours and events should be made intelligible as 'violations' and thus delineated those facts that are of concern to the network. At the same time, law also defined the distinction between what should be regarded by governments as information and those utterances which transgressed law's formally recognised codes and should thus be dismissed as potentially dangerous noise. A positivistic epistemology and positive law thus combined to delineate the legitimate site of contemporary human rights interventions, constructing the movement as an informational project that dispels forms of political contestation that stray beyond unambiguous limits.

Informational Logic

For human rights organisations, the issue of politics (as noise) has often been understood 'immanently' as a kind of bias, or a preference for or against certain governments. As we have already glimpsed, the potential for accusations of bias by the governments AI addressed was a problem frequently discussed within the organisation. Rafts of policies were developed to zealously guard its perceived impartiality. AI's meticulous cross-checking of facts, efforts to balance its informational work across different geographical regions and ideological lines, and creation of an internal 'borderline committee' to ensure the impartiality of its approach were all designed to combat the immanent threat of political bias and the subsequent distortion of its information.[146]

But there is also another sense of politics inhabiting the epistemic closures inherent in human rights information which deserves more focus here. The exclusionary embrace of 'auto-effective' facts that reifies human rights information qua information also disbars the critical lines of reasoning that subject norms, values and ends to interrogation or attempt to uncover and overturn the power relations and ideological frames that structure the social. Forms of systematic thinking, critical theorising and speculative worldmaking that are central to, for example, the Marxist, anticolonial and Third Worldist movements which defined earlier traditions of activism are excluded from the informational project of human rights. Insofar as these forms of knowledge production depart from positivistic concerns with physically observable behaviour and utilise methods of interpretive analysis that both question social formations and imagine them otherwise, they are treated with suspicion and dismissed as politically dangerous noise.[147]

The position taken by the French humanitarians which rose to prominence in the late 1970s crystallises these epistemological and political exclusions and their place in the contemporary movement. Influenced by the Nouveaux Philosophes and their acerbic denunciation of Marxism, the activists clustered around Médecins Sans Frontières explicitly defined their work as a turn to '"human realities"'.[148] 'Reality', as Whyte has demonstrated, was directly opposed to 'structural economic analyses', which were simply dismissed as 'utopian messianic ideologies'.[149] This opposition between the supposed 'real' of human suffering and forms of critical and systemic thought articulates something important about the epistemic commitments that shape the politics of the contemporary human rights movement. The dismissal of 'messianic' thought demarcates the exclusionary borders of human rights information and, concomitantly, an epistemological resistance to the interpretive and theoretical modes of knowing that are required for radical politics which is built right into the foundations of the contemporary movement.

The alignment(s) between the contemporary movement and cybernetic capitalism thus resides in an informational logic that is bound up with their shared conceptualisation of the world in terms of informational dynamics and systems. In a world composed of networks, information has become a form of 'containment', as Terranova might suggest, that upholds safe limits on critique, ensuring that the kinds of claims made in the name of human rights do not transgress the ideological and discursive boundaries of late capital.[150] Consequently, while Turchin never predicted the demise of socialism, his desire for a depoliticised practice of human rights as a central aspect of a cybernetic society has seemingly come to fruition. Through the very cybernetic thinking that shaped Turchin's own politics, the now hegemonic project of human rights has been 'contained', depoliticised so that it functions neatly within the limited imaginaries of a social world shaped by cybernetic capitalism. The challenge that I take up in the next chapters is to follow the informational logic of human rights as it has been made and remade, reproduced and transformed, in specific material practices that have been crucial in the development of the human rights movement. As these cases gradually take us to the present, it will be possible to clarify how the informational logic of human rights operates today.

Notes

1. Valentin Turchin, *The Inertia of Fear* (New York: Columbia University Press, 1981).
2. Turchin, *The Inertia of Fear*, 133.
3. Turchin, *The Inertia of Fear*, 133.
4. Turchin, *The Inertia of Fear*, 124.
5. Turchin, *The Inertia of Fear*, 147.
6. For example, the key argument of Hayek and his followers was that market organisation was a superior cybernetic device for organising society than the state. As Seb Franklin suggests, this kind of argument is also common for progenitors of the kinds of horizontal and networked forms of management and corporate organisation that have proliferated under neoliberalism. Stafford Beer, for instance, saw the crisis of the 1970s as a cybernetic rather than socio-economic and political problem, one that could be resolved by properly engaging with cybernetic onto-epistemologies. See Friedrich Hayek, 'The Use of Knowledge in Society', *The American Economic Review* 35, no. 4 (1945): 519–30; Seb Franklin, 'Repetition; Reticulum; Remainder', *Novel* 50, no. 2 (2017): 157–75; Stafford Beer, *Platform for Change* (Chichester: John Wiley & Sons, 1975).
7. Turchin, *The Inertia of Fear*, 283.
8. Samuel Moyn, *The Last Utopia: Human Rights in History* (Cambridge, MA and London: Harvard University Press, 2010), 121. See also Robert Horvath, '"The Solzhenitsyn Effect": East European Dissidents and the Demise of the Revolutionary Privilege', *Human Rights Quarterly* 29, no. 4 (2007): 879–907.
9. On the one hand, Dardot and Laval have shown that understanding not only neoliberal thought but the various strands within it and their impact on our contemporary world requires an investigation of early neoliberal ideas as they emerged around the middle of the twentieth century. At the same time, Whyte has shown that an understanding of how human rights have been neoliberalised rests on understanding the different ways neoliberal thinkers have conceptualised human rights

since the post-war period. See Pierre Dardot and Christian Laval, *The New Way of the World: On Neoliberal Society* (London and New York: Verso, 2013); Jessica Whyte, *The Morals of the Market: Human Rights and the Rise of Neoliberalism* (London and New York: Verso, 2019).

10. See, for example, Nick Dyer-Witheford, *Cyber-Marx: Cycles and Circuits of Struggle in High-Technology Capitalism* (Chicago: Illinois University Press, 1999); Philip Mirowski, *Machine Dreams: Economics Becomes a Cyborg Science* (Cambridge and New York: Cambridge University Press, 2002).

11. Dyer-Witheford, *Cyber-Marx*, 3. See also Charles Babbage, *On the Economy of Machinery and Manufactures* (Cambridge: Cambridge University Press, 2010).

12. Dyer-Witheford, *Cyber-Marx*, 3.

13. For more on the profound social impact of cybernetics, see Orit Halpern, *Beautiful Data: A History of Vision and Reason since 1945* (Durham, NC and London: Duke University Press, 2014); John Beck and Ryan Bishop, 'Introduction: The Long Cold War', in *Cold War Legacies: Systems, Theory, Aesthetics*, ed. John Beck and Ryan Bishop (Edinburgh: Edinburgh University Press, 2016), 4–5.

14. Norbert Wiener, *Cybernetics: Or, Control and Communication in the Animal and Machine* (Cambridge, MA: MIT Press, 1948), 40.

15. Wiener, *Cybernetics*, 42.

16. Seb Franklin, *Control: Digitality as Cultural Logic* (Cambridge, MA: MIT Press, 2015), 43.

17. Nick Dyer-Witheford, *Cyber-Proletariat: Global Labour in the Digital Vortex* (London: Pluto Press, 2015), 43.

18. In fact, it is well known that the labour undermining capacities of cybernetics deeply troubled Wiener's own humanistic principles. It is a dystopian potential that Wiener directly addressed in the opening chapters of *Cybernetics*. Dyer-Witheford gives a fuller account of Wiener's fears in *Cyber-Proletariat*, 39–41.

19. John Johnston, *The Allure of Machinic Life: Cybernetics, Artificial Life, and the New AI* (Cambridge, MA: MIT Press, 2008), 6–7.

20. For an account of the Macy Conferences and how they enabled cybernetic ideas to move into new disciplines, see N. Katherine Hayles, *How We Became Posthuman: Virtual Bodies in Cybernetics, Literature, and Informatics* (London and Chicago: Chicago University Press, 1999).

21. Peter Galison, 'War against the Center', *Grey Room* 4, no. 4 (2001): 29.

22. See N. Katherine Hayles, *My Mother Was a Computer* (Chicago: University of Chicago Press, 2005).

23. It is a strange and notable paradox that cybernetic ideas have had such an extensive influence even as the term itself became increasingly unfashionable. Though the confines of space do not allow a discussion of this issue, Ronald Kline has provided an insightful overview of this paradox. See Ronald Kline, *The Cybernetics Moment: Or Why We Call Our Age the Information Age* (Baltimore, MD: Johns Hopkins University Press, 2015). See also Beck and Bishop, 'Introduction: The Long Cold War'.

24. Mirowski, *Machine Dreams*, 233–41.
25. Hayek, 'The Use of Knowledge in Society'.
26. Friedrich Hayek, 'The Sensory Order after 25 Years', in *Cognition and Symbolic Process* (Hillsdale, NJ: Erlbaum, 1982), 326.
27. Mirowski, *Machine Dreams*, 238.
28. Mirowski, *Machine Dreams*, 236.
29. Mirowski, *Machine Dreams*, 235.
30. Maxime Ouellet, 'Cybernetic Capitalism and the Global Information Society: From the Global Panopticon to a "Brand" New World', in *Cultural Political Economy*, ed. Jacqueline Best and Matthew Paterson (London: Routledge, 2010), 177–96; Quinn Slobodian, *Globalists: The End of Empire and the Birth of Neoliberalism* (Cambridge, MA and London: Harvard University Press, 2018), 218–62.
31. Philip Mirowski, 'Defining Neoliberalism', in *The Road from Mont Pèlerin: The Making of the Neoliberal Thought Collective*, ed. Philip Mirowski and Dieter Plehwe (Cambridge, MA and London: Harvard University Press, 2009), 417–56; William Davies, 'The New Neoliberalism', *New Left Review* 101 (September–October 2016): 121–34.
32. Franklin, *Control*, xxi–xxii.
33. Slobodian, *Globalists*, 218–62.
34. John Roberts and Jonathan Joseph, 'Beyond Flows, Fluids and Networks: Social Theory and the Fetishism of the Global Informational Economy', *New Political Economy* 20, no. 1 (2015): 12–13.
35. Luc Boltanski and Eve Chiapello, *The New Spirit of Capitalism* (London and New York: Verso, 2005).
36. Franklin, *Control*, 80.
37. Franklin, *Control*, 80.
38. McKenzie Wark, *Capital Is Dead: Is This Something Worse?* (London and New York: Verso, 2019), 80.
39. Tiqqun, *The Cybernetic Hypothesis* (Los Angeles, CA: Semiotext(e), 2020); Dyer-Witheford, *Cyber-Proletariat*.
40. One of the most interesting findings of Noble's detailed and important work was that the automation systems adopted by industry were not necessarily the most efficient but did provide opportunities to undermine labour. As Noble details, the Numeric Control (N/C) system was a much more complex affair than a rival programming technique, the Record Playback (R/P) system, but the former was taken up because it could be programmed by managers and thus wrested control of the factory floor from labour and put it in the hands of capital. See David F. Noble, *Forces of Production: A Social History of Automation* (New York: Alfred A. Knopf, 1984).
41. Dyer-Witheford, *Cyber-Proletariat*, 49.
42. Noble, *Forces of Production*, 325–32.
43. Noble, *Forces of Production*, 328.
44. Dyer-Witheford, *Cyber-Proletariat*, 84.
45. For a good outline of how containerisation has contributed to the globalisation of production, see Marc Levinson, *The Box: How the*

Shipping Container Made the World Smaller and the World Economy Bigger (Princeton, NJ: Princeton University Press, 2006). See also Edna Bonacich and Jake Wilson, *Getting the Goods: Ports, Labor, and the Logistics Revolution* (Ithaca, NY: Cornell University Press, 2008); Jasper Bernes, 'Logistics, Counterlogistics and the Communist Project', *Endnotes* 3 (2013): 172–201.

46. This asymmetry is best described by Maurizio Lazzarato in his work on debt. See Maurizio Lazzarato, *The Making of the Indebted Man: An Essay on the Neoliberal Condition* (Los Angeles, CA: Semiotext(e), 2012); Maurizio Lazzarato, *Governing by Debt* (South Pasadena, CA: Semiotext(e); Cambridge, MA: MIT Press, 2015).

47. Michel Feher, *Rated Agency: Investee Politics in a Speculative Age* (New York: Zone Books, 2018).

48. As Franklin suggests, each of these technologies is deeply indebted to advances that emerged out of cybernetics. See Franklin, *Control*, 70.

49. Michael Castelle, 'Relational and Non-Relational Models in the Entextualization of Bureaucracy', *Computational Culture* 3 (2013): 23–4. For more on the intimate relationship between finance and information technologies, see also Dyer-Witheford, *Cyber-Proletariat*.

50. Dyer-Witheford, *Cyber-Proletariat*, 84.

51. Wark, *Capital Is Dead*, 78.

52. Maurizio Lazzarato, 'Immaterial Labour', in *Radical Thought in Italy: A Potential Politics*, ed. Michael Hardt and Paolo Virno (Minneapolis and London: University of Minnesota Press, 2006), 133.

53. Lazzarato, 'Immaterial Labour', 135.

54. Tiziana Terranova, 'Free Labor: Producing Culture for the Digital Economy', *Social Text* 18, no. 2 (2000): 33–58.

55. David Harvey, *A Brief History of Neoliberalism* (Oxford: Oxford University Press, 2007), 159.

56. Tiqqun, *The Cybernetic Hypothesis*.

57. In *The Stack*, Benjamin Bratton provides another way to describe these intertwined aspects of cybernetic capitalism when he argues that 'the economic history of the second half of the twentieth century is largely unthinkable without computational infrastructures and superstructure', such that 'so much of what is referred to as neoliberalism are interlocking political-economic conditions within the armature of planetary computation'. See Benjamin Bratton, *The Stack: On Software and Sovereignty* (Cambridge, MA and London: MIT Press, 2016), 56.

58. Tiziana Terranova, *Network Culture: Politics for the Information Age* (London: Pluto Press, 2004), 7. For more on the permeation of network logic as a socio-cultural phenomenon, see Alexander R. Galloway and Eugene Thacker, *The Exploit: A Theory of Networks* (Minneapolis and London: University of Minnesota Press, 2007).

59. Ronald E. Day, *The Modern Invention of Information: Discourse, History and Power* (Carbondale: Southern Illinois University Press, 2001), 60.

60. Claude Shannon and Warren Weaver, *The Mathematical Theory of Communication* (Urbana: University of Illinois Press, 1963).

61. Shannon and Weaver, *The Mathematical Theory of Communication*, 3.
62. Hayles, *How We Became Posthuman*, 53–4.
63. Shannon and Weaver, *The Mathematical Theory of Communication*, 106.
64. Shannon and Weaver, *The Mathematical Theory of Communication*, 95–8.
65. See Wiener, *Cybernetics*; Norbert Wiener, *The Human Use of Human Beings* (London: Free Association Books, 1989); Karl Deutsch, *The Nerves of Government: Models of Political Communication and Control* (New York: The Free Press of Glencoe, 1963); Stafford Beer, 'What Has Cybernetics to Do with Operational Research?', *Journal of the Operational Research Society* 10, no. 1 (1959): 1–21.
66. Hayles, *How We Became Posthuman*.
67. Shunya Yoshimi, 'Information', *Theory, Culture & Society* 23, no. 2–3 (2006): 272.
68. Scott Lash, *Critique of Information* (London: SAGE Publications, 2002).
69. Ronald E. Day, 'The "Conduit Metaphor" and the Nature and Politics of Information Studies', *Journal of the American Society for Information Science and Technology* 51, no. 9 (2000): 805.
70. Day, 'The "Conduit Metaphor"', 808.
71. Day, 'The "Conduit Metaphor"', 810.
72. Day, 'The "Conduit Metaphor"', 810.
73. Day, *The Modern Invention of Information*, 114.
74. These kinds of arguments can be found, for example, in the Marxist critical theory of Theodor Adorno and Max Horkheimer, the postcolonial theory of Edward Said and Gayatri Chakravorty Spivak, as well as in feminist critiques of technoscience from authors such as Donna Haraway and Isabelle Stengers.
75. Donna Haraway, 'Situated Knowledges: The Science Question in Feminism and the Privilege of Partial Perspective', *Feminist Studies* 14, no. 3 (1988): 575.
76. Day, *The Modern Invention of Information*, 77.
77. Jonathan Beller, *The Message Is Murder: Substrates of Computational Capital* (London: Pluto Press, 2017), 75.
78. See Franklin, *Control*.
79. Terranova, *Network Culture*, 25.
80. Yoshimi, 'Information'.
81. Patrick William Kelly, 'The 1973 Chilean Coup and the Origins of Transnational Human Rights Activism', *Journal of Global History* 8, no. 1 (2013): 167.
82. Terranova, *Network Culture*, 15.
83. For some interesting histories of Amnesty International, see Tom Buchanan, '"The Truth Will Set You Free": The Making of Amnesty International', *Journal of Contemporary History* 37, no. 4 (2002): 575–97; Stephen Hopgood, *Keepers of the Flame* (Ithaca, NY: Cornell University Press, 2006).
84. On the reconceptualisation of the organisation's structure, see 'Report of the Crash Committee (CCC) appointed to advise on AI Development

and Planning', Agenda item no. 14, IEC meeting, July 1977. Folder 118, Amnesty International. International Secretariat Archive. International Institute of Social History, Amsterdam.

85. For example, arguments for decentralisation were often justified in terms of giving more responsibility to national sections as a means of enabling a more 'egalitarian' information flow and making it possible to 'rechannel information back to source countries'. See 'Report on the Seminar on Information Handling within the AI Movement, 11–12 March', 21 April 1978, DOC 01/02/78. Microfilm 118, Amnesty International. International Secretariat Archive. International Institute of Social History, Amsterdam, 2–3.

86. Odile Garros, 'Proposal to establish a Documentation Centre to handle, process, and retrieve information needed for the work of Amnesty International', Agenda Item 8, IEC Meeting, 11–13 April 1975, 1. Folder 91, Amnesty International. International Secretariat Archive. International Institute of Social History, Amsterdam.

87. Odile Garros, 'Proposal to establish a Documentation Centre', 1–2.

88. Odile Garros, 'Proposal to establish a Documentation Centre', 6.

89. 'Seminar on Information Handling within the AI movement', letter from International Secretariat to the National Sections, 15 December 1977, DOC 01/03/77. Microfilm 116, Amnesty International. International Secretariat Archive. International Institute of Social History, Amsterdam.

90. 'AI Seminar on Information Handling', DOC 15/01/78. Folder 132, Amnesty International. International Secretariat Archive. International Institute of Social History, Amsterdam; 'Introductory Note on AI Information', IEC Subcommittee on Information Techniques, 19–20 January 1979, ACT 81/IEC 04/79. Folder 142, Amnesty International. International Secretariat Archive. International Institute of Social History, Amsterdam. See also Amnesty International, *Amnesty International Annual Report 1978*, POL 10/0001/1978 (London: Amnesty International, 1978), 7, <https://www.amnesty.org/download/Documents/POL100011978ENGLISH.PDF> (last accessed 24 February 2022).

91. 'Report on the Seminar on Information Handling within the AI Movement, 11–12 March', 21 April 1978, DOC 01/02/78. Microfilm 118, Amnesty International. International Secretariat Archive. International Institute of Social History, Amsterdam.

92. 'Report of the Crash Committee (CCC)', 19.

93. Amnesty International, 'The "Disappeared" of Argentina: List of Cases Reported to Amnesty International November 1974–December 1979' (London: Amnesty International, 1980), AMR 13/06/80. See also the evaluation of the Argentina computer project by Tricia Feeney, head of AI's Latin America Research. While she noted a number of problems, Friederike Knabe argued that computerisation 'has already been of insatiable value to my department'. See Tricia Feeney and Friederike Knabe, 'A Brief Assessment of the Argentina Computer Project', AMR 13/IEC/01/79. Folder 149, Amnesty International. International Secretariat Archive. International Institute of Social History, Amsterdam.

94. Amnesty International, *Information Technology: A Manual for Sections* (London: Amnesty International, 1985), DOC 02/01/85. Folder 478, Amnesty International. International Secretariat Archive. International Institute of Social History, Amsterdam.

95. 'Report of the Crash Committee (CCC)', 8.

96. The guidelines for responsible handling of information were first developed by Martin Ennals, Secretary General of Amnesty International, in 1978. The guidelines would provide new categories for different kinds of information and their level of sensitivity, as well as policy guidelines on the storage of documents. See 'IEC and Security/Responsible Handling of Information', report from Martin Ennals to IEC members and IS Staff, 17 May 1978. Folder 132, Amnesty International. International Secretariat Archive. International Institute of Social History, Amsterdam. Training for staff began in 1978 but an extensive training plan for members became part of the plans set out for the organisation in 1980–2. Moreover, the publication of a large, comprehensive *Amnesty International Handbook* for groups for the first time in 1977 was a result of discussions on the need for further training and professionalisation of its work. See 'Draft plan 1980–82', agenda item 21(a), IEC meeting, 5–8 April 1979. Folder 143, Amnesty International. International Secretariat Archive. International Institute of Social History, Amsterdam; Amnesty International, *Amnesty International Handbook*, ORG 20/001/1977 (London: Amnesty International, 1977), <https://www.amnesty.org/en/documents/ORG20/001/1977/en/> (last accessed 24 February 2022).

97. Kenneth Cmiel, 'The Emergence of Human Rights Politics in the United States', *Journal of American History* 86, no. 3 (1999): 1231–50; Peter Slezkine, 'From Helsinki to Human Rights Watch: How an American Cold War Monitoring Group Became an International Human Rights Institution', *Humanity: An International Journal of Human Rights, Humanitarianism, and Development* 5, no. 3 (2010): 345–70.

98. 'Report of the Crash Committee (CCC)', 19.

99. Lazzarato, 'Immaterial Labour', 135.

100. 'Seminar on Information Handling within AI', Agenda item no. 56a, IEC meeting, 25–7 November 2020. Folder 123, Amnesty International. International Secretariat Archive. International Institute of Social History, Amsterdam.

101. As the report on the seminar clarifies, the agenda was eventually made by its participants and centred on more practical issues such as 'standardisation', 'decentralisation' and the 'responsible handling of information', but such questions do revolve around the need to construct an AI information system. See 'Report on the Seminar on Information Handling within the AI Movement, 11–12 March', 21 April 1978, DOC 01/02/78. Microfilm 118, Amnesty International. International Secretariat Archive. International Institute of Social History, Amsterdam.

102. See Alexander R. Galloway, 'Are Some Things Unrepresentable?', in *The Interface Effect* (Cambridge: Polity Press, 2012), 78–100;

Ulises Ali Mejias, *Off the Network: Disrupting the Digital World* (Minneapolis and London: University of Minnesota Press, 2013); Franklin, *Control*, 89–100.

103. For a sense of how cybernetic diagrams owe a genealogical debt to earlier practices, see David Mindall's work on 'proto-cybernetic' practices that emerged in the earlier part of the twentieth century. See David Mindall, *Between Human and Machine: Feedback, Control and Computing before Cybernetics* (Baltimore, MD: Johns Hopkins University Press, 2002).

104. Franklin, *Control*, 94, 97.

105. 'AI Seminar on Information Handling – Working Paper', Seminar on Information Handling, 11–12 March 1978, Amnesty International London. Microfilm 118, Amnesty International. International Secretariat Archive. International Institute of Social History, Amsterdam.

106. Policy recommendations that emerged from the 1978 information handling seminar argued that the strengthening of national sections and the deconcentration of functions from the IS into national sections would be fundamental 'to the future AI information system'. See 'Report on the Seminar on Information Handling within the AI Movement, 11–12 March', 21 April 1978, DOC 01/02/78. Microfilm 118, Amnesty International. International Secretariat Archive. International Institute of Social History, Amsterdam.

107. See Amnesty International, 'Structure and People', <https://www.amnesty.org/en/about-us/how-were-run/structure-and-people/> (last accessed 24 February 2022).

108. 'Proposal for a Press and Communications Strategy', ORG 03/01/77, Amnesty International, London. Microfilm 118, Amnesty International. International Secretariat Archive. International Institute of Social History, Amsterdam. Confirmation that the parameters set out in the paper were endorsed as policy is given in a paper on the 'Policy and Structure of the Press & Communications Department', presented at the International Executive Committee meeting, November 1977. See 'Policy and Structure of the Press & Communications Department', agenda item 50 and 51, IEC meeting, 25–7 November 1977, London. Folder 124, Amnesty International. International Secretariat Archive. International Institute of Social History, Amsterdam.

109. 'Quadrennial Report, 1973–1977, Submitted by Amnesty International, a Non-Governmental Organisation in Consultative Status with the Economic and Social Council'. E/C.2/H.49/add.101, UN Economic and Social Council, 2 December 1977. Microfilm 118, Amnesty International. International Secretariat Archive. International Institute of Social History, Amsterdam.

110. 'Warren Christopher proposes International H.R. CLEARINGHOUSE', *Human Rights Internet Newsletter* 3, no. 5–6 (March 1978): 13. CSD ZK 55939, Amnesty International. International Secretariat Archive. International Institute of Social History, Amsterdam.

111. 'HURIDOCS: Project to Consider the Establishment of a Human Rights Documentation Service', *Human Rights Internet Newsletter 5*, no. 6 & 7 (April 1980): 1, 10. CSD ZK 55939, International Institute of Social History, Amsterdam.
112. 'HURIDOCS: Project to Consider the Establishment', 1.
113. As the Ford Foundation, which initially funded the working group, reported, 'during the first grant period [. . .] the initial concept for an International Human Rights Information and Documentation Service (HURIDOCS) evolved from the idea of a single center for the collection, compilation and dissemination of data to a decentralized network of international facilities with a system of regional link-ages'. See Stephen Marks, 'Human Rights Internet: Human Rights Information and Documentation Service (HURIDOCS) – Closeout Evaluation'. Ford Foundation Interoffice Memorandum, 20 December 1984. Microfilm 4224, Ford Foundation Grant Files, Rockefeller Archive Center, Sleepy Hollow, New York.
114. Asbjørn Eide, 'Technical Considerations regarding the Proposed Human Rights Documentation Service', presented by Martin Ennals to Amnesty International's IEC Meeting, 2 December 1979. Folder 155, Amnesty International. International Secretariat Archive. International Institute of Social History, Amsterdam.
115. Eide, 'Technical Considerations'.
116. Bjørn Stormorken, 'Human Rights Information Handling: Choice of Technological Levels', in *A Guide to Establishing a Human Rights Documentation Centre: Report of a UNESCO-UNU International Training Seminar on the Handling of Documentation and Information on Human Rights*, ed. Laurie S. Wiseberg (Ottawa: Human Rights Internet, 1988), 24. BRO 2477/10 fol., International Institute of Social History, Amsterdam.
117. For examples of this triumphalism, see Margaret E. Keck and Kathryn Sikkink, *Activists beyond Borders: Advocacy Networks in International Politics* (Ithaca, NY: Cornell University Press, 1998); James Ron, Howard Ramos and Kathleen Rodgers, 'Transnational Information Politics: NGO Human Rights Reporting, 1986–2000', *International Studies Quarterly* 49, no. 3 (2005): 557–88. The degree to which HURIDOCS prefigured a form of networked organisation central to the human rights movement can be seen in its similarity to later human rights networks such as the International Office of Human Rights Action on Colombia, which formed in the late 1990s to coordinate a network of Colombian and European NGOs. Like HURIDOCS, as Winifred Tate suggests, 'the Coordination was specifically designed to prevent the network from becoming another NGO; instead, the technical secretary was restricted to organizing events and ensuring information flow. [. . .] According to activists involved in the founding of the Coordination, the initiative was generated as a response to general concern about redundant work (including receiving multiple urgent actions from different organizations on the same case), the lack of follow-up, and insufficient or unclear

information. [. . .] "The main purpose of the office was to improve the quality and fluidity of information," one of the office's founders told me. "People say that the information flow doesn't work because of emergencies and the stress that everyone works under, but that is not all true; it's also because people don't understand the value of information, how to produce information."' See Winifred Tate, *Counting the Dead: The Culture and Politics of Human Rights Activism in Colombia* (Berkeley: University of California Press, 2007), 120–1.

118. Terranova, *Network Culture*, 14–15.
119. Gregory Bateson, *Steps to an Ecology of Mind: Collected Essays in Anthropology, Psychiatry, Evolution, and Epistemology* (Chicago: University of Chicago Press, 1972).
120. Terranova, *Network Culture*, 15.
121. Terranova, *Network Culture*, 15.
122. Thomas Hammarberg, 'Preface', in *Amnesty International Report 1978*, 2.
123. Whyte, *The Morals of the Market*, 158–9.
124. Amnesty International, *Handbook*, 29.
125. The collection of impartial facts as key to Amnesty's work is relayed in Hammarberg's prefaces to the 1977 and 1978 annual reports. For more on human rights epistemology today, see Claire Moon, 'What One Sees and How One Files Seeing: Human Rights Reporting, Representation and Action', *Sociology* 46, no. 5 (2012): 876–90; Joel R. Pruce and Alexandra Cosima Budabin, 'Beyond Naming and Shaming: New Modalities of Information Politics in Human Rights', *Journal of Human Rights* 15, no. 3 (2016): 408–25.
126. Human Rights Watch, *About Us* (2020) <https://www.hrw.org/about/about-us> (last accessed 24 February 2022).
127. 'Amnesty International: The Impartial Defence of Human Rights', presented at the International Executive Committee meeting, 25–7 November 1977, London. Folder 125, Amnesty International. International Secretariat Archive. International Institute of Social History, Amsterdam. See also Hammarberg, 'Preface', 2.
128. David Heaps, 'Brief Notes on Conference, Ford Foundation, September 25, 1978', 28 September 1978. Microfilm 4224, Ford Foundation Archives. Rockefeller Archive Center, Sleepy Hollow, New York.
129. Moon, 'What One Sees', 879. Similar ideas have also been developed in Richard Ashby Wilson, 'Representing Human Rights Violations: Social Contexts and Subjectivities', in *Human Rights, Culture and Context: Anthropological Perspectives*, ed. Richard A. Wilson (London: Pluto Press, 1996), 134–60; Andrew Herscher, 'Surveillant Witnessing: Satellite Imagery and the Visual Politics of Human Rights', *Public Culture* 26, no. 3 (2014): 469–500.
130. Mary Poovey, *A History of the Modern Fact* (Chicago: University of Chicago Press, 1998), xii. See also Elizabeth Adams St. Pierre, 'The Appearance of Data', *Cultural Studies – Critical Methodologies* 13, no. 4 (2013): 223–7.

131. Wiener, *The Human Use of Human Beings*, 105, 110.
132. Wiener, *The Human Use of Human Beings*, 107, 109.
133. Mireille Hildebrandt, 'Law as Information in the Era of Data-Driven Agency', *Modern Law Review* 79, no. 1 (2016): 1–30.
134. Turchin, *The Inertia of Fear*, 177.
135. Paul O'Connell, 'Marxism and Public Law', *SSRN*, 17 January 2021, 355–7, doi.org/10.2139/ssrn.3732346; Rosemary Hunter, 'Contesting the Dominant Paradigm: Feminist Critiques of Liberal Legalism', in *The Ashgate Research Companion to Feminist Legal Theory*, ed. Margaret Davies and Vanessa Munro (London and New York: Routledge, 2016), 25–42.
136. Kurt Waldheim, Remarks on the 25th Anniversary of the Universal Declaration of Human Rights (speech, General Assembly, 28th Session, 2195th Plenary Meeting, New York, 10 December 1973), <https://media.un.org/en/asset/k1g/k1g22grjjq> (last accessed 27 February 2022).
137. In regard to the political and ideological contestation of human rights in the writing of the UN Declaration, see Jessica Whyte, 'The Fortunes of Natural Man: Robinson Crusoe, Political Economy, and the Universal Declaration of Human Rights', *Humanity: An International Journal of Human Rights, Humanitarianism, and Development* 5, no. 3 (2014): 301–21. In regard to the political contestation over the meaning of rights, particularly the NIEO's contestation of the right to self-determination, see Adom Getachew, *Worldmaking after Empire: The Rise and Fall of Self-Determination* (Princeton, NJ: Princeton University Press, 2019); Bradley R. Simpson, 'Self-Determination, Human Rights, and the End of Empire in the 1970s', *Humanity: An International Journal of Human Rights, Humanitarianism, and Development* 4, no. 2 (2013): 239–60.
138. Day, *The Modern Invention of Information*, 77.
139. 'Amnesty International: The Impartial Defence of Human Rights'.
140. Margo Picken, 'Strategy, Structure and Planning of AI work at the UN', presented at the International Executive Committee, London, 2–4 June 1978. Folder 132, Amnesty International. International Secretariat Archive. International Institute of Social History, Amsterdam.
141. Picken, 'Strategy, Structure and Planning'.
142. In some accounts, the rights commitments embedded in the Helsinki Final Act are given a large and causal role in the demise of communism. See, for example, Daniel C. Thomas, *The Helsinki Effect: International Norms, Human Rights, and the Demise of Communism* (Princeton, NJ: Princeton University Press, 2001).
143. Helsinki Watch, *Annual Report 1982*, New York, 1982. Box IX I Folder 6, Human Rights Watch Archives, Columbia University Rare Book and Manuscript Library, New York.
144. Slezkine, 'From Helsinki to Human Rights Watch', 356.
145. Picken, 'Strategy, Structure and Planning'.

146. 'Amnesty International: The Impartial Defence of Human Rights'.
147. Day, 'The "Conduit Metaphor"', 808.
148. Whyte, *The Morals of the Market*, 200–3.
149. Whyte, *The Morals of the Market*, 202.
150. Terranova, *Network Culture*, 24.

Chapter 2

Seeing Violations as Events: Technologies of Capture and Cutting

> Processes of capture, definition, optimization and filtering [. . .] necessarily implement a distinction between those aspects of the world that are intended and included within a given digital representation and those that are excluded or filtered out.
>
> – Seb Franklin, *Control*

'Information is an important prerequisite for human rights action', one-time General Secretary of Amnesty International Martin Ennals argued at a UNESCO meeting of experts in teaching human rights in 1983, a year after becoming the founding president of HURIDOCS. 'We have to address, therefore, the question of how to ensure that relevant information can be identified by those who need it.'[1] The success of human rights, Ennals concluded, hinged on the development of new information infrastructures 'to standardise and regularise the free flow of information about human rights, their existence, [. . .] their protection and their violation'.[2] The construction of 'agreed terminology, classification and information retrieval techniques' was seen as a vital task.[3] Insofar as HURIDOCS formed as an international NGO network precisely to develop information systems for the still nascent human rights movement, Ennals's speech might be read as a manifesto for the organisation. His argument sets out HURIDOCS' future work as a vital component of an informational project that relied upon the accurate documenting and communication of human rights violations.

One decade later, the seeds of the project outlined by Ennals had blossomed into ambitious, concrete results. Though sadly Ennals died just as its contents were being finalised, the publication in 1993 of the Events Standard Formats – a tool for documenting human rights violations by HURIDOCS – was a major achievement for an organisation guided by the desire to systemise human rights information.[4]

The document outlined a set of informational standards which, HURI-DOCS argued, could facilitate efficient recording and communication of 'information about [. . .] those types of human rights violations which have become world-wide phenomena', namely violations of civil and political rights such as 'torture, arrests, detention; deaths and killings; displacements and destruction of property; disappearances; as well as deportation, external exile and banishments'.[5]

At its heart, the Events Standard Formats provided a standardised, yet flexible, data model for accurately recording instances of human rights abuse that could be used by a range of organisations to scaffold their informational practices, filing systems and databases. This Events Method or Model, so called because it maps violations as discrete 'events', was designed to support manual filing systems and, embracing the new technologies of the information age, could also be implemented on computerised systems. The sense of technological momentum attached to the Formats is clearly visible in its relationship to HURIDOCS' own in-house specialised database software for recording violations, 'Evsys', which was released around the same time and was structured around the Events Model. In its various iterations, the Events Model has continued to provide the structure for much of the specialist database software released by HURIDOCS up until today.

If, as we have already seen, the human rights movement that emerged in the 1970s largely crystallised around new informational practices of recording and circulating facts about human rights violations, then the Events Standard Formats (and Evsys) provided a critical step towards what Ennals envisaged as the 'free flow of information about human rights'.[6] The modelling tools elaborated in the Formats were valuable insofar as they delivered an infrastructure capable of identifying, defining and linking together the key informational elements required to have accurate information about violations but that could also be adapted to fit the particular needs of any given organisation. Consequently, both the Formats and Evsys were promoted as the benchmark for effectively monitoring violations of civil and political rights. It has largely been for this purpose that the Events Model has been deployed (though it was later argued that it could be utilised, albeit in a limited way, to document economic, social and cultural (ESC) rights violations, an issue that I return to in the next chapter on the development of indicators for socio-economic rights).

The Events Standard Formats is an interesting and important object of study inasmuch as it outlines a standardised way for NGOs and activists to 'see' human rights abuses across the diverse contexts of their happening. The concept of seeing that I invoke here is deployed with a specific tenor in mind. Drawing on Ian Hacking's account of seeing atoms with an electronic microscope, Karen Barad has argued that seeing 'is not a matter of simply looking – of passively gazing on something as a spectator – but an achievement that requires a complex set of practices to accomplish'.[7] I therefore suggest that the development of the Events Model and the mode of seeing violations that it makes available should be understood as an accomplishment forged through a meshing of socio-technical practices. I take it as axiomatic that the 'images' of violations seen through the Events Model 'are not snapshots of what awaits us but rather condensations or traces of multiple practices of engagement'.[8]

The form of 'seeing' materialised in the Events Model is particularly crucial not simply because it represents a set of standards for reporting violations but also because, in both its development and subsequent use, the Formats crystallise a consensus regarding how abuses should be recorded. On the one hand, the design of the Events Standard Formats drew from existing practices developed by human rights NGOs as well as several UN agencies, notably UNESCO and the High Commissioner for Refugees (UNHCR). The Events Model thus reflected a standardisation of human rights information that was both based on and intended to further develop existing best practices.[9] On the other hand, the Events Model has been widely implemented and shown a remarkable stability and longevity in its use. The various iterations and computerised implementations of the Events Model, many of which will be outlined within this chapter, have been used to record violations in a multitude of contexts.[10]

In this respect, though the Formats have by no means been universally adopted by the human rights community, they nevertheless represent and bring together the combined efforts of many organisations to develop appropriate methods for recording information about rights violations. Mediating between the needs for flexibility and standardisation, the Events Model is thus somewhat akin to what sociologists of infrastructure call 'boundary objects'. Boundary objects, as Susan Leigh Star argues, are infrastructural elements that move across and facilitate knowledge production and communication between different communities.[11] To do so, boundary objects are more 'weakly structured' at the abstract level and maintain a 'common identity' even as they cut across organisational boundaries but become more 'strongly structured' as they are mobilised within, and adapted to, particular institutional sites and local practices.[12] Imbued with this same quality of straddling both the abstract and the particular, the Events Model represents a method for seeing human rights that distils the key needs and dilemmas shared by the movement as an informational project. The model is thus a paradigmatic example of the informational practices that have defined much of the human rights movement since its rise to prominence in the 1970s.

This chapter analyses the Model developed within the Events Standard Formats as a socio-technical device that provides a crucial way of seeing violations as information. Having first outlined both the organisational processes and dilemmas that animated the development of the Events Standard Formats, the chapter centres on a close examination of the Events Model as a crucial part of the information infrastructures through which the informational logic of human rights has materialised in practice. Drawing from a range of theoretical tools borrowed from software studies, STS and digital sociology, this chapter reads the Events Model as a practice of 'capture' that has been employed to construct depoliticised information. Capture, I suggest, employs processes of discretisation, filtration and exclusion to produce bare or 'brute' (and thus seemingly objective) facts about human rights violations, crystallising them around positivistic, empirical data. Such facts, I demonstrate, emerge only because more transformative political concerns that bring questions around violence into relation with the socio-economic structures in which they are situated are filtered out by the Model. It is in this sense, I conclude, that the Events Model provides an informatised way of seeing human rights that operates within both the imaginary and the discursive limits of cybernetic capitalism.

The Networked Imaginary of HURIDOCS

As we saw in Chapter 1, HURIDOCS began with a working group formed at a Ford Foundation conference organised in 1979. But the organisation was only later formalised at a founding assembly in Strasbourg in 1982, where it restated its commitment to the vision of a networked movement articulated by Asbjørn Eide. Loosely following the ideas set out by Eide, HURIDOCS' early ambition was to organise the movement as a 'computer-supported network' with a series of regional substructures. In laying out these plans, Ennals conceded that such proposals might seem too 'remote and futuristic' to many organisations. But he was optimistic about their realisation in the future. 'The development in information and computer technology', he argued, 'will make such an approach feasible in the near future even for organisations with modest funds.'[13] A myriad of plans for the movement's network infrastructure would eventually unfold over the course of the 1980s as HURIDOCS responded to the increasingly informatic world around it and the fast-changing informational dynamics of the human rights movement. Key members of the organisation such as Hans Thoolen and Bjørn Stormorken would flesh out and develop this networked imaginary in different directions. The possible use of information 'brokers' designed to mediate information exchanges between human rights organisations as well as plans to organise the network around a universally accessible, decentralised human rights database are just two examples of these developments.[14]

Though many of these ideas provided a utopian sketch of a networked future more than they did a concrete set of plans, and none of them were realised as HURIDOCS intended, they are nevertheless indicative of the organisation's preoccupation with the possibilities of information systems and networks. Crucially, these same concerns also drove the more tangible contributions that HURIDOCS made to the movement as network. Alongside its more conceptual work, HURIDOCS was also occupied by more practical concerns with the development of information infrastructures – tools, technologies and, above all, standards – for 'the coding and transmitting of [. . .] information through many hands'.[15] For HURIDOCS, standardisation was a matter of creating templates and codes designed to format human rights information for its effective transmission. This was seen as a vital project; standardised information was central to the creation of a 'universal communication system' for human rights, without which 'valuable information [would] be wasted, existing international machinery [would] not function, and implementation [would] not be monitored'.[16]

HURIDOCS' quest for the standardisation of information is indicative of the degree to which ideas rooted in the cybernetic sciences had passed into the organisation's own understanding of the work necessary to render the movement as network. From a cybernetic perspective, of course, processes of standardisation are inherent within any talk of information and communication systems. As I argued in the previous chapter, when cybernetic systems become the model for social and cultural processes the requirements of information control mean that the latter are increasingly shaped into standardised forms so that signals can effectively be moved between sender and receiver (and, conversely, 'noise' can be excluded). Standards that shape the form and content of information are one precondition for making information predictable in both its reception and intended effects and are thus essential to effective communication and control. It is largely for this reason that, as Benjamin Bratton contends, standards have multiplied as critical infrastructures for the planetary networks of contemporary capitalism and, insofar as they engender problems of inclusion (signal) and exclusion (noise), also become potential sites of political contestation.[17]

With this in mind, I raise the broader work to develop informational standards undertaken by HURIDOCS not only because it provides the context in which the Events Standard Formats emerged; taking a closer look at some of the organisation's earlier attempts to standardise information also foreshadows some of the socio-political issues that necessarily inhabit these standardising endeavours. HURIDOCS' first major project, designed to develop 'bibliographic control tools', a set of common standards for the 'recording and retrieving of information to facilitate sharing and exchange', is a case in point.[18] Culminating in the publication of the not so pithily titled *Standard Formats for the Recording and Exchange of Information on Human Rights* in 1985, the bibliographic standards it contained were envisaged as central to the functioning of the movement as information system. As HURIDOCS clarified in its preface to the book, 'the lack of agreed formats for the recording and retrieving of information is a major obstacle to the rapid use of information upon which activists and organisations depend for their effectiveness'.[19] This being the case, the set of standards developed in the book were 'a step in the direction of making the free flow of [. . .] information easier'.[20]

The array of standards brought together on the pages of the Recording and Exchange Formats was, and remains, truly impressive. There were standards for recording the names of persons (specified for different contexts such as Korea or Europe), human rights organisations and centres, geographical locations, and index terms for organising human rights information, to name just some. Each of these amounted to a set of controlled vocabularies, a standardised language for organising human rights documents designed to make information easy to identify and retrieve across the network. The Recording and Exchange Formats were promoted by HURIDOCS as a vital tool that supported 'documentation for action'.[21] HURIDOCS' bibliographic tools, in other words, represented more than the skeleton of a filing system; they were understood as vital to the movement because information was inseparable from human rights action.

Of course, the development of standards needs to be understood as an information control process designed to 'render the world legible', as information, and thus facilitate clear communication.[22] But it should also be remembered that any informational standard is also a method for filtering out whatever does not coincide with its numeric and linguistic constructs, and is thus de facto exclusionary. As Day argues, while a controlled vocabulary 'might be desirable for accurate information retrieval in a narrow sense', when such techniques are expanded to encompass processes and representations of the social world the control exerted over 'the limits and possibilities of meaning' is not simply a technical problem but also a social and political one.[23]

HURIDOCS' compilation of standards for geographical terms from 'internationally recognised countries', for instance, was justified in technical terms as the most effective way 'to cater for the needs of "documentation for action"'.[24] But as the invocation of 'recognition' (by whom and in what way?) implies, such lists are not constructed through a view from nowhere. Rather, HURIDOCS' incorporation of 'recognised countries' is a reminder that what passes as 'informational' is often simply that which is given within a dominant order of discourse at the expense of an opportunity for further engagement and contestation. Justification of their choices in terms of technical efficacy does not dispel the political problems that they pose; using 'Burma' instead of 'Myanmar' or 'the Occupied West Bank Territories (Palestine)' but not 'Palestine' as such points to the inescapably socio-political geography of power that undergirds what it means to receive recognition.

Formulating Events Formats: Information for Action

By the mid-1980s, several infrastructural practices and technologies had emerged within the human rights movement in order to construct and transmit information about human rights violations. Amnesty International's Prisoner Dossier and Casesheet, which provided 'a record of a human being deprived of fundamental rights', used for shuttling information from its research department to its local groups.[25] The case files developed by Vicaría de la Solidaridad (VS) in Chile and its *Sábana* – 'a kind of handmade data spreadsheet' – were utilised to register patterns of disappearances under Pinochet and develop a 'synoptic view'.[26] The violations database constructed by Comisión de Derechos Humanos de Centroamérica (CODEHUCA) compiled information about violations across several countries in Latin America.[27] Each of these describes a set of socio-technical devices and practices rooted in the particularities of the organisation that developed it. Taken together, they demonstrate the idiosyncratic nature of information systems in this period, which all tended to be deeply embedded in the practices of specific human rights groups.[28]

But while these earlier approaches to documenting civil and political rights violations arose from quite specific organisational needs, the development of HURIDOCS' Events Model signalled a very different, even oppositional, infrastructural strategy. Against the specificity and embeddedness of practice, the standardising approach to recording and documenting violations at stake in the Events Standard Formats speaks directly to the same informational imaginary that defined HURIDOCS' work from its inception in the early 1980s. Most of all, the Events Model seemed to harbour new possibilities for meaningful action by ensuring that information could be passed quickly through the movement. In his role as chairperson of HURIDOCS, Kumar Rupesinghe would later argue that as part of 'the development of new communication systems and [. . .] networks', the standards 'would have considerable consequences for the protection of human rights. There had already been some instances where quick dissemination of information to alert the international community had prevented human rights violations.'[29] What the Formats promised, then, was the possibility of a well-configured network in which information could flow in order to 'make a difference'.[30]

The origins of the Events Standard Formats lay in a 1986 conference in Rome on 'Communications, Development and Human Rights', co-organised by HURIDOCS, Interdoc, the Inter Press Service (IPS) and the Society for International Development (SID). The conference brought together individuals representing seventy organisations working in both the Global North and South and focused on a number of issues at the core of HURIDOCS' work. Reflecting HURIDOCS' *raison d'être*, the collection of activists, legal experts, information specialists and technologists gathered in Rome sought to discuss ways they might work towards 'common infrastructures for information exchange'.[31]

For HURIDOCS, the conference provided important impetus to continue and expand its work on standards, largely by bringing the Global South into sharper focus as its key area of concern. Discussions at the conference appeared to clarify that much of its future work lay 'outside of Europe', where 'the link between information and action is better understood as is the crucial effect of systematic reporting and monitoring information for action and as a basis for change'.[32] But recognition that the Global South was the site where efforts to record and transmit information about human rights violations should now centre also posed critical problems regarding the competence, capacity and professionalism of organisations based there. The notion that the South lacked, and thus required, competence became an important problem that HURIDOCS saw as its function to resolve. As Rupesinghe would later argue, '[t]he HURIDOCS idea [. . .] stresses the need for confidence- and competence-building in the Southern hemisphere'.[33] Within HURIDOCS, the perceived demand for 'common techniques', and 'competence-building', in the South translated into a need to develop more informational standards.[34] Among the proposals, the need for new standard formats for documenting violations became the most pressing.

The foregoing discussions are obviously nestled within the dense thicket of difficult, if contradictory, postcolonial relations that afflicts much of the contemporary human rights movement.[35] Even if HURIDOCS described the demand for competence building as originating from organisations based in the Global South, the mapping of postcolonial distinctions between North and South onto a set of anxieties about the quality and ambiguities of information – the worry that signal might be mistaken for noise – is certainly noteworthy. It hints at some of the material ways that the contemporary movement has captured human rights as a Western project.[36] Focus on the Global South as both the space of concern for HURIDOCS and the site for intervention with regard to developing practices, competencies and technologies reflects and reinscribes some of the ways that the broader human rights movement has figured the South (in rather paternalistic ways) as the object of its intervention.[37] The exclusionary narrowing of competence around a form of informational work completely elides that the Global South had been a (though admittedly different and more radical) site for a vibrant set of human rights knowledges and expertise built up through the anticolonial projects of the mid-twentieth century.

That said, the practical, technical development of the Events Standard Formats also paints a slightly more complicated picture of North–South relations. In 1988, HURIDOCS formally commissioned Judith Dueck, a Canadian with experience working for Al-Haq in Palestine, to head a taskforce to produce a generalisable set of formats for collecting and communicating information about violations of civil and political rights. The taskforce drew its team from both the North and South and acknowledged the need for Southern expertise. Indeed, Ricardo Cifuentes, a Chilean human rights documentalist at CODEHUCA who had already developed its database for recording violations, would become a key member of the team. Even if the South remained inscribed as the site of human rights violations, the lack of professionalisation and competence building certainly was not always attributed to the South in a monolithic way. Though it was perhaps because the South had been figured as the site of human rights violations that a select few organisations based there were acknowledged to have the necessary informational expertise.

Following the convening of a specialised taskforce, the Events Standard Formats were developed slowly over a period of five years.

Embracing a decentralised approach, the taskforce aimed not to create and then impose an entirely new set of standards but to draw from the experiences within its network. In 1990, as the Events Model entered the testing phase, HURIDOCS was keen to emphasise that its approach was 'based on existing forms, stated requirements, extensive discussion within the HURIDOCS Task Force and network as well as input from other experts in the field of human rights documentation'.[38] In practice, the Formats were developed from the expertise and existing practices of organisations such as CODEHUCA and Taskforce Detainees (Philippines). Conscious of the need for interoperability, the Taskforce also received input from larger organisations such as Amnesty International and UN agencies, mainly so that the model was compatible with their existing systems.

Following a prolonged period of development and testing, the publication of the Events Standard Formats in 1993 marked the official arrival of the Events Model. The Model combined a rigorous approach to configuring standardised information with the flexibility needed to scaffold the growing number of informational practices in the arsenal of the human rights movement. Concurrently, the development of a computerised implementation of the Events Model, Evsys, programmed by Cifuentes and released around the same time as the Standard Formats, provided new tools for databasing. Not only did it help pave the way for the electronic storage, retrieval and exchange of standardised human rights information, it also had a profound effect on the movement's capacity to 'perform analyses that are not possible on a case-by-case basis'.[39] Evsys was thus highly significant because it made new kinds of statistical analysis widely available and thus promised to deliver new forms of information that emerged from patterns in data.

Reformulating Events Formats: Databasing Violations

Given the possibilities of scale vis-à-vis data that Evsys seemed to make possible, it is perhaps unsurprising that large data projects such as those underpinning the South African Truth and Reconciliation Commission (SATRC) and efforts to map the Rwandan genocide were some of the first to use computerised implementations of the Events Model.[40] The thousands of violations mapped and counted by both projects appear to attest to the Model's capacity to operate at large scales. But the ambition of these projects also revealed the Model's inherent limits. A key issue was that while the representational schema of the Events Model '[made] sense in a paper system', when it was used to structure a database it harboured data redundancies, where data is recorded more times than is necessary, creating ambiguities.[41] It was often difficult, for example, to determine whether victims and perpetrators of the same name were in fact the same person.[42] Though the combined release of the Events Standard Formats and Evsys in the early 1990s was a key landmark in the development of standard tools for documenting (largely civil and political) rights violations, there was a growing realisation that the Events Model would need revision.

Collaboration with the American Association for the Advancement of Science (AAAS) became an important catalyst for these revisions. In July 1994, a meeting in Washington DC brought together a taskforce of representatives from HURIDOCS, Amnesty International and AAAS, resulting in the development of a more definite set of standards for designing human rights databases. The design decisions that came out of that meeting were outlined in *A Definition of Database Design Standards for Human Rights Agencies*, a publication written largely by Patrick Ball, then a consultant at AAAS.[43] The project aimed to resolve precisely the ambiguities or 'noise' that seemed to occur when the Events Model was deployed as the structure of a database, particularly within large-scale data projects like the SATRC. But while Ball et al. expressed that their objective was to 'establish design standards for the implementation of human rights databases compatible with the HURIDOCS formats',[44] it is perhaps more accurate to say the inverse is true. Given the ways they would call for the reshaping of the Events Model itself, the Design Standards provided more of a rethinking of the HURIDOCS formats through 'modelling ideals [. . .] for representing particular formations of information necessary in the work of a human rights agency' within a database.[45]

The specific socio-technical transformations of the Events Model following the intervention of AAAS are dealt with in the sections below, but here I want to stay with the broader organisational process through which the model was reshaped. By 1996, HURIDOCS put together a working group, the Evsys Design team, to work on its future development largely by responding to the issues which Ball's text had clarified. The result was a new iteration of Evsys, 4.1, published in 1998. The new iteration of the software was built around a data structure that significantly diverged from the original model laid out in the first edition of the Formats. Evsys 4.1 did so precisely because it embedded the Database Design Standards developed alongside AAAS.[46] The changes made to Evsys would eventually cascade into a rewriting of the Events Model itself. The second edition of the Events Standard Formats, published in 2001, was both driven by and modelled directly on the data structure that was used in Evsys 4.1.[47]

The process of revising the Events Standard Formats outlined above already hints at some of the ways that 'seeing' violations is not simply a matter of transparently discovering facts by passively gazing at the real, but an accomplishment that is configured and, importantly, constrained by the apparatuses and technologies that construct and mediate our vision. But at the same time, the process of transforming the Events Model is also suggestive of the ways that the computational forms which proliferate under cybernetic capitalism have increasingly folded into and shape how social processes and events are seen and understood. Insofar as the Formats were progressively remodelled to better fit the structure(s) of databases (rather than, say, the other way around), the evolution of the Events Model perhaps speaks to some of the 'grey' ways that a computational vision, particularly through the idiom of databasing, is ever more tightly woven into our perception of socio-cultural processes.[48]

Interestingly, the second edition of the Events Standard Formats would be the last major revision to the model, even though it would go on to be used frequently over the next two decades. Subsequent modifications would largely be to the computerised implementations of the model, 'articulation work' that maintained its operability and functionality in response to the perpetually shifting socioeconomic and technical sands moved by the ever fluctuating tides of cybernetic capitalism.[49] First, WinEvsys was released in 2001 alongside the second edition of the Formats. It made Evsys compatible with Windows by building the new data structure onto Microsoft Access. The next iteration, OpenEvsys, was a free, open-source web-based implementation of the Events Model released in 2009. The fact that neither WinEvsys nor OpenEvsys departed from the second edition of the Events Standard Formats, however, is significant. The longevity of the second edition of the Formats highlights the degree to which they provided a form of seeing that was adequate to the needs of the human rights movement. But it might also attest to the extent to which the Formats represented a form of vision made entirely compatible with the logical structures and computational syntax that inheres within databases; an inherently computational mode of seeing violations.

It is only very recently that HURIDOCS has begun phasing out OpenEvsys in favour of a more flexible system, Uwazi Reveal. Taken from the Swahili word for 'openness', Uwazi Reveal is an open-source software platform that makes use of the latest in NoSQL database tools and new capacities to store and manipulate multimedia resources.[50] But this has not spelled the end of the Events Model. Uwazi Reveal is designed to handle implementations of the Events data structure and, moreover, the time I have spent with human rights organisations indicates that the Events Model continues to be used in this new software platform.[51] In this respect, the media history set out above is testament to the remarkable stability and longevity of the Events Standard Formats as a socio-technical device for human rights work, one which makes it possible to 'see' phenomena that are of concern to the human rights movement as information. But this also raises the question of precisely what and how the Events Model allows one to see.

Reticular Sight/Databased Vision

Though the concept of the database owes a debt to Cold War military technologies, specifically the SAGE anti-aircraft command and control network, databases as we now know them first emerged in the late 1960s through Database Management Systems created by General Electric and IBM. As Thomas Haigh notes, the data 'base' was first imagined as the 'pools of shared data' underpinning the firm whose organisation and integration promised greater managerial control over organisational and commercial processes.[52] What would subsequently be understood as database software emerged as a way of compiling and manipulating this data for the purpose of management. Database Management Systems thus provided one of the material ways that the concept of information control, first applied to problems of military organisation, moved into commercial applications concerned with the control of the firm.

With the burgeoning of the information economy in the 1970s, databases proliferated through the corporate world, taking several different forms. The first databases, hierarchical databases that organised data into a vertical tree-like structure, were eventually superseded by the relational database first designed by Edgar 'Ted' Codd.[53] By the beginning of the twenty-first century, relational databases, which organise data more flexibly into non-hierarchical entity tables that are linked or 'related' together, had become the dominant paradigm for data organisation in both commercial and governmental organisations. Their dominance has only recently been challenged by the emergence of even more flexible database types over the last decade such as graph databases, which have no fixed structure but offer the possibility of constantly mapping and remapping new data points and their relations.

Though database types differ, the critical point to note is that they all engender what Jannis Kallinikos calls a 'computational rendition of reality' that is neither a transparent nor straightforward 'transposition of reality to electronic medium'.[54] Computation involves, as Kallinikos notes,

> the far-reaching decomposition of the unity, coherence and complexion of things and social processes as the outcome of its inescapable and comprehensive analytic predilection [. . .] Thus disaggregated reality is reassembled by passing through the bottleneck of coding, and [its] rules and procedures.[55]

The crucial point, argued by Hayles, David Berry and others, is that computation requires the parsing of reality, which might otherwise be conceptualised as analogue and continuous, through a digital logic that 'captures' the world by breaking it down into discrete elements, objects and processes.[56]

With this in mind, any database needs to be understood as a particular kind of 'grey' mediation, as Matthew Fuller and Andrew Goffey would argue, replete with technical operations that serve to discretise the aspects of the world that are of concern and render them computationally legible.[57] Databases construe and construct information through predefined and structuring forms or classifications that are inherently discrete. For instance, databases often concern themselves with data entities or objects, the well-defined relationships that can be forged between them, and often, though not always, similarly discrete properties or attributes of which entities might be composed. The ways these different forms are construed and interact as well as the relative importance of each depend on the type of database that is being used.

The rise of database software thus brings new design problems, primarily how one might model and represent the relevant social and organisational processes and objects within the discretising structure of a database. In the late 1960s, General Electric's Charles Bachman codified the data structure diagram (DSD), a graphical representation or modelling device that diagrams the real world as information by breaking it down into two graphical forms 'the block, to represent an entity class; and the arrow'.[58] Bachman's original approach was extended and refined into the entity-relationship diagram (ERD) first codified by Peter Chen in the late 1970s. At varying degrees of abstraction, the ERD similarly constitutes social and organisational information as a disaggregated cluster of boxed entities linked by lines of relation. An entity 'car' would thus be represented as a box connected to another entity, 'owner', by a relationship line.[59] (Depending on the diagram's granularity, the car might also be broken down into a set of attributes – colour, model, registration, etc. – represented through a further set of boxes connected by relation lines.) Though various approaches to diagramming data structures have been developed over the last five decades, what they tend to share with the ERD and the DSD is this splitting of social processes into boxed elements and lines of relation. This is largely because it is operationally efficacious, mapping onto the ways many database types disaggregate and reassemble their objects.

The ways that data diagrams organise the real world into database-compatible forms are highly consequential. As Fuller and Goffey argue, such diagrams provide 'a rough and ready sketch of the ontology of the entity or entities modelled [. . .] that is usually glossed as a "universe of discourse"'.[60] Insofar as such diagrams attempt to capture the ontological aspects of processes and entities, or at least all that is worth knowing about them, they are a window into the mode of vision made available by databases and their construction of the world as data. Crucially, in diagramming the social as boxed elements or entities and lines of relation that connect them, data diagrams disclose an abstract (and abstracting) mode of seeing social processes and/or forms which is strikingly similar to the kinds of modelling originally proffered by the cyberneticians. The informational vision of data diagrams is little different to the black boxes and connecting lines of communication, the flat ontology of nodes and edges, of the network diagram. The representational schemas of data diagrams are often a commitment to seeing the world as composed of 'networks' of atomic, discrete entities related to each other in specific ways.[61]

As a template for rendering human rights violations as information, the Events Model utilises a similarly reticular lens. From its first, multipurpose but database-compatible iteration to its second iteration more finely attuned to the technical structures of databases, the Events Model is presented in both editions of the Events Standard Formats through a series of diagrams that, while not named as such, greatly resemble simple data model diagrams. Central to the Model, then, is a mode of seeing which arranges human rights violations as a 'network' of discrete nodes linked by specific lines of relation. A close reading of the Events Model through these diagrams and their explication in the Events Standard Formats thus provides important opportunities to explore how the Model provides a way of seeing violations as it has become ever more tightly bound up with the properties of databases over the course of its evolution.

Seeing Violations as Events

As its title might imply, a good way into the Events Model is to begin with its principle organising unit, the 'Event' entity. In the 1993 edition of the Formats, the Event refers to either 'a single isolated incident' or 'a grouping of incidents' that are of concern to human rights organisations, a somewhat euphemistic and slippery definition that is indicative of some of the difficulties encountered in trying to parcel up the social processes as useable information.[62] The Event is an abstraction formed to encompass either a violation or a cluster of interrelated violations where their separability is not straightforward. As abstraction, the Event provides the basic spatiotemporal unit of the model, concretising it and thus providing a plane of consistency for the other entities. It is for this reason that the Event is described in the first edition of the Formats as the 'Master Record' which 'provides reference to all records and documents related to the event'.[63] In other words, the Event entity both frames and links together all the other entities that are required to 'see' human rights violations. The ways these elements interact are given in Figure 2.1, which diagrams the model as a 'network' of entities.

The other entities within the model are the 'Victim' of the incident(s); the '(alleged) Perpetrator' of the Event; the 'Source' from which the information came; and the 'Intervention' – information

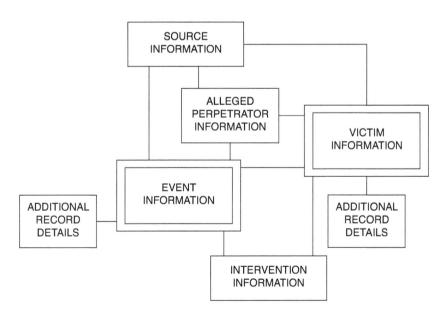

Figure 2.1 Basic data model from *Events Standard Formats* (1993). © HURIDOCS.

about what the organisation and/or other organisations have done in response. This range of entities introduced in the first edition of the Standard Formats, and the task of configuring the relations between them, has been a consistent part of the Events Model through both of its iterations. Though the diagram is not fine-grained enough to show it, each entity is comprised of a set of attributes or properties. Possible attributes for each entity are outlined in the Standard Formats. For example, a Victim might be made up of a list of personal identifiers such as name, age, gender, ethnicity; an Event might be composed of 'event type', date, location, number of victims, and so on.[64] One should thus bear in mind that the Formats not only map a model that relates the entities required to see violations but also delineate substantive definitions of the content of these entities through their attributes. In this way, the Formats shape entities, even if somewhat flexibly, into standardised forms.

Of the entities detailed above, the first edition of the Events Standard Formats posed the Victim and the Perpetrator as the two most important vis-à-vis the construction of violations (alongside the Event). Their importance is reflected in the structure of what the 1993 Formats calls 'Short Formats', pared down, skeletal versions of the full Model designed to provide flexibility for the array of situations in which it might be used. In the two Short Formats described in the 1993 edition, the Event entity is used alongside either only the Victim entity (as in Short Formats I) or the Victim and Perpetrator entity (in Short Formats II).[65] In this sense, while its approach may seem obvious to human rights groups today, the fundamental insight that crystallised in the Events Model was the identification of the most basic elements and their relationships required to capture human rights abuses as information. 'Seeing' violations was figured primarily as a matter of identifying 'Events' and their discrete 'network' of Perpetrators and Victims.[66]

Whether configured in full or as either of the Short Formats, the Model's capturing of entities and their relationships in a variety of different combinations of one-to-many relations (for example, one Victim could be part of many Events or vice versa) made it possible to capture various kinds of violations at multiple scales. The Model could, in theory at least, just as easily capture the illegal detention of an individual as larger and more complex incidents of mass violence. Figures 2.2 and 2.3, taken from the Events Standard Formats, are pedagogical tools designed to show how an organisation might model two complex set of Events with multiple Victims. What is particularly striking here is that the way the diagram disaggregates the violations into a 'network' of entities functions as a proposition or instruction about how such complex situations might be disentangled and made

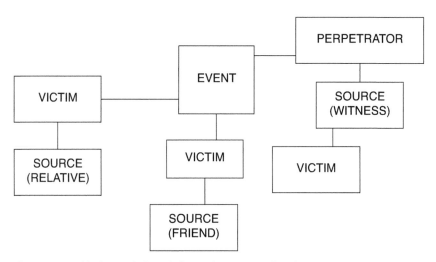

One event with three victims. Information concerning the perpetrator, the event and one victim was supplied by a witness. Other sources supplied information concerning the other victims.

Figure 2.2 Modelling an Event with multiple victims from *Events Standard Formats* (1993). © HURIDOCS.

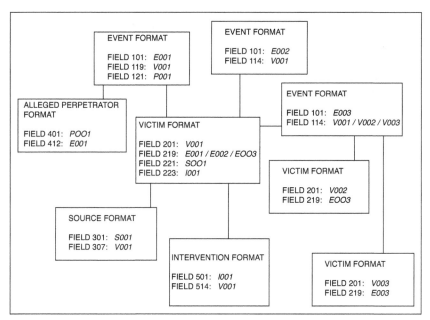

There were three events: one (E001) with one victim (V001); another (E002) with the same victim; a third (E003) with the same victim plus two others (V002 and V003).

There is information about the alleged perpetrator of the first event. There is a record of intervention on behalf of the first victim, and there is also a record of the source of information about this victim.

Figure 2.3 Coded model of an Event with multiple victims from *Events Standard Formats* (1993). © HURIDOCS.

sense of. Insofar as it demonstrates how the Events Model can be used to conceptualise violations, the diagram is indicative of the degree to which the Model harbours, and therefore disseminates, a fundamentally reticular vision. When the Model becomes a tool for thinking about violations, then mapping and thus seeing violations becomes a matter of correctly parsing them as an assemblage of discrete nodes and edges.

The shift from the first to the second edition of the Events Standard Formats, which was intended to better integrate the Model into the structure of databases, would complicate this vision largely by attending to the 'structural problems of some data having complex relations to other data'.[67] As noted earlier, the Database Design Standards that developed out of the collaboration between HURIDOCS and AAAS strongly shaped the 2001 revision of the Events Standard Formats. The strategy of the collaboration was to reduce data redundancies and the ambiguity that the first edition of the Events Model introduced when utilised as the structure of a database. To do so, both 'disambiguation' and 'parsimonious rulemaking' became the philosophy of those who drew up database standards in response to these issues. The goal, as Ball et al. argued, was 'to develop structural rules which represent the simplest, or most atomic, relations between basic entities', an ambition, I would suggest, that reflects the kinds of computational decomposition (as Kallinikos might put it) necessary to render information about violations amenable to databases.[68]

The disaggregation and discretisation at work in Ball et al.'s Database Design Standards shaped the second edition of the Events Formats in several specific ways. First, the Design Standards disambiguated the definition of the Event entity. The problem was that, in its original definition as 'an incident' or 'incidents', the Event did not contain adequate rules to distinguish between one violation or a group of violations. In response, the 1994 Database Design Standards introduced a new element, the 'Act'. Defining the Event as 'the context or frame an agency uses to make sense of a sequence of concrete acts', the Act was defined as 'a concrete, indivisible occurrence between two NAMEd [sic] entities [. . .] something very precise which happened in the world'.[69] This distinction between Event and Act became central to the second edition of the Formats, which no longer defined an Event as an 'incident' but as 'something that happens, with a beginning and an end, and which progresses until its logical conclusion [. . .] a single act, a series of related acts, or a combination of related acts happening together'.[70] The Event thus remained the main 'organisational unit' of the model but could be disaggregated into a reticulum of connected Acts. Additionally, the second edition introduced the 'Chain of Events' as a way of relating together several Events that, for instance, might make up part of the same conflict.

The introduction of the Act helped to clarify a growing sense about the fundamental entities and relations that defined information about violations. 'Precise' information, as the 1994 taskforce put it, must identify 'who committed which violations against whom'.[71] This 'who did what to whom' framework recognised that a violation is fundamentally 'a combination of two people – a perpetrator and a victim – who are related by a particular type of violence'.[72] That is, the perpetrator (the who) 'acts' upon and violates (the what) the victim (the whom). This seemed to confirm an intuition about the relative importance of the victim and perpetrator entities developed in the 1993 Events Standard Formats, whilst also introducing the Act as the node which mediated them. The Act became the entity which linked information about the Victim and the Perpetrator to the Event in the second edition of the Standard Formats because, as Ball argued, any other arrangement would '[leave] open the possibility of confusing who did what to whom' (Figures 2.4 and 2.5).[73]

Finally, the Database Design Standards addressed the major informational ambiguities introduced by the original Standard Formats. As I touched upon earlier, in cases of mass violence where an individual might be a Victim in one event but a Perpetrator in another, the original model might require information about that individual to be recorded twice (once as Victim and once as Perpetrator in each Event). Not only did this create an unnecessary duplication of work but, more importantly, it could also lead to confusion about whether the individual listed in each Event was the same person. To address these ambiguities, the Database Design Standards introduced the 'Person' entity, which was made distinct from a person's role in a

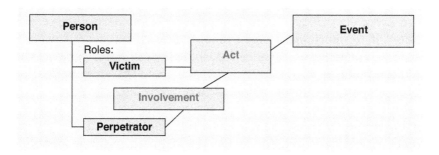

Figure 2.4 'Who did what to whom', Events Model for OpenEvsys (2009). © HURIDOCS.

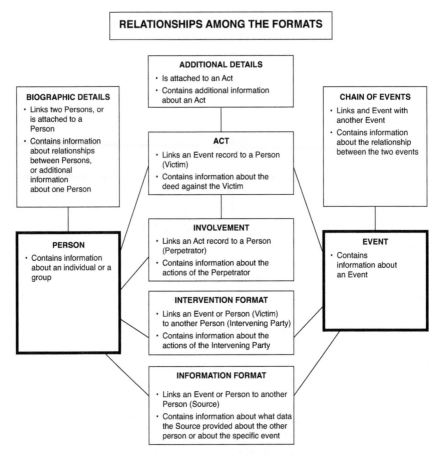

Figure 2.5 Full Events Model (2001). © HURIDOCS.

violation. A 'Person' entity could be made up of attributes such as name, gender, ethnicity, place and date of birth, and so on. But they could only occupy a limited number of roles, largely Victim or Perpetrator (but also Source and Intervention), which would link them to an Event via the Act.[74] This innovation became part of the second edition of the Formats. In an Events database, this would make it possible to unambiguously identify all the Events that a single person had been involved in and in what capacity, and therefore to develop more sophisticated forms of statistical analysis.

With the introduction of the Act and the distinction between Persons and their roles, the way of 'seeing' violations enabled by the Events Model had been somewhat reconfigured. Now it identified (Chains of) Events made up of discrete Acts involving Persons in their roles as either Victims or Perpetrators. There can be no doubt that these changes add greater complexity to the Model with the obvious pay-off of improving the data's clarity and stability. But changes in the degrees of complexity between each iteration of the model should not be confused with a change in kind. What remains central, as Figures 2.4 and 2.5 clarify, is a fundamentally reticular vision, albeit one more tightly bound to the needs and structures of the database as computational form. There might be more nodes and more edges, but they are nodes and edges all the same.

Events Models as Capture

For its part, HURIDOCS was bullish about the role that the Model could play within the broader human rights movement. The improved second edition of the Events Model, it argued, was a 'tool in the quest for truth', which made it possible not only 'to compile comprehensive data that tell in the most minute of detail what became of a single victim' but 'equally [. . .] to compile comprehensive data that tell what happened to a whole country'.[75] In a meaningful sense, then, the Events Model was understood as a technical device that could help to provide the Truth (with a capital 'T') of the myriad of contexts it would attend to at both micro and macro scales. Such claims cannot help but be read as an assertion about the Model's level of completeness and, consequently, the possibilities it furnished for collecting comprehensive information about a human rights situation. That is, the invocation of truth is an argument that everything one could want or need to know about rights violations can be captured by the Model.

Undoubtedly, truth claims made on behalf of the Events Model rest in part on an assumption about the way that the data model, as noted earlier, seemingly provides an 'ontology of the entity or entities modelled'.[76] As the word 'ontology' denotes, the configurations of objects and processes performed by databases are often understood as a more or less faithful rendering of those objects themselves, the capture of some kind of essence. But crucially these assumptions are in turn reinforced by the strategic and instrumental possibilities that a model affords for users of the database. As Berry notes, the power of any data model is located in the capacities engendered by its discretising and 'subtractive methods' to 'produce new knowledges and methods for the control of reality (techne)'.[77] The levels of control and utility proffered by a database tend to stand in as markers of a model's completeness insofar as they indicate precisely that everything worth knowing about the entities modelled has been captured.

Truth and related notions of completeness are thus directly connected to the Events Model's function as a kind of techne that not only promises to make the kind of 'brute' facts in which human rights groups are interested visible but also provides opportunities for further insights through their subsequent aggregation and organisation. At the micro level, the minutiae of the victim and their experience are constructed through classifications of specific Acts (murder, torture, etc.) and information about victims as Persons comprised of known attributes: age, sex, ethnicity, and so on. At the macro level, 'Truth' is implicitly constituted as Chains of Events, themselves made up of Victims, Perpetrators and the Acts that unite them, which can be nested inside each other at different scales. Something like a conflict can, in theory, be captured as a meta-event made up of chains of smaller, discrete events. Subsequent sorting, querying and filtering provide greater analytical purchase by identifying additional patterns in the data. A sense of mastery that legitimises the truth claims made by HURIDOCS emerges from the possibility of aggregating similar kinds of act to see whether particular patterns of violence occur in specific regions or, alternatively, finding patterns of victimhood by sorting events according to attributes of related victims (ethnicity, country of birth, and so on).

One of the key insights of the tradition of critique developed within the humanities, however, is that it is often a mistake to conflate notions of utility and efficacy with truth and totality. As this sensibility has diffused into critical analyses not only of computational forms but, more broadly, their place in informatic capitalism, there has been an increased focus on the gaps that inevitably open up between digital, computational modes of representation and the altogether more continuous and complex realities of social existence. Approaches from digital sociology, software studies and related fields demonstrate that the forms of capture involved in the constitution of a data model require choices about what might be included and excluded and on what terms.[78] As capture, a data model is thus constructed through processes of discretisation, disaggregation and reassembly that, as the epigraph of this chapter indicates, distinguish 'between those aspects of the world that are intended and included within a given digital representation and those that are excluded or filtered out', which are denied a 'functional existence'.[79] The Events Model is no exception to this problem.

How might we conceptualise the line that cleaves that which is included and that which is excluded? In his insistence that the network diagram provides cybernetic capitalism with its paradigmatic mode of representation, Franklin contends that such diagrams can, in and of themselves, tell us much about the inherent limits of digital capture. The lines of network diagrams, Franklin suggests, are direct markers of the threshold between inclusion and exclusion: 'only black boxes (standing in for neurons, computers, workers or what have you) and their interconnections (or inputs and outputs) can be included'. Anything either 'inside' the black boxes or lying beyond the lines that construct them and their interconnecting inputs and outputs 'fall[s] out of representation altogether'.[80] The capture of social processes within the lines of network diagrams has consequences for which parts of such processes are included or filtered out. Like the opacifying black box concept that shapes their logic, network diagrams flatten social worlds into assemblages of surfaces, often capturing only positively observable entities and behaviours in their webs of communicative action. In mapping the social, these diagrammatic forms thus tend to render visible the forms of positive knowledge that can be glossed as 'informational' at the expense of other ways of knowing the world such as those deeper textural interpretations that, as Orit Halpern might put it, concern 'hidden truths, invisible elements or psychological depths'.[81]

My own argument is that the inclusion/exclusion enacted by the Events Model can similarly be traced through its own 'flat' reticular diagrams. The 'cut' between inclusion and exclusion is, in other words, legible in the lines that mark out both the boxed entities known by the Model and the relations which connect them. As with the form of capture that characterises network diagrams, the flat (and flattening) ontology assembled by the lines of the Events Model folds into and undergirds the positivistic inclinations of human rights as an informational project. It thus brings forth the matters of (brute) fact that concern human rights groups, not only by composing their constituent entities but, perhaps more importantly, by arranging them in relations that stabilise and make visible positively observable and thus apparently objective notions of causality: 'who did what to whom'; perpetrator acts upon victim. But the Model does so only insofar as it has already filtered out anything that might cut across and intrude upon the lines of the diagram, including the kinds of texture and depth hidden within, or even pushing beyond, the limits of its boxes, and which consequently might disrupt, complicate or entirely unravel the Model.

On this basis much indeed could be said about what is excluded by the Events Model. But staying with the issue of causality brings some of the crucial issues at stake to the fore. Certainly, the Events Model's network of relations enables one to see a chain of causality that appears, contra Barad, as an unmediated vision of a reality that seems to speak for itself: a murders b, x tortures y. These insights emerge with such clarity, however, because the Model's network of entities excludes and thus forecloses nagging and altogether more disquieting questions about agency and causality that connect violence to issues of political economy, particularly the iniquitous structures of the global economy. Grasping human rights from this perspective may call for a denunciation of violations that is inseparable from a structural understanding of social exploitation, foregrounding a set of expressly political demands for the transformation of socioeconomic structures in ways that challenge the ideological, discursive limits of contemporary capitalism. Such possibilities are, nevertheless, safely foreclosed by the 'nodocentrism', as Mejias might put it, of the Model's diagrammatic form.[82]

An example helps to clarify this issue. One could, for instance, readily use the Model to record the endemic violence suffered by Black Americans at the hands of the police which has now been brought to the forefront of public attention by the #BlackLivesMatter movement. Using the Model, each case of police brutality would be recorded as an Event containing an Act, a Victim and a Perpetrator. One could even statistically aggregate these Events in any number of ways to demonstrate the scale of the violence. These practices would surely enable one to 'see' the violations in ways that human rights groups are interested in. Given that the problem of how little Black lives do seem to matter has long been occluded, the practice of recording these events may, in and of itself, be no bad thing. But if, as activists and scholars such as Keeanga-Yamahtta Taylor argue, the issue of police brutality in America is inextricable from the iniquitous structures of racialised capitalism it is situated in, then it is extremely difficult to see how the Model enables one to develop this kind of understanding. Nor is it easy to imagine how it would support the articulation of political demands equal to the problem.[83] In fact, framing the issue as a 'chain' of events could serve to mystify these connections by isolating incidence of brutality as fact whilst filtering out the rest.

It is also unclear how the Model could be modified to address this problem. The addition of another box, 'racialised capitalism', might literally forge a relation between police brutality and contemporary capitalism, but the flattening of the latter as one entity or node among others does not lend itself to an analysis of how the structures of capital shape, constitute and thus flow through state violence. In this sense, the problem is not the Model's level of 'granularity' but the violence of reticular abstraction, which, as Mejias bemoans, excludes anything that cannot be rendered as a node.[84] Consequently, getting at the issue of racial capitalism would almost certainly require a fundamentally different idea of, and engagement with, information (a proposition I attempt to take up in the final chapter of this book). With this being the case, the example of #BlackLivesMatter demonstrates the model's limits in ways that, perversely, bring into focus its value as a means of 'informatising' and thus depoliticising human rights issues. Through its arraying of violations as nodes and edges, the Events Model facilitates the production of facts as signal precisely by filtering out the noise of politics. It is in this sense that the Events Model might be understood as a materialisation of the informational logic of human rights as practice.

The Ends of Events: Capture as Cutting

In early 2003, a newsletter celebrating the twentieth anniversary of HURIDOCS provided the opportunity for past members of the organisation such as Bjørn Stormorken to reflect upon the organisation's development. For Stormorken, the Events Standard Formats was the crowning achievement of HURIDOCS: the organisation 'became most relevant [. . .] with the standards and methodologies for recording events'. This was, in his mind, a concrete contribution to 'improving the infrastructure upon which activism can be built'.[85] Even though it is important to reiterate that the Events Standard Formats were never universally adopted, Stormorken is no doubt correct to insist that their impact has been profound. Indonesia, Sri Lanka, the Philippines, Rwanda, South Africa, Burundi, Liberia, Croatia, Turkey, Zimbabwe, Mexico and Guatemala are just some of the places where NGOs have used the Events Model to document violations of civil and political rights in the three decades since its first edition was published. The Model is also used by large international NGOs such as Global Witness, who have documented the killing of environmental activists as Events.[86]

But more than that: in representing a particular informational paradigm, the Events Model reflects some of the ways that the contemporary human rights movement has materialised as an informational project. While human rights information is often naturalised as that which can be transparently discovered when one simply looks at the real, a careful reading of the Model demonstrates that seeing violations is a complex achievement that crystallises through 'multiple practices of engagement'.[87] In its engagements with the world, I would argue that the Events Model is simultaneously a form of capture and cutting, or, at least, a form of capture where what is captured appears as such largely because of what has been cut away from it. Making this point is not intended as a criticism of the value of the Model in terms of its efficacy for human rights groups in their informational work but it does direct us towards what is lost through such practices. In cleaving empirical acts of violence from the social processes, exploitations and deprivations which flow into and constitute them, modelling injustice as an issue of discrete events is generative of a human rights project made more amenable to the ideological and discursive limits of late capitalism.

Importantly, observing the specific way of splitting informational signal from political noise engendered by the Events Model has implications for the arguments mobilised across this book. In particular, this chapter demonstrates that the discretising vision of digital computation readily binds to the radical positivism of human rights in ways that reinforce the movement's informational logic. Insofar as computational practices have been all but universalised in human rights work (and much else besides) under contemporary capitalism's digital turn, the Model is an important object of analysis because it anticipates a way of thinking about and 'seeing' human rights that has now become ubiquitous and, perhaps for this reason, taken for granted. The task now is to examine how this mode of seeing is articulated differently across the range of informational practices that gather under the banner of human rights.

Notes

1. Martin Ennals, 'Exchange of Information in the Field of Human Rights Ways and Means', *Bulletin of Peace Proposals* 14, no. 1 (1983): 26.
2. Ennals, 'Exchange of Information in the Field of Human Rights', 24.
3. Ennals, 'Exchange of Information in the Field of Human Rights', 34.
4. The original publication of the standard formats contains a dedication to Ennals which notes that 'Martin Ennals, the Founding President of HURIDOCS, died in Saskatoon, Canada on 5 October 1991, while the [Events Standard Formats] Task Force was holding its final sessions in Lima, Peru.' See Judith Dueck, *HURIDOCS Standard Formats: A Tool for Documenting Human Rights Violations* (Oslo: HURIDOCS, 1993), iii.
5. Judith Dueck, 'Human Rights Violations and Standard Formats: An Introduction', *HURIDOCS News*, no. 9 (1990): 5. IISG ZK 53725, International Institute of Social History, Amsterdam.
6. Ennals, 'Exchange of Information in the Field of Human Rights', 24.
7. Karen Barad, *Meeting the Universe Halfway: Quantum Physics and the Entanglement of Matter and Meaning* (Durham, NC and London: Duke University Press, 2007), 51. See also Ian Hacking, *Representing and Intervening: Introductory Topics in the Philosophy of Natural Science* (Cambridge: Cambridge University Press, 1983).

8. Barad, *Meeting the Universe Halfway*, 53.
9. The original publication of the Events Standard Formats contains a list of over thirty organisations whose own work supported the development of the Events Model. See Dueck, *HURIDOCS Standard Formats*, viii.
10. Looking at the training log left on the HURIDOCS website is instructive in getting a sense of the scope of where it has been implemented. See HURIDOCS, *Training Log*, 2009, <http://web.archive.org/web/20110408045138/http://www.huridocs.org/training-logbook/> (last accessed 27 February 2022).
11. Susan Leigh Star and James R. Griesemer, 'Institutional Ecology, "Translations" and Boundary Objects: Amateurs and Professionals in Berkeley's Museum of Vertebrate Zoology, 1907–39', *Social Studies of Science* 19, no. 3 (1 August 1989): 387–420.
12. Star and Griesemer, 'Institutional Ecology, "Translations" and Boundary Objects', 393.
13. Ennals, 'Exchange of Information in the Field of Human Rights', 29
14. Hans Thoolen, 'Human Rights Databasing: Why HURIDOCS Could Make Sense', *SIM Newsletter* 14 (1986): 3–14.
15. Bjørn Stormorken and Annie McMorris, *HURIDOCS Standard Formats for the Recording and Exchange of Information on Human Rights* (Dordrecht: Martinus Nijhoff, 1985), vii–viii. A similar argument was also made in 1983 in a single-paged flyer, where the fledgling organisation argued that 'HURIDOCS facilitates the identification, location, and free flow of public information through the linking of participants in the network.' See Appendix 3, Summary Report, European Co-Ordination Committee on Human Rights Documentation, 4th meeting, 28 January 1983, DH INFO-CO (83)1, <https://ecchrd.files.wordpress.com/2015/03/report-4-1983-strasbourg.pdf> (last accessed 27 February 2022).
16. Taken from the following quote: 'The rapid increase of interest in human rights coincides with the rapid development of information technology. Unless a common and universal system of communication is evolved, valuable information will be wasted, existing international machinery will not function, and implementation will not be monitored.' Attributed to Martin Ennals, this passage appears on a number of newsletters and other promotional materials developed by HURIDOCS.
17. Benjamin Bratton, *The Stack: On Software and Sovereignty* (Cambridge, MA and London: MIT Press, 2016).
18. Stormorken and McMorris, *HURIDOCS Standard Formats for the Recording and Exchange of Information on Human Rights*, v, ix.
19. Stormorken and McMorris, *HURIDOCS Standard Formats for the Recording and Exchange of Information on Human Rights*, vi.
20. Stormorken and McMorris, *HURIDOCS Standard Formats for the Recording and Exchange of Information on Human Rights*, vii.
21. Stormorken and McMorris, *HURIDOCS Standard Formats for the Recording and Exchange of Information on Human Rights*, 1.

22. Seb Franklin, *Control: Digitality as Cultural Logic* (Cambridge, MA: MIT Press, 2015), xix–xx.
23. Ronald E. Day, 'The "Conduit Metaphor" and the Nature and Politics of Information Studies', *Journal of the American Society for Information Science and Technology* 51, no. 9 (2000): 808.
24. Stormorken and McMorris, *HURIDOCS Standard Formats for the Recording and Exchange of Information on Human Rights*, 145.
25. Amnesty International, *Prisoner Dossier: General Instructions*, ACT 10/016/1978 (London: Amnesty International, 1978), <https://www.amnesty.org/download/Documents/204000/act100161978eng.pdf>.
26. Oriana Bernasconi, Elizabeth Lira and Marcela Ruiz, 'Political Technologies of Memory: Uses and Appropriations of Artefacts that Register and Denounce State Violence', *International Journal of Transitional Justice* 13, no. 1 (2019): 18.
27. Ricardo Cifuentes, 'CODEHUCA American Information and Documentation Network on Human Rights: A Brief Description of the Project', in HURIDOCS, *Communication, Development and Human Rights: Final Report of a Conference*, vol. 1 (Utrecht: HURIDOCS, 1986), 1–13.
28. For example, the CODEHUCA database described by Cifuentes almost certainly influenced the design of the Events Formats and Evsys.
29. Kumar Rupesinghe, quoted in Elizabeth Lapham and Bert Verstappen, 'Human Rights Violations and Standard Formats: Towards Compatibility in Recording and Transferring Information Conference Report', *HURIDOCS News*, no. 9 (1990): 18. IISG ZK 53725, International Institute of Social History, Amsterdam.
30. Gregory Bateson, *Steps to an Ecology of Mind: Collected Essays in Anthropology, Psychiatry, Evolution, and Epistemology* (Chicago: University of Chicago Press, 1972), 386.
31. Cifuentes, 'CODEHUCA American Information and Documentation Network on Human Rights', 10.
32. Cifuentes, 'CODEHUCA American Information and Documentation Network on Human Rights', 11.
33. Kumar Rupesinghe, 'The Role of HURIDOCS', in *A Guide to Establishing a Human Rights Documentation Centre: Report of a UNESCO-UNU International Training Seminar on the Handling of Documentation and Information on Human Rights*, ed. Laurie S. Wiseberg (Ottawa: Human Rights Internet, 1988), 11. BRO 2477/10 fol., International Institute of Social History, Amsterdam.
34. Cifuentes, 'CODEHUCA American Information and Documentation Network on Human Rights', 11; HURIDOCS, 'Conclusions and Recommendations – Rome Conference', in *Communication, Development and Human Rights*, vol. 1, 24–7.
35. See Kiran Kaur Grewal, *The Socio-Political Practice of Human Rights: Between the Universal and the Particular* (London and New York: Routledge, 2017); Upendra Baxi, *The Future of Human Rights* (Oxford: Oxford University Press, 2008).

36. Joseph R. Slaughter, 'Hijacking Human Rights: Neoliberalism, the New Historiography, and the End of the Third World', *Human Rights Quarterly* 40, no. 4 (2018): 735–75.

37. For more on this, see the following excellent analyses: Tshepo Madlingozi, 'On Transitional Justice Entrepreneurs and the Production of Victims', *Journal of Human Rights Practice* 2, no. 2 (2010): 208–28; Makau Mutua, 'Savages, Victims, and Saviors', *Harvard International Law Journal* 42, no. 1 (2001): 201–46; Obiora C. Okafor, 'International Human Rights Fact-Finding Praxis in Its Living Forms: A TWAIL Perspective', *The Transnational Human Rights Review* 1, no. 1 (2014): 59–105; Jessica Whyte, 'Powerless Companions or Fellow Travellers? Human Rights and the Neoliberal Assault on Post-Colonial Economic Justice', *Radical Philosophy* 2, no. 2 (2018): 13–29. One might also note, on this front, that by 1988 HURIDOCS had decided that its 'main emphasis' would be 'to strengthen information and documentation centres in the Third World'. See HURIDOCS, 'Introduction', *HURIDOCS News*, no. 5 (1988): 1. IISG ZK 53725, International Institute of Social History, Amsterdam.

38. Dueck, 'Human Rights Violations and Standard Formats', 5.

39. Comments made regarding the new possibilities of human rights databases by the American Association for the Advancement of Science (AAAS) following a meeting at which HURIDOCS and Amnesty International were invited to showcase their database models. See Daniel Salcedo, 'Computer Applications to Document Human Rights Abuses', *Report on Science & Human Rights* 15, no. 2 (1994): 6, <https://www.aaas.org/sites/default/files/1994-Vol.-15-Issue-2.pdf> (last accessed 24 February 2022).

40. In a 1998 issue of *HURIDOCS News*, HURIDOCS brings together some of the ways that both Events Formats and Evsys have been used. The adaptation of the Formats for the South African and Rwandan context are two of the larger examples given. See Manuel Guzman and Bert Verstappen, 'International Conference on Computerised Documentation of Human Rights Events: Mexico City, 11–13 November', *HURIDOCS News*, no. 22 (1998): 11–13. IISG ZK 53725, International Institute of Social History, Amsterdam.

41. Patrick Ball et al., *A Definition of Database Design Standards for Human Rights Agencies* (Washington DC: American Association for the Advancement of Science, 1994), 6, <https://hrdag.org/wp-content/uploads/2013/01/Definition_of_Database_Design_Standards_1994.pdf> (last accessed 24 February 2022).

42. These concerns were reported to HURIDOCS at a conference in Mexico City in July 1997, where some of those responsible for using Evsys to support the work of the SATRC outlined their experiences. See Lydia Levin, Polly Dewhirst and Brandon Hamber, 'The Use of Evsys for Preparing a Human Rights Database for Presentation to the Truth and Reconciliation Commission (TRC) in South Africa', presented at HURIDOCS Conference, Mexico City, 11 November 1997, <https://www.csvr.org.

za/the-use-of-evsys-for-preparing-a-human-rights-database-for-presen-tation-to-the-truth-and-reconciliation-commission-trc-in-south-africa/> (last accessed 27 February 2022); Guzman and Verstappen, 'International Conference on Computerised Documentation of Human Rights Events'.

43. Ball et al., *A Definition of Database Design Standards*. See also Patrick Ball, *Who Did What to Whom: Planning and Implementing a Large Scale Human Rights Data Project* (Washington DC: American Association for the Advancement of Science, 1996), <https://hrdag.org/who-didwhattowhom/contents.html> (last accessed 27 February 2022).

44. Ball et al., *A Definition of Database Design Standards*, 1.

45. Ball et al., *A Definition of Database Design Standards*, 2.

46. Guzman and Verstappen, 'International Conference on Computerised Documentation of Human Rights Events'.

47. As Manuel Guzman, then Executive Director of HURIDOCS, argued at the 1997 conference in Mexico City, 'revision of the Standard Formats on events [is] driven by the changes which the EVSYS software is going through'. See Guzman and Verstappen, 'International Conference on Computerised Documentation of Human Rights Events', 13.

48. The way that databasing structures our understanding of the world has been covered by Paul Dourish, Melissa Mazmanian and Ed Finn. See Paul Dourish, 'No SQL: The Shifting Materialities of Database Technology', *Computational Culture* 4 (2014): 1–37; Paul Dourish and Melissa Mazmanian, 'Media as Material: Information Representations as Material Foundations for Organizational Practice', in *How Matter Matters: Objects, Artifacts, and Materiality in Organization Studies*, ed. Paul R. Carlile, Davide Nicolini, Ann Langley and Haridimos Tsoukas (Oxford: Oxford University Press, 2013), 92–118; Ed Finn, *What Algorithms Want: Imagination in the Age of Computing* (Cambridge, MA and London: MIT Press, 2017).

49. For more on the concept of articulation work, see Geoffrey C. Bowker, Karen Baker, Florence Millerand and David Ribes, 'Toward Information Infrastructure Studies: Ways of Knowing in a Networked Environment', in *International Handbook of Internet Research*, ed. Jeremy Hunsinger, Lisbeth Klastrup and Matthew Allen (Dordrecht: Springer, 2009), 97–117.

50. Kristin Antin, 'Starting at the Source: Introducing Uwazi Reveal', HURIDOCS, 16 May 2018, <https://huridocs.org/2018/05/starting-at-the-source-introducing-uwazi-reveal/> (last accessed 24 February 2022).

51. Antin, 'Starting at the Source'.

52. Thomas Haigh, '"A Veritable Bucket of Facts": Origins of the Data Base Management System', *SIGMOD Record* 35, no. 2 (2006): 33–49. See also Thomas Haigh, 'How Data Got Its Base: Information Storage Software in the 1950s and 1960s', *IEEE Annals of the History of Computing* 31, no. 4 (2009): 6–25.

53. E. F. Codd, 'A Relational Model of Data for Large Shared Data Banks', *Communications of the ACM* 13, no. 6 (1970): 377–87.

54. Jannis Kallinikos, 'On the Computational Rendition of Reality: Artefacts and Human Agency', *Organization* 16, no. 2 (2009): 189.

55. Kallinikos, 'On the Computational Rendition of Reality', 189.

56. David M. Berry, *The Philosophy of Software: Code and Mediation in the Digital Age* (Basingstoke and New York: Palgrave Macmillan, 2011); N. Katherine Hayles, *My Mother Was a Computer* (Chicago: University of Chicago Press, 2005); Seb Franklin, *Control*, 80.

57. Matthew Fuller and Andrew Goffey, *Evil Media* (Cambridge, MA: MIT Press, 2012).

58. Charles W. Bachman, 'Data Structure Diagrams', *Data Base* 1, no. 2 (1969): 4–10.

59. Peter Pin-Shan Chen, 'The Entity-Relationship Model – Toward a Unified View of Data', *ACM Transactions on Database Systems* 1, no. 1 (1976): 9–36.

60. Matthew Fuller and Andrew Goffey, 'Digital Infrastructures and the Machinery of Topological Abstraction', *Theory, Culture & Society* 29, no. 5 (2012): 325.

61. Interestingly, this reticular mode of representation is briefly touched upon by Jon Agre as appearing across multiple fields in computation and database research. The ERDs developed to render business management systems, Agre notes, 'resemble nothing so much as the "semantic networks" employed in AI knowledge representation research'. See Philip E. Agre, 'Surveillance and Capture: Two Models of Privacy', *The Information Society* 10, no. 2 (1994): 101–27.

62. Dueck, *HURIDOCS Standard Formats*, 5.

63. Dueck, *HURIDOCS Standard Formats*, 5.

64. See chapter 5 of Dueck, *HURIDOCS Standard Formats* for an outline of the attributes.

65. Dueck, *HURIDOCS Standard Formats*, 7–8.

66. Even though the schema inherent within the Events Model might now be taken be taken for granted as obvious by many human rights organisations, the disaggregation and recombination of information as related entities that inheres in the Events Model has not always been so. For example, in the 'case files' developed by Vicaría de la Solidaridad, these entities bleed together, crisscrossing in paper-based forms that place a victim's details together with a written narrative of their *relato* or story of their victimisation. In this sense, while the Events Model might have been shaped by a growing consensus about how violations are seen, the mode of seeing that it crystallised was also just one way of seeing violations among others. See Oriana Bernasconi, Marcela Ruiz and Elizabeth Lira, 'What Defines the Victims of Human Rights Violations? The Case of the Comité Pro Paz and Vicaría de la Solidaridad in Chile (1973–1992)', in *The Politics of Victimhood in Post-Conflict Societies: Comparative and Analytical Perspectives*, ed. Vincent Druliolle and Roddy Brett (Cham: Palgrave Macmillan, 2018), 101–31.

67. Ball et al., *A Definition of Database Design Standards*, 3.

68. Ball et al., *A Definition of Database Design Standards*, 4.

69. Ball et al., *A Definition of Database Design Standards*, 5.
70. Judith Dueck, Manuel Guzman and Bert Verstappen, *HURIDOCS Events Standard Formats: A Tool for Documenting Human Rights Violations*, 2nd edn (Versoix: HURIDOCS, 2001), 8.
71. Ball et al., *A Definition of Database Design Standards*, 4.
72. Ball, *Who Did What to Whom*, ch. 3.4.2.
73. Ball, *Who Did What to Whom*, ch. 2.2.3.
74. Guzman et al., *Events Standard Formats*, 9–10. Interestingly, persons could also occupy the role of a Source.
75. Dueck et al., *HURIDOCS Events Standard Formats*, v.
76. Fuller and Goffey, 'Digital Infrastructures and the Machinery of Topological Abstraction', 325.
77. Berry, *The Philosophy of Software*, 15.
78. See, for example, Berry, *The Philosophy of Software*; Alexander R. Galloway, *The Interface Effect* (Cambridge: Polity Press, 2012).
79. Franklin, *Control*, xix–xx, 94.
80. Franklin, *Control*, 95.
81. Orit Halpern, *Beautiful Data: A History of Vision and Reason since 1945* (Durham, NC and London: Duke University Press, 2014), 84.
82. Ulises Ali Mejias, *Off the Network: Disrupting the Digital World* (Minneapolis and London: University of Minnesota Press, 2013).
83. Keeanga-Yamahtta Taylor, *From #BlackLivesMatter to Black Liberation* (Chicago: Haymarket Books, 2016). For more excellent work on this issue, see César 'Ché' Rodríguez, '"The Whole Damn System Is Guilty": Urban Violence, the Principal Contradiction of Racial Capitalism, and the Production of Premature Death in Oakland, California', *Critical Sociology* 46, no. 7–8 (2020): 1057–74. The term racialised or racial capitalism, it should also be noted, owes much to the pioneering work of Cedric Robinson. See Cedric J. Robinson, *Black Marxism: The Making of the Black Radical Tradition* (Chapel Hill: University of North Carolina Press, 2000).
84. Mejias, *Off the Network*.
85. Bjørn Stormorken, quoted in 'Other Pioneers Recall the Early Years', *HURIDOCS News*, no. 26 (2003): 10. IISG ZK 53725, International Institute of Social History, Amsterdam.
86. The model was used as the basis of a report on the killing of environmental activists. See Global Witness, *Defenders of the Earth: Global Killings of Land and Environmental Defenders in 2016* (London: Global Witness, 2017).
87. Barad, *Meeting the Universe Halfway*, 53.

Chapter 3

Doing Rights as Indicators: Informatising Social and Economic Rights

[Human rights statistics] are nothing less than a quest for a science of human dignity. [. . .] What are needed are solid methodologies, careful techniques, and effective mechanisms to get the job done.

– Mary Robinson, UN High Commissioner for
Human Rights, Montreux, September 2000

In 1976, Harold Laswell and fellow political scientists Richard C. Snyder and Charles F. Hermann published a paper outlining their proposals for a global monitoring system that would 'appraise the effects of government on human dignity'.[1] Indebted to Deutsch's and John Weltman's pioneering development of cybernetic approaches to political science, Laswell and his collaborators aimed to design a 'continuous, open, visible, and self-correcting' cybernetic system through which governments could weight the effects of their policies in relation to universal standards and 'steer' accordingly. Embodying the cybernetic concept of feedback, the primary component of the proposed system would be a network of policy scientists who would 'employ standardized procedures' to collect information and continuously appraise the impact of government actions 'on the attainment and distribution of basic human values'.[2] In turn, the information collected by the monitors was to be periodically provided to governments who would themselves use it to evaluate and potentially shift public policy to better advance basic public goods.

Interestingly, Laswell et al. deployed the Universal Declaration of Human Rights (UDHR) to fill in their definition of human dignity. Echoing the informational conception of law propounded by cyberneticists such as Turchin and Wiener, the UDHR was assumed to represent a transparent and clear consensus about human values that, in theory at least, all government action could be measured against. Taking the full gamut of rights enshrined in the Declaration, the monitoring system's vision of human dignity not only included issues of democratic participation and other civil and political rights but placed a particular emphasis on social and economic rights, especially in relation to issues such as education and health.[3]

But the question remained of how social and economic rights might be operationalised as measures of human dignity. For Laswell and his co-authors, the answer lay in another field greatly influenced by cybernetics and systems theory: social indicators. Though undoubtedly an heir to the statistical biopolitics that emerged in the eighteenth century, the social indicators movement was nevertheless shaped by cyberneticians such as Raymond Bauer and concerned itself with constructing an 'over-all societal information system' for measuring human development.[4] A reaction against purely economic measures of development such as gross national product (GNP) that dominated national and international policy discussions, the movement attempted to develop statistical indicators in areas such as health, social welfare and quality of life, as broader and more effective measures of how policy affected social 'systems'. For Laswell et al., this growing array of statistical measures was thus seen as an ideal source for the quantitative information that their proposed monitoring system could use to measure human dignity.

Only one year later, and while not exactly as Laswell and his co-authors had planned, their utopian vision of a global monitoring system underpinned by human rights would be at least partially realised by Jimmy Carter's presidency and his embrace of a human rights-based foreign policy. Mobilising its own network of foreign service workers and embassies (rather than policy scientists), the Carter administration began compiling information on the human rights performance of countries across the world into its annual *Country Reports on Human Rights Practices*. In a move which is suggestive of the ways that human rights were weaponised against the Global South, the information contained in the *Reports* was then used to make determinations regarding foreign aid allocations. Recipient countries with poor human rights records were, in theory at least, to be left without US aid.[5] Crucially, among the information collected to make such decisions, the State Department gradually deployed social indicators as a principal method for monitoring social and economic rights within the *Country Reports*.

Admittedly, the *Country Reports* tended to emphasise civil and political rights issues, and where socio-economic rights were concerned the information collected by the State Department had been less than ideal.[6] But in mid-1980 the US State Department invited Judith Innes de Neufville, a leading figure in the social indicators movement, to develop statistical indicators as 'a more objective and meaningful way to prepare [the social and economic rights] section of the report'.[7] Prioritising areas such as health, education and nutrition, Innes de Neufville recommended the US State Department utilise a number of statistical indicators such as life expectancy, literacy rates, infant mortality, and school enrolment. Though cautioning that such indicators 'represented merely what appear to be the best, current, widely available indicators', Innes de Neufville nevertheless hoped that they represented a first step in a 'self-perpetuating learning process' through which better indicators could be developed.[8] For its part, the US State Department appeared to agree; Innes de Neufville's recommendations were integrated into the *Country Reports* beginning in 1981, although the project would quickly be derailed by the Reagan administration, which denied the existence of socio-economic rights.[9]

Despite this setback, the human rights indicators developed by Innes de Neufville are a significant precursor to later events. Following the establishment of the UN Committee on Economic, Social and Cultural Rights in 1985, enthusiasm for social indicators resurfaced as more attention was given to questions of how to realise socioeconomic rights and monitor state compliance. By the early 1990s this growing consensus about the value of indicators in human rights work had developed into a set of concerted attempts to develop universal measures for social and economic rights both within the UN system and beyond.[10] And while, as this chapter shows, their development has been far from straightforward, social indicators continue to be understood as a central tool in the fight for human rights.

Though the influence of cybernetics on social indicators, like much of our cybernetic heritage, now operates as a largely unmarked discourse, the integration of social indicators into the struggle for social and economic rights is nevertheless revealing. Not only is it yet more evidence of the extent to which cybernetic ideas have diffused over the last seven decades; I would also suggest that the ongoing enthusiasm for indicators to measure social and economic rights is a key marker of the ways they embody the informational logic of human rights. Following this trajectory, this chapter develops a critical reading of social indicators, which counterposes them to earlier and avowedly political struggles for social and economic rights, especially those prosecuted by the non-aligned countries of the Third World. I suggest that social indicators responded to ongoing anxieties about these political visions and uses of social and economic rights with an informational mode of 'doing' human rights designed to defang and depoliticise them. Indicators, I contend, bind social and economic rights claims to, and thus contain them within, technical practices that readily cohabit with the principles of economic growth and national competition that define late capitalism.

The Other Human Rights: Radical Activism(s) before 1980

In her recent book, Susan Marks turns back to the political movements of English peasants and serfs from the fifteenth to the seventeenth centuries in order to trace a radical history of human rights. Unearthing a motley crew of Diggers and Levellers, Marks demonstrates that the language of rights was often invoked in this period to try to secure the social and economic needs of ordinary people against the deleterious enclosures of early capitalism.[11] In doing so, Marks recovers a genealogy of rights that has often been obscured in the oft-exalted Western teleology of the rights of man and its idealisation of the bourgeois revolutions of the eighteenth century as the foundation and origin of human rights. Against the civil and political rights claims that the emerging bourgeoisie saw as central to their capitalist societies, the earlier rights movements of the Diggers and Levellers offered a different model of social and economic rights that was purposefully antagonistic to the advent of capitalism. In excavating this history, Marks's work is an important reminder that long 'before the US and old European colonial powers rediscovered human rights in the 1970s [. . .] human rights were an uncertain and unstable discourse that covered a hugely varied collection (or better, dispersion) of principles and promises'.[12]

Joseph Slaughter's recovery of some of the many occluded human rights claims of subaltern peoples provides an even more expansive account of their discursive instability. From African American abolitionists to Latin American anti-imperialists, Slaughter insists, all manner of radical movements reside within the obfuscated history of human rights.[13] Perhaps one of the most compelling places to look for an alternative vision of human rights is in the anti- and postcolonial struggles that rose to prominence in the middle decades of the twentieth century. Certainly, the human rights credentials of the anticolonial movement have often been contested, largely because its claims fall outside the narrow, depoliticised version of human rights that dominates today. But as Bonny Ibhawoh contends, the anticolonialism of the South can (and should) be seen as a human rights movement that understood 'political struggle as the paramount human rights question in the colonial context'.[14] Indeed, Ibhawoh sits alongside a growing body of scholars who suggest the antico-lonial struggles articulated an expansive and radical vision of rights that was not only antithetical to but also eventually challenged and superseded by the now hegemonic mode of human rights activism articulated in the 1970s.[15]

Following Adom Getachew, I suggest that the concept of 'world-making' provides the best way of grasping the anticolonialist mobili-sation of human rights and the ways it is epistemologically and politically distinct from the informational (anti)politics of human rights today. As Getachew contends, anticolonialism was driven by 'an expansive account of empire', which problematised colonial-ism not simply as a problem of alien rule but as an 'international structure of unequal integration and racial hierarchy'.[16] In response, Getachew argues, the anticolonial struggles recognised that over-coming colonialism required a similarly global project of 'reordering the world' to 'undo the hierarchies that facilitated domination'.[17] It is this speculative and political process of not only reimagining the international order but intervening in, transforming and/or creating its legal, economic and political institutions to secure postcolonial justice that Getachew understands as 'worldmaking'. As Getachew points out, the right to self-determination became both a central means and end of anticolonial worldmaking that manifested differ-ently in two key phases: the institutionalisation of the right to self-determination at the United Nations and, later, the demand for a New International Economic Order.

The first phase emerged out of the post-war international order through institutions like the United Nations and its subsequent Universal Declaration of Human Rights. Over the course of the 1950s and 60s, and in a context where both the UN Charter and the Declaration had either downplayed or ignored the question of self-determination, the anticolonial nationalists sought to use their growing power within the UN to 'reinvent' the principle of self-determination as a right. Driven by anticolonial leaders such as Kwame Nkrumah, the construction of self-determination as a right was built on an understanding that, on its own, national independence would not necessarily resolve the problems of international domination and hierarchy. As Getachew notes, the right to self-determination 'functioned as the juridical component of nondomination. It created [. . . a] vision of an international order, premised on the independence and equality of states.'[18] This 'expansive vision of an egalitarian world order' was advanced by the eventual inclusion of the right to self-determination as the first article of both International Covenants on Civil and Political Rights, and Economic, Social and Cultural Rights.[19] And the passing of UN Resolution 1514 in 1960, the 'Declaration on the Granting of Independence to Colonial Countries and Peoples', which called on states 'to promote the realization of the right to self-determination', reaffirmed its importance within the UN agenda.[20]

Crucially, the anticolonial nationalists did not see the right to self-determination in isolation but, refracted through their critique of colonialism, as the foundation of all other rights. As Getachew observes, proponents of self-determination saw the unequal international hierarchy created by colonialism as a system in which colonial peoples were kept in conditions of servitude akin to slavery. Like the enslaved, the people of the South were not only denied collective social and economic rights but 'experienced a violation of the rights of citizenship and personhood that denied them human dignity'.[21] Only through the undoing of colonial hierarchy and the creation of a world system of nondomination could individual rights be fully realised. In this sense, the worldmaking project of the anticolonial struggle created an ecosystem of different rights that, in responding to a careful critique of colonial order, imaginatively forged connections between them.

This vision of self-determination as the basis of all other rights received perhaps its greatest endorsement following the UN's Teheran Conference on Human Rights in 1968. With the countries of the Third World able to exert much greater leadership over the human rights agenda, the discussion and tone of the conference was imbued with the worldmaking ambitions of the South. The main document to emerge from this meeting, the Teheran Proclamation, argued that 'since human rights and fundamental freedoms are indivisible, the full realisation of civil and political rights without the enjoyment of economic, social and cultural rights is impossible'.[22] Furthermore, sowing the seedbed for what would later become the New International Economic Order, the Proclamation asserted that 'the widening gap between the economically developed north and the developing countries impedes the realization of human rights in the international community [. . . all countries must] make the maximum possible effort to close this gap'.

As the second passage from the Teheran Proclamation indicates, the next phase of the anticolonial articulation of human rights came from a growing realisation that securing nondomination necessitated a new project to tackle the socio-economic inequalities of the emerging postcolonial order. By the late 1960s, the project of decolonisation had seen many countries of the South granted formal independence. But formal independence did not take account of the ways that ongoing social and economic dependence on a global economy configured for the benefit of the North stultified development and, with it, the realisation of human rights in the South.[23] The reliance on aid and debt would, in fact, eventually trap many Southern countries in deleterious and persistent indebtedness. Seeing this problem as one of what Nkrumah had termed 'neo-colonialism', Getachew demonstrates that postcolonial leaders such as Jamaica's Michael Manley and Tanzania's Julius Nyerere sought to rethink 'the vision of political economy that was concomitant with the project of anticolonial self-determination'.[24] Self-determination was reconceived as requiring a 'radical form of economic and political equality between [all] states', and the emerging postcolonial states began articulating demands for what would become known as a New International Economic Order (NIEO), promulgated as a UN Declaration and Charter in 1974.

It is important to stress, as Julia Dehm does, that what was at stake in the NIEO was not the construction of an anti-capitalist global order.[25] Rather, it sought to reconfigure capitalist relations in ways that demanded global redistribution from North to South and a new legal architecture to govern these relations. The Declaration's emphasis on 'Full permanent sovereignty of every State over its natural resources and all economic activities', as well as its demands for 'regulation and supervision of the activities of transnational corporations' and '[p]referential and non-reciprocal treatment for developing countries [. . .] in all fields of international economic co-operation', underscore the redistributive nature of this project.[26] Nevertheless, Nyerere's framing of the NIEO as 'international class war' waged by the proletarian states of the South is also indicative of not only the antagonisms it sought to engage but also the real threat that it posed to the interests of the capitalist North.[27]

This is not of course to idealise anticolonial self-determination as entirely free from contradictions or moral ambivalences. It bound together a diverse range of projects, from the socialist humanisms of Nyerere and Manley to other avowedly capitalist or sometimes disconcertingly authoritarian national projects. Given both this and the emphasis on an externally facing, national form of self-determination, the anticolonial movement did inevitably come with some major blind spots regarding the internal state of human rights in the South. For instance, anticolonial nationalists were largely antagonistic, as both Ibhawoh and Getachew pick up on, to sub-national struggles for self-determination such as in Biafra and Katanga which appeared to threaten the integrity of their statist projects.[28] Subsequently, sub-national claims for self-determination were not only rejected by Third World states but often brutally suppressed at the cost of many violations of human rights. As I demonstrate in the next section, inconsistencies like this would be eagerly pounced upon by the capitalist North. But this should not detract from the achievement of the Third World. The non-aligned movement created a coherent and radical project, which mobilised human rights not as a means of smoothing off some of the rougher edges of the world as it does today but as a claim against the racialised and (post)colonial structures of the world which demanded they be fundamentally reconfigured.

Against the NIEO

Capital's eventual defeat of the postcolonial project of self-determination was the result of a strategy that embraced a number of tactics. On the one hand, the material basis of self-determination would be undermined by the strategic shift in the role of the IMF over the 1970s. As Sundhya Pahuja has demonstrated, while the IMF was largely set up to 'manage a system of stable exchange rates between industrialised nations', a series of legal and policy shifts over the 1970s enabled the Fund to exert greater interest in, and power over, the postcolonial states.[29] Through the construction of an extensive informatics of surveillance, she argues, the IMF laid the groundwork for an apparatus that would be able to exert greater control over the economic policies of postcolonial states. This would be taken advantage of with spectacular results following the decision of the US Federal Reserve to raise interest rates, which plunged postcolonial states into a debt crisis. The IMF's subsequent embrace of structural adjustment loans and their attendant policy conditionalities became a mode of informatic governance that would undermine self-determination by forcibly reshaping much of the South according to the homeostatic imperatives of cybernetic capitalism's global market.

But the undermining of postcolonial self-determination was also effectuated through the North's own appropriation of human rights discourses and their weaponisation against the Third World. Alongside the explosion of new organisations like Amnesty International, the embrace of human rights by the US under Carter is often understood as a catalyst for the rise of human rights as we understand them today. Several competing reasons are often offered for why Carter chose to emphasise human rights in his foreign policy proposals, including the perception of the declining moral standing of the US following Vietnam and the Watergate scandal. But as Courtney Hercus suggests, the growing power of 'the NIEO must also be considered as a significant factor that shaped US human rights policies in the late

1970s'.[30] As she suggests, the Carter administration's turn to human rights was part of a strategy that aimed to 'defuse the activism of the Third World', which threatened the profitability of American multinational corporations.[31]

Hercus's argument is corroborated by scholars such as Slaughter, who argue even more forcefully that human rights were part of the US strategy to roll back the Third World. This barely concealed goal of US human rights policy, Slaughter shows, is made explicit in a 1976 letter from the then UN ambassador, Daniel Moynihan, to the US State Department: 'colonialism is over', Moynihan declared, and in its wake 'human rights is our secret weapon'.[32] Crucially, these sentiments were not confined to the US government but also came to be echoed within other parts of the human rights movement. As Whyte demonstrates, the rather spiky rhetoric of the new humanitarians that gathered around the French section of Médecins Sans Frontières (MSF) in the 1980s also weaponised human rights in order to delegitimise a Third World that it saw as corrupt and authoritarian.[33]

What is quite remarkable is the degree of alignment between the aims and strategies pursued both in US foreign policy and by the French humanitarians. Within both arenas one clear objective was to quash the worldmaking rights claims of the NIEO by disconnecting questions regarding economic conditions in the Global South from considerations regarding the uneven structure of the global economy. For the new humanitarians of MSF, the aim was to undermine Third Worldism by developing the argument that the 'underdevelopment' of the South was determined by 'the burden of human error and bad local political decisions, rather than external elements'.[34] Similarly, in US foreign policy circles, Moynihan argued that the economic hardships of the Global South were 'of their own making and no one else's' and that 'no claim on anyone else arises in consequence'.[35] In this sense, opponents of the NIEO shared a distaste for 'the anticolonial insistence that international political and economic relations were deeply implicated in domestic politics', and instead connected human rights discourses to their attempts to frame 'question of political and economic crisis as matters of internal capacity'.[36]

The development of the State Department's *Country Reports on Human Rights Practices*, which, as I noted earlier, had tied evidence of human rights violations to foreign aid decisions, should be considered as part of this strategy. Taking advantage of some of the moral ambivalences and contradictions of postcolonial regimes, the *Country Reports* brought the internal policies of Third World states into critical focus and gave civil and political rights claims a central place in the broader 'repudiation of the Third World agenda'.[37] In effect, the strategy was to chip away at the moral and political legitimacy of the redistributive human rights discourses developed in the Global South, undercutting the human rights credentials of postcolonial governments with evidence of the violence and 'totalitarian' abuse they perpetrated inside their own countries. The growing mountain of information about human rights abuses, in this sense, was mobilised to weaken Third World claims for an NIEO and, along with it, the connections forged between human rights, the (neo-)colonial international order and global inequalities.

For the French humanitarians, 'the language of human rights' was even more crucial to their efforts 'to shift responsibility for poverty onto Third World states'.[38] As Whyte points out, the human rights discourse mobilised by key figures in MSF was not only deployed to delegitimise regimes as abusive and totalitarian. Rights violations also came to be understood as symptomatic of, and signifiers for, the broader illiberalism of Third Worldism, especially the 'bad local policy decisions' that vitiated the economic development of Southern countries. In this respect, the civil and political rights activism that defined organisations such as Amnesty International was not simply an alternative model of human rights to the NIEO; it was enrolled in efforts to reorient attention away from Third Worldist claims for global justice and towards the failings of the postcolonial state. The informational politics of human rights readily combined with the informatics of structural adjustment as two prongs of an attempt to roll back the Third World.

Accordingly, the late 1970s came to be marked by a kind of dichotomy that set the civil and political rights of individuals emphasised by the capitalist North against the challenge of the anticolonial struggle and its accounts of self-determination, development and, more broadly, social and economic rights. This dichotomy only hardened as the US government's already modest inclusion of social and economic rights under Carter's foreign policy agenda was explicitly disavowed by the reheated anticommunism of the Reagan administration. While Ronald Reagan embraced the idea that civil and political rights were vital pillars of democracy, socio-economic development was rejected as a right and was subordinated to the market. Indeed, as Zachary Manfredi has recently argued, 'the Reagan administration was actively engaged in efforts to discredit the [ICESCR] domestically and internationally', and the avowed position of the administration brought US policy into line with neoliberal thinkers like Hayek who 'vehemently reject[ed] human rights to food, housing, and education'.[39]

Combined with the reality that the NGOs that shaped the human rights agenda in this period largely ignored social and economic rights issues, Reagan's rejection of social rights seemed to bolster the idea that human rights meant the negative freedoms of civil and political rights. The neoliberal reconfigurations of the global economy would only further ossify this exclusionary dichotomy. As the deleterious effects of structural adjustment would fracture and break the solidarities and power of the Third World, its influence over the meaning of human rights subsequently waned. Human rights came to be largely confined to the definitions shaped within the capitalist North.

It would be a mistake, however, to see the movement's prioritisation of civil and political rights as signalling the total exclusion of their social and economic counterparts. Against the Reaganite rejection of socio-economic rights, the 1980s also saw the development of a project that, though admittedly secondary and stop-start, nevertheless intended to rehabilitate and reintegrate them within the contemporary movement. A revival of Third World radicalism this was not; rather than providing a radical challenge to neoliberal order, the development of economic and social rights in this period represented an attempt to cleanse them of their political connotations. In other words, this amelioratory project was designed to informatise social and economic rights, to expunge their political content, transform them into signal, and thus realign them to the emerging contours of cybernetic capitalism. Indicators, as I will soon demonstrate, represented the material and infrastructural configuration of this project to informatise social and economic rights.

Reformulating Rights: Legalistic Informatisation

In 1987 Philip Alston became the first rapporteur for the newly minted UN Committee on Economic, Social and Cultural Rights, whose establishment to monitor the implementation of the ICESCR was the source of some hope for long-suffering proponents of social and economic rights. That same year, Alston published a paper with Gerard Quinn which sought to understand the 'Nature and Scope of States Parties' Obligations under the International Covenant on Economic, Social and Cultural Rights'.[40] As Manfredi has recently argued, the paper remains representative of 'mainstream' attempts to rehabilitate social and economic rights by assuaging neoliberal concerns.[41] Interestingly, Alston and Quinn presented their approach as a return to the legal framework of social and economic rights as a means of clearing up 'the fallacies and misperceptions which in the past have too often served to distort and obfuscate the debate'.[42]

Invoking the informational quality of law and its apparent capacity to clear up distortions or 'noise', then, the underlying logic of Alston and Quinn's argument is already suggestive of a project driven by the informational logic of human rights.

Against neoliberal critics, Alston and Quinn insisted on counteracting the perception that socio-economic rights are 'of a deeply ideological nature, [. . .] necessitate an unacceptable degree of intervention in the domestic affairs of states', and are 'inherently incompatible with a free market economy'.[43] Emphasising the Covenant's 'realism', Alston and Quinn make several interlocking arguments in order to demonstrate that it 'does not purport to impugn any particular socioeconomic system or state ideology as such'.[44] Of these arguments, perhaps the most vociferous is against the suggestion that the implementation of the ICESCR would require states to adopt totalitarian, communistic forms of economic management and thus destroy the free market. Quickly demolishing this suggestion, Alston and Quinn argue that this contention only really holds water if one subscribes to a 'libertarian philosophical analysis, according to which any redistributive action on the part of a government is unacceptable'.[45] But, they continue, it would be 'bizarre' and 'detached from reality' to denounce even limited involvement in social and economic planning by the state given that it is 'so universally accepted in practice'. Moreover, the fact that such complaints were not raised by the many states with free market and mixed economies who ratified the covenant suggests that 'the Covenant has never been interpreted by any governmental or intergovernmental body in such a way as to lend even the least bit of credence to the assertions cited above'.[46]

At the same time, Alston and Quinn moved quickly to head off concerns that the Covenant would create legal obligations that would require wealth redistribution from the North to the South, noting that 'there is no precise legal obligation of [that] kind [. . .] to be found specifically in the covenant'.[47] With important echoes 'of debates about the NIEO and post-colonial states' demands for redistribution of global resources', Manfredi astutely argues that Alston and Quinn's attempt to tackle this may have been designed to reassure 'anxious western actors [. . .] that the ICESCR could not be used to resuscitate the projects of the post-colonial rivals they had so recently vanquished'.[48] I would go one step further and suggest that this is where the ideological and political orientation of the mainstream social and economic rights project appears from behind the veil of political neutrality. Where the non-aligned movement had utilised the right to self-determination as a means of anchoring a speculative and imaginative project of global transformation, figures like

Alston attempted to reconcile the meaning of social and economic rights to the world as it already was. Assuaging neoliberal critics, the task of 'mainstream' advocates for socio-economic rights was to render them as signals compatible with the ideological and material contours of late capitalism.

This project of informatising socio-economic rights centred on supplanting the speculative vision of self-determination with an 'informational' reading of law anchored by the concept of progressive realisation written into the ICESCR. The first article of the Covenant put postcolonial claims centre stage by asserting that '[a]ll peoples have the right of self-determination'.[49] But it was article 2(1), with its insistence that each state should 'take steps [. . .] to the maximum of its available resources, with a view to achieving progressively the full realization of the rights recognised in the present Covenant by all appropriate means', that was centralised in attempts to rehabilitate social rights. Alston and Quinn once again articulate this shift by suggesting that 'the concept of progressive achievement is the linchpin of the whole Covenant. Upon its meaning turns the nature of state obligations.'[50] Accordingly, a significant portion of their work is given over to 'an analysis of the words and phrases used in article 2(1)'.[51]

Though Alston and Quinn are keen to insist that the ICESCR does create binding legal obligations, their interpretation of 'achieve progressively' and 'to the maximum of its available resources' is intended to support their supposed ideological 'neutrality', largely by reading these phrases as providing for a wide degree of state discretion. Affirming that 'achieve progressively' denotes a process of incremental improvement, Alston and Quinn contend that it is 'the state of a country's economy that most vitally determines its obligations', and that deference ought to be paid to state assessments of available resources and possible allocations.[52] This provides, as Alston and Quinn themselves suggest, wiggle room for states to determine what portion of their resources are available, giving much scope for governments won over, for instance, to neoliberal orthodoxies to defend their choices on economic grounds.

But more than that, this mainstream reading of article 2(1) constructs a set of connections between states and the global economy that presents a very different image of the world to that of anticolonial worldmaking. Whilst it brings the state into focus as the subject of obligations, the state's capacities are immediately subordinated to its economy, whose condition is in turn naturalised as a constraint that is unevenly distributed across different states. The double move at work here is to centre the state whilst also implicitly subjecting it to the unequal relations of the global economy, which are simply taken as an unmarked given rather than as a crucial frame of reference for ESC rights and a possible site of intervention. In stark contrast to the transformative demands of postcolonial self-determination, Alston and Quinn's informational reading of progressive realisation reinforces arguments which reject the colonial dynamics underpinning global inequality (such as those made by Moynihan and the new humanitarians of MSF), by naturalising postcolonial inequality. They articulate a state-centred, incrementalistic vision of socio-economic rights compatible with neoliberal conceptions of 'normal development', driven by economic growth and 'the efficiency of the market economy', rather than global redistribution.[53]

Alston and Quinn's work represented a new consensus where 'the obligation to progressively realize [social and economic] rights "to the maximum of a state's available resources" is understood to be at the heart of their realization'.[54] As this consensus on progressive realisation began to take shape, attention quickly turned to the question of its measurement, of how incremental improvements in social rights might be observed and monitored. Reflecting the broader informational project of human rights which, as AI put it, hinges on 'information received, evaluated, processed, transformed into new information and disseminated', this new vision of economic and social rights required the development of appropriate information infrastructures.[55] It was in this context that the use of quantitative methods and, in particular, social indicators quickly gained traction as promising mechanisms for measuring progressive realisation.

Making Indicators Work

Across the late 1980s, the possibility of using indicators to monitor economic and social rights began to percolate in academic debates. Scholars like Frances Stewart and Asbjørn Eide had already begun to assume that indicators based on literacy rates, primary health care and nutrition rates would be part of an effective framework for monitoring the realisation of socio-economic rights.[56] And while remaining generally critical of quantitative approaches to human rights, Robert Justin Goldstein declared in 1986 not only that economic and social rights were more suitable for quantification than their civil and political counterparts but also that the Physical Quality of Life Index (PQLI) had become a widely accepted indicator of their realisation.[57] By 1990, the idea that indicators would be central to socio-economic rights work had seemingly been confirmed by the first UN Special Rapporteur on the Realization of Economic, Social and Cultural Rights, Danilo Türk, who was appointed in 1989.

Türk's work as rapporteur centred on responding to practical issues regarding the realisation of social and economic rights as well as exploring the possibilities of a unified approach across all organs of the UN. His recognition of the value of indicators came to the fore in a series of reports published between 1989 and 1992 and was given a particular focus in a *Progress Report* published in 1990. Noting that the issue of indicators was 'extensive, complex and intricate', Türk argued nevertheless that their use 'within the field of economic, social and cultural rights can, if applied in a precise and systematic manner, contribute to the realization of these rights in a variety of ways'. With an inherent capacity 'to measure both a certain situation and changes to that situation over time', indicators could 'provide one means of assessing progress over time towards the "progressive realization" of these norms'. Even if indicators could bring 'imperfections' such as the lack of available and/or reliable statistics and would also need to be disaggregated by age, ethnicity and income, Türk maintained they could act as a 'yardstick' for governments to compare their progress with others and help to establish 'minimal thresholds' for social and economic rights.[58]

Though Türk did not wish to minimise the potential difficulties of establishing standard indicators, his *Progress Report* also recognised that several UN bodies had already established various indicators that might be used to monitor social and economic rights. Canvassing existing indicators used by the International Labour Organization, UNESCO and the Children's Fund (UNICEF), he suggested that it would be possible to discern a set of core indicators that could be used by human rights bodies. Türk's *Progress Report* singled out and proposed nine such core indicators: under-five mortality rate; per capita GNP for the poorest 40 per cent of the population (including the existence of a 'poverty line' and criteria for this line); the PQLI; overall literacy rate; access to primary health care; percentage of population (or number of persons) suffering from acute malnutrition; percentage of population (or number of persons) inadequately housed; disaggregated indicators for each right by gender, race, descent, national or ethnic origin, age, income level, etc.; and per capita GNP (for comparative purposes). Like Innes de Neufville before him, then, Türk made a serious contribution to how indicators for socio-economic rights might work in practice.

The groundwork set out by Türk was to be further developed at a seminar on 'Appropriate Indicators to Measure Achievement in the Progressive Realization of Economic, Social and Cultural Rights' held at the UN World Conference in Vienna in 1993.[59] At the seminar, Türk gathered experts on indicators and human rights to discuss the practical development of indicators with the ultimate aim of 'setting ideal indicators for each of the substantive economic, social and cultural rights', a fact reflected in the seminar's original agenda.[60] But things did not quite go to plan. As Judith Welling has noted, what first appeared as a moment of triumph for indicators became a moment of crisis. Those present at the seminar could not agree on the indicators which the UN Committee could use to measure socioeconomic rights.[61] With unanswered questions not only about how best to measure the progressive realisation of rights but also about whether ESC rights had been sufficiently conceptualised in order to measure them at all, the participants at the seminar agreed that it was too early to make any pronouncements about ideal or universal standards in regard to indicators.[62]

These difficulties reveal one of the main cleavages that has continued to plague social and economic rights. On the one hand, as Manuel Guzman, then director of HURIDOCS, argued in 2001, there was a consensus that the 'indicators-based methodology' was 'especially suited for monitoring violations of economic, social and cultural rights, such as in determining the level of enjoyment of the right to education by a given population'.[63] Indicators, moreover, could 'assist states parties in better understanding the current situation, including the consequences of current policies', and emphasise 'areas for future policy change'.[64] On the other hand, even while the dream for many has been the development of universal international indicators, precisely what kind of measures might be used to monitor ESC rights has remained a stubbornly open question, resulting in a certain degree of fragmentation. In different circumstances, both the PQLI and the Human Development Index (HDI) have been deployed as indicators of social and economic rights.[65] At the same time, however, the UN Committee on Economic, Social and Cultural Rights largely allowed states to develop and submit their own indicators for reporting purposes, posing new problems regarding the standardisation of monitoring and reporting.[66]

By 2006 the Office of the United Nations High Commissioner for Human Rights (OHCHR) renewed its efforts to standardise international indicators.[67] However, the OHCHR's approach did not deliver a universal set of indicators for socio-economic rights, instead providing guidance about appropriate indicators in the form of the Structure, Process, Outcome framework. According to this framework, monitoring should use indicators that aggregate states' compliance with international treaties (Structure), the resources mobilised to realise them (Process), and the realisation of rights through measures like infant mortality and literacy rates (Outcome).[68] This has been followed up with further guidance for those wishing to use human rights indicators such as its implementation guide published in 2012.[69]

Despite these efforts, the approaches to indicators used for monitoring socio-economic rights have continued to proliferate, with a growing number of NGOs and academics developing their own indicators. For instance, the Social and Economic Rights Fulfilment (SERF) Index, developed by Sakiko Fukuda-Parr and her colleagues, has emerged as a rival to more recognised indexes like the HDI.[70] The SERF Index collates statistics on health, education, access to food, and so on into composite scores for countries all across the world, but unlike the HDI it uses different approaches for 'low- and middle-income countries' and 'high-income countries', as an attempt to better reflect global disparities. The Centre for Social and Economic Rights (CESCR) has similarly developed its own Outcome, Policy Efforts, Resources, Assessment (OPERA) framework, which has been heralded as a promising new way forward for NGOs and activists.[71] For its proponents, what makes the OPERA framework particularly useful is that it combines traditional statistical indicators for measuring progressive realisation (outcomes) with forms of budgetary analysis designed to measure whether 'maximum available resources' are being deployed by states. In doing so, it promises a more systematic picture of compliance.

Other approaches have attempted to address specific geographical locations or a particular cluster of rights. The Right-to-Education Project, for instance, focuses on educational rights and has put together a range of 150 indicators with linkages to relevant and, where possible, disaggregated data that individuals and organisations can select and use. Indicators include: the adult literacy rate; pupil/textbook ratio; education expenditure ratio; and out-of-school children rate.[72] Conversely, the Egypt Social Progress Indicators (ESPI) project brings together a range of indicators on education, health, food, water and agricultural land, and more to measure the progressive realisation of social and economic rights in Egypt.[73] Indicators on health, for example, include student/teacher ratios and pre-primary enrolment rates that can be disaggregated according to gender, ethnicity and income. ESPI collates indicators on each area into a colour system: red (no progress), orange (weak progress), yellow (partial progress) and green (good progress).

Though the examples above by no means paint an exhaustive picture, they do helpfully demonstrate an important point about indicators for human rights. Like the Events Model we explored in the previous chapter, indicators are also a kind of boundary object, which remains abstract at a 'global' level and achieves a more concrete iteration in particular organisations and circumstances. But the plurality of approaches to indicators suggests a boundary object that is more weakly structured than the Events Model, which coagulates around the structuring power of HURIDOCS' Events Standard Formats. It might be understood as what Susan Leigh Star called an 'ideal type', a form of boundary object that is 'abstracted from all domains', and thus 'fairly vague', but 'provides a sufficient roadmap for all parties'.[74] Hence, the challenge of analysing indicators that the next sections take on is one of straddling the abstract and the particular, of defining the general stakes of their usage whilst paying careful enough attention to specific practices and the issues their particularities might raise.

Informatising Rights: Indicators as Technical Project

The systems of global governance that have emerged since capitalism's triumph at the end of the Cold War, which, as Margaret Satterthwaite and AnnJanette Rosga note, has generalised the use of indicators to 'audit' and govern the behaviour of states, provides a crucial context for the development of indicators in human rights.[75] Rights-based indicators are part of a broader array of statistical composites and other numerical forms that have become key tools within institutions with which to capture the performance of states in relation to a particular issue and to monitor their progress over time. Accordingly, the monitoring of ESC rights has, as Bal Sokhi-Bulley contends, emerged alongside and as part of a growing mode of 'informational governance' promoted by institutions like the UN, World Bank and the IMF.[76] Echoing the kind of world cybernetic system imagined by Laswell and his co-authors, an array of indicator-based systems – from the World Bank's 'ease of doing business index' to measures of vaccination rates and primary education attainment – subject states to forms of evaluation, comparison, ranking and competition intended to modify and/or discipline state behaviour.

In many respects, however, the forms of informational governance constructed through social and economic rights indicators have much in common with the earlier forms of informational politics carried out by the new human rights NGOs that came to the fore in the late 1970s. Remembering that cybernetics is etymologically rooted in the Greek *kybernētēs* meaning 'governor' or 'steersman', both projects are, in the final instance, efforts to use informational feedback as a means of shaping or 'governing' state behaviour. Moreover, in both approaches NGOs, international governmental organisations and states are all integrated nodes within their respective systems. Where they differ is on questions of recognition, of signal and noise. As we have seen, the movement's rise to prominence in the 1970s congealed around an empirical epistemology based on positive facts cleaved from thorny issues of politics and social structure. But given the issue of political economy is a much more intractable one for social and economic rights, transforming them into information obviously requires a different strategy. The crucial question, then, is what epistemological resources indicators deploy as practice to respond to this problem and embody the depoliticising informational logic of human rights.

The use of indicators in socio-economic rights issues has long attracted critical attention in academic debates, and the work of authors such as Satterthwaite and Rosga, Sally Engle Merry and David McGrogan provides substantial ground upon which to develop my own analysis. These critics reinforce the notion that the turn to indicators embodies a faith in the informational power of quantification. As McGrogan notes of the OHCHR's contribution to the development of human rights indicators, 'the preference is for the quantitative over the qualitative'.[77] These 'objective indicators', as the OHCHR puts it, 'are verifiable and can be easier to interpret when comparing the human rights situation in a country over time and across populations'.[78] The allure of indicators, as Merry contends, is that they produce numbers as 'simple descriptors of phenomena', which 'resist the biases of conjecture and theory because they are subject to the invariable rules of mathematics', and 'appear free of interpretation and to be neutral and descriptive'.[79] Indicators, in other words, lay claim to objectivity through the structure of what Poovey calls the 'modern fact'.[80] In leaning on the supposedly objective qualities of quantitative knowledge, indicators represent a strategy to defend social and economic rights from the political.

Moreover, the emphasis on quantitative indicators radically attenuates the capacity for political judgement by concentrating debates about rights on technical issues. As Satterthwaite and Rosga contend, normative judgement is suspended by questions of measure, an issue which displaces 'contestation over substantive rights issues onto seemingly bureaucratic or technical decisions about choice of indicators'.[81] The debates that have dominated the operationalisation of indicators, forensically traced by Todd Landman and Edzia Carvalho in *Measuring Human Rights*, are a case in point.[82] Concerns with whether statistics used to measure welfare and development are accurate enough measures of human rights standards and obligations and can thus be transposed from one arena to another, for instance, reflect the way a technics of measurement takes centre stage. Such discussions tend to foreclose 'political struggles over what human rights mean', by submerging them beneath 'technical questions of measurement [and] criteria'.[83] Indeed, this 'sovereignty of technique', as McGrogan calls it, means that 'even where scepticism is raised about the possibility of measuring human rights performance empirically [. . .] there usually remains a sense that what are needed are simply better indicators used in different ways'.[84]

What existing critical analyses of indicators have missed, however, is that the ways in which indicators transmute issues of political and normative 'judgement' into technical matters reflects what critical scholars understand to be a broader tendency of neoliberal governance. In her recent work on neoliberalism, Wendy Brown has argued that one of the ways neoliberalism serves to depoliticise the social is to transform politics into a space of technical management, which 'brackets off [. . .] conflict and deliberation about common values or ends'.[85] Discourses associated with neoliberal governance tend to function through a post-ideological emphasis on 'what works' and, in doing so, 'eliminates from discussion politically, ethically, or otherwise normatively inflected dimensions of policy, aiming to supersede politics with practical, technical approaches to problems'.[86] In this context, the technical application of numbers that characterises much of the quest for indicators for socio-economic rights aligns with a 'neoliberal' strategy that dispels the political contestation of social and economic issues through technical objects such as econometrics, statistical distributions, Laffer curves, GDP, and so on.

But if, as I have argued, neoliberal governance makes up one aspect of a 'larger' social formation that I have been calling cybernetic capitalism, then the 'neoliberal' embrace of technical solutions might also be read as symptomatic of capital's informatic turn. From this perspective, the use of indicators to measure social and economic rights looks more like another trajectory of cybernetic capitalism's informational logic as it has been instantiated within the field of human rights. As informational and informatising devices, indicators provide a technical and seemingly objective discourse that can help social and economic rights to achieve systemic recognition by excluding political noise. Indicators are thus 'communicative instruments', as one World Bank study put it;[87] or, as the AAAS argued in its work on the right to health, '[i]ndicators are signals that make it possible to determine the extent to which a particular obligation or standard has been, or is being, attained'.[88]

Formatting States as 'Discrete States'; or, Effacing the Global

Arguing that the technical submerges the political, however, is not to imply indicators are simply objective referents for the social world that are without politics. As discussed in Chapter 1, the universalist claims of objectivity elide the ways that all forms of knowledge are configured by and within exiting relations of power and social authority. In its traditional Western form, objectivity is a kind of epistemic 'god trick' that obfuscates the ways that particular perspectives – and the political claims necessarily attached to them – are able to leverage existing power relations so that the specificity of their viewpoint remains unmarked, appearing as a god's-eye view 'of everything from nowhere'.[89] With this in mind, it is important to remember that the technical form of indicators both reflects while it simultaneously veils the social and political assumptions embedded within them. To extend Bruno Latour's famous aphorism slightly: '[data] science is politics by other means'.[90]

My argument is that indicators realise as practice the kinds of incremental, state-centric project developed by 'mainstream' practitioners of social and economic rights such as Alston. In other words, they materialise a way of thinking about these rights intended to make them compatible with the material and imaginary limits of late capitalism. The incrementalism of 'progressive realisation', which as noted earlier is well suited to a vision of development through market-led economic growth rather than a more radical and redistributive project, is embodied within the logic indicators that measure statistical changes in progress over time. Indeed, because indicators make no claims on how a state might make incremental improvements on specific measures but simply track changes over time, they reflect the 'ideologically neutral' vision of rights that is now mainstream. One should not forget, however, that the apparent ideological neutrality embedded in indicators is a pretext for forms of measurement and monitoring that are compatible with market-led notions of development that predominate today, a context where the postcolonial economy of global capitalism is rarely challenged.

Indicators also lend themselves to practices such as benchmarking and target-setting which reinforce incremental logics. Indeed, the OHCHR and CESCR strongly favour benchmarking since, '[o]n their own, indicators are inconclusive. They say nothing without clear reference points against which to judge performance and assess the adequacy of achievements or progress over time.'[91] As McGrogan notes, where statistical indicators provide the implicit end goal of 100 per cent achievement, benchmarking works against this by transforming statistics into targets – a benchmark might be used to improve literacy rates from 25 per cent of the population to a base level of 30 per cent , for instance.[92] In this way, benchmarks dispel the political contestation of social and economic rights even further by entrenching incremental targets that lessen expectations and by reinforcing a logic of measurement that leaves little room for more imaginative questions about values, means and ends. This is especially true when one observes that benchmarks are usually set according to what constitutes a 'realistic' achievement and a state's 'existing level of development'.[93] Benchmarks further settle the incremental fulfilment of economic and social rights within the constraints of contemporary capitalism and do not engage with the possibility of more imaginative, transformative and redistributive agendas. From this perspective, benchmarked indicators reconcile us with the world as it is rather than as it could be.

Indicators also bolster the state-centric approach of the mainstream social and economic rights project. The numeric forms produced by indicators make visible the internal functioning of national spaces, opening them up as the primary site of human rights practice, and subjecting states to the measurement, observation and evaluation made available by literacy rates, educational attainment, doctors per capita, and so on. The implication, of course, is that the state is responsible for the outcomes measured by indicators and is thus figured as the key agent for the realisation of social and economic rights. Through policy measures or the prioritisation of specific economic sectors, it is assumed that the state can and will effectuate incremental improvement. The OHCHR's emphasis on developing what it calls 'structural' and 'process' indicators further inscribes the agency of the state by measuring 'commitments and acceptance of international human rights standards (structural indicators) [and] efforts being made to meet the obligations that flow from the standards (process indicators)'.[94]

Importantly, the state's inscription in indicators materialises through a somewhat 'digital' vision of social and economic rights, or at least one that is compatible with digital forms, which captures the world as a set of discrete and autonomous nation-states that can be measured temporally across a set of similarly discrete intervals. Indicators reproduce discrete States as discrete states. This digitally is perhaps not that surprising given that many of the complex calculations that undergird statistical indicators require support from computational machines. It should be remembered, however, that the discretising process of the digital only constitutes its entities and agential/causal arrangements by 'cutting' them away from and excluding others. Indicators stabilise and foreground the agency of the state through an array of 'cuts' and their attendant exclusions; their binding of social and economic issues into the interiority of the state is a consequence of a constitutive cut that excludes and thus renders invisible the dynamic agency of the global economy and the causal dynamics it exerts not only over states' capacities but also over forms of dispossession, exploitation and inequality in local spaces.[95]

Unlike the project of the NIEO, then, indicators provide absolutely no way to see and therefore act upon the postcolonial economy of global capitalism, and, moreover, it is difficult to see how they might be reformed to do so. If the global economy can be glimpsed at all, it is through indexes like SERF and the HDI which, in placing discrete nation-states next to each other in rankings and other modes of comparison, make it possible to glimpse the effect of the postcolonial economy within numerical disparities between states. But rather than problematise these disparities, the cross-national comparisons and rankings that are an intrinsic part of these indexes simply reinscribe a logic of competition that naturalises inequality. After all, as the sociologist William Davies has argued, competition itself assumes unequal outcomes and thus displaces any desire for substantive equality with the objective of improving a state's score in relation to its rivals.[96] In this way, global inequality in itself becomes no obstacle to the realisation of rights; in fact, inequality is implicitly reconfigured as one possible driver of realisation.

This is especially true in the case of the SERF index, which separates what it calls 'core countries' from 'high income OECD countries' and measures them according to distinct standards that are deemed appropriate for each grouping.[97] While the logic of doing so is laudably one of not overburdening poorer countries (and, conversely, 'under-burdening' richer ones), because the indicators lock measurement into the logic of the nation-state, this form of two-track system reinscribes the division between the Global North and South.[98] Postcolonial inequality is reinscribed under the auspices of creating seemingly 'fairer' parameters for comparison between states, making uneven development simply a given that escapes problematisation. In this way, indicators constitute a reversal of earlier anticolonial projects for socio-economic rights and exclude, if not entirely efface, questions of the global transformation and redistribution of resources as a rights issue.

What Alternatives for Social and Economic Rights?

Though indicators have continued to be developed as an informational solution to the problems posed by social and economic rights, as this chapter has hinted at, they have also faced consistent questions about their feasibility. The quest for rights indicators has had to confront not only recurring methodological questions around what it is that specific indicators measure but also the huge practical problem that effective monitoring 'requires an enormous amount of good quality data'.[99] This is by no means a new problem; in designing their global cybernetic system for monitoring human dignity, Laswell and his co-authors noted that one 'danger' was the problem of 'over-conceptualization' which would leave 'the need [. . .] for data to fill a void'.[100] But in a world driven by cybernetic capitalism where, to borrow from Jonathan Beller, digital computation 'announces the universal generalization of ever more granular accounting', the perceived lack of necessary data is an ever closing horizon.[101] Indeed, this chapter has shown that the more pressing danger might be what Laswell et al. called 'technological lock-in – the commitment to a given type of data, method of analysis, and technology for supporting interpretation'.[102] As the informational reading of the ICESCR, with its incrementalism and centring of the state, becomes locked into the information infrastructures, data types and particular computational methods associated with indicators, the worry is that possibilities for thinking economic and social rights otherwise sink even further.

In fact, the only real alternative to indicators has come from those who, seeing the methodological and practical difficulties outlined above, have attempted to develop a way of doing social and economic rights that treats them much like their civil and political counterparts. An important strand of this alternative trajectory emerged out of an AAAS project on economics and social rights led by Audrey Chapman in the mid-1990s, which aimed to move towards what she termed a 'violations approach' for social and economic rights.[103] Carefully reading the ICESCR, Chapman argued that it is possible to distinguish between those economic and social rights subject to progressive realisation and other parts of the Covenant that engender immediate obligations such as duties to prevent discrimination according to gender, race, sexuality, etc. For Chapman, these immediate obligations provided opportunities to make ground in the fight for social and economic rights because issues such as discrimination represented tangible rights violations that could be remedied using existing tools developed to defend civil and political rights. Focusing on more immediate obligations, Chapman insisted, would enable NGOs to treat social and economic rights as 'events' and deploy familiar weapons such as naming and shaming which would make monitoring 'more feasible and more manageable than progressive realization alone'.[104]

Chapman's perspective has been reinforced by prominent members of the NGO community such as Kenneth Roth, the executive director of Human Rights Watch. In 2004, Roth published a commentary on how NGOs might address long-neglected social and economic rights issues. His argument was that progressive realisation posed difficulties for human rights NGOs largely because it does not readily comport itself into the naming and shaming methodology and the absolute clarity it provides with regard to 'violation, violator, and remedy'.[105] If human rights organisations are to take on economic and social rights issues, Roth argued, it would be better to focus on 'arbitrary or discriminatory conduct' that crystallises a clear 'violation [. . .,] violator (the government or other actor through its arbitrary or discriminatory conduct), and [. . .] remedy (reversing that conduct)'.[106] It is unsurprising, then, that the violations approach to social and economic rights outlined by Chapman has continued to grow alongside indicators. As Eitan Felner has recently noted, 'monitoring efforts by UN Treaty Bodies of specific State Parties, field investigations by NGOs, and adjudication by courts of concrete cases' have made more ground on protecting immediate obligations, particularly 'discriminatory laws or practices carried out by public officials, such as doctors, teachers, etc.'[107]

In focusing on that small subset of rights issues which can be readily rendered as events, however, the violations approach neither unpicks the informational logic of progressive realisation nor does it provide a more expansive account of social and economic rights. If anything, it represents a much narrower vision that is even better attuned to late capitalism. Principles like non-discrimination embody a kind of formal equality before the law that, as Gillian MacNaughton contends, has very little to say about and thus 'fail[s] to challenge the gross economic and social inequalities in the world today'.[108] Formal equality is crucial for a cybernetic social world whose representational schema is the flat nodes and edges of the network diagram; it is the protocol by which individuals come to look like identical nodes in the totalising network of the market, helpfully hiding the ways that bodies and communities are unequally constituted and distributed in the social. Little wonder that, as Whyte demonstrates, non-discrimination principles have often been celebrated by neoliberal ideologues because they can play a 'role in perpetuating existing inequalities'.[109] Stressing the formal equality embedded in non-discrimination principles has become part of a strategy 'to prevent redistribution for the purpose of greater substantive or socio-economic equality, and to rule out demands for foreign aid, support for industries of former colonies, or reparations'.[110]

The approaches to social and economic rights which predominate today provide few opportunities for emancipatory change. Developing a vision of human rights equal to cybernetic capitalism will require moving beyond the notion of ideological neutrality and the limits of formal equality by refusing to ignore wealth distribution as a global issue. But any attempt to move in this direction and radically shift the terrain upon which social and economic rights is fought will first require a refusal of the informational logic of human rights, its depoliticising pursuit of 'signal', and the technological lock-in of its current informational practices. The task, which I reflect on in the final chapter of this book, is to invent and mobilise a concept of information whose 'granular accounting', as Beller puts it, confronts the human cost – in all its raced, classed and gendered permutations – of cybernetic capitalism. It is under these conditions that human rights might begin to develop pathways beyond the miseries of the present.

Notes

1. Richard C. Snyder, Charles F. Hermann and Harold Laswell, 'A Global Monitoring System: Appraising the Effects of Government on Human Dignity', *International Studies Quarterly* 20, no. 2 (1976): 221–60.
2. Snyder et al., 'A Global Monitoring System', 222
3. Snyder et al., 'A Global Monitoring System'.
4. Raymond Bauer (ed.), *Social Indicators* (Cambridge, MA: MIT Press, 1966), 13. It is worth further noting that alongside Bauer other leading figures in the social indicators movement such as Charles Austin explicitly saw their work on indicators as, first and foremost, a form of social cybernetics.
5. Antony Anghie, 'Whose Utopia? Human Rights, Development, and the Third World', *Qui Parle* 22, no. 1 (2013): 63–80; Joseph R. Slaughter, 'Hijacking Human Rights: Neoliberalism, the New Historiography, and the End of the Third World', *Human Rights Quarterly* 40, no. 4 (2018): 735–75.
6. In a 1977 presidential memorandum, the US approach to human rights was outlined in the following terms: 'While "internationally recognized human rights" would include, inter alia, all of the rights in the Universal Declaration of Human Rights [. . .] with the concept of "gross violations," Congress intended to cover mainly the right to be free from governmental violation of the integrity of the person, i.e., the first group of [civil and political] rights discussed above.' Consequently, while less acknowledged, social and economic rights were on the

agenda throughout all of the *Country Reports*. However, As Innes de Neufville explained, a lack of social policy expertise in the US Foreign Service workforce that compiled information for the *Country Reports*, and a wariness of embarrassing the countries that hosted them, often meant that 'these sections of the reports were frequently laden with subjective language, vague impressions, and individual opinions'. See Courtney Hercus, *The Struggle over Human Rights: The Non-Aligned Movement, Jimmy Carter, and Neoliberalism* (London and Lanham, MD: Lexington Books, 2019), 89; Judith Innes de Neufville, 'Social Indicators of Basic Needs: Quantitative Data for Human Rights Policy', *Social Indicators Research* 11, no. 4 (1982): 385.

7. Innes de Neufville, 'Social Indicators of Basic Needs', 385.
8. Innes de Neufville, 'Social Indicators of Basic Needs', 401–2.
9. United States Department of State, *2015 Country Reports on Human Rights Practices* (Washington DC: Government of the United States, 2016).
10. Margaret L. Satterthwaite and AnnJanette Rosga, 'The Trust in Indicators: Measuring Human Rights', *Berkeley Journal of International Law* 27, no. 2 (2009): 253–315.
11. Susan Marks, *A False Tree of Liberty: Human Rights in Radical Thought* (Oxford: Oxford University Press, 2019).
12. Slaughter, 'Hijacking Human Rights', 755.
13. As Slaughter points out, 'the words were being used by African American and abolitionist newspapers in both the North and the South in the middle of the nineteenth century, almost weekly, in Frederick Douglass's The North Star; by Spanish-language newspapers in the North to elaborate José Martí's anti-imperial vision of "Nuestra América" in the late nineteenth century.' See Slaughter, 'Hijacking Human Rights', 747.
14. Bonny Ibhawoh, 'Testing the Atlantic Charter: Linking Anticolonialism, Self-Determination and Universal Human Rights', *International Journal of Human Rights* 18, no. 7–8 (2014): 842–60.
15. Recent examples include: Julia Dehm, 'Highlighting Inequalities in the Histories of Human Rights: Contestations over Justice, Needs and Rights in the 1970s', *Leiden Journal of International Law* 31, no. 4 (2018): 871–95; Bradley R. Simpson, 'Self-Determination, Human Rights, and the End of Empire in the 1970s', *Humanity: An International Journal of Human Rights, Humanitarianism, and Development* 4, no. 2 (2013): 239–60; Slaughter, 'Hijacking Human Rights'.
16. Adom Getachew, *Worldmaking after Empire: The Rise and Fall of Self-Determination* (Princeton, NJ: Princeton University Press, 2019), 2.
17. Getachew, *Worldmaking after Empire*, 2.
18. Getachew, *Worldmaking after Empire*, 74.
19. Getachew, *Worldmaking after Empire*, 74.
20. United Nations General Assembly Resolution 1514 (XV), 'Declaration on the Granting of Independence to Colonial Countries and Peoples', 14 December 1960.

21. Getachew, *Worldmaking after Empire*, 89.

22. Proclamation of Teheran, Final Act of the International Conference on Human Rights, Teheran, 22 April to 13 May 1968, UN Doc. A/CONF. 32/41, 3. For more on the Teheran Proclamation and its shaping of a Third World human rights agenda, see Roland Burke, 'From Individual Rights to National Development: The First UN International Conference on Human Rights, Tehran, 1968', *Journal of World History* 19, no. 3 (2008): 275–96.

23. For instance, Getachew argues that Julius Nyerere did not just see the unequal international order as a detriment to social and economic rights. Insofar as the global economy subordinated some individuals to others, it meant that the equal citizenship formalised in law would always be eroded by the reality of socio-economic inequality. In this sense, civil and political rights remained, at least for some, an integral part of the idea of self-determination. See Getachew, *Worldmaking after Empire*, 154–5.

24. Kwame Nkrumah, *Neo-Colonialism: The Last Stage of Imperialism* (London: Thomas Nelson & Sons, 1965); Getachew, *Worldmaking after Empire*, 143.

25. Dehm, 'Highlighting Inequalities in the Histories of Human Rights'.

26. United Nations General Assembly Resolution 3201 (S-VI), 'Declaration on the Establishment of a New International Economic Order', 1 May 1974.

27. Julius Nyerere argued in fact that the choice available to the North was 'an economic revolution effected in an orderly and planned manner, or violent revolution'. Nyerere, quoted in Getachew, *Worldmaking after Empire*, 160.

28. Ibhawoh, 'Testing the Atlantic Charter'; Getachew, *Worldmaking after Empire*.

29. Sundhya Pahuja, 'Technologies of Empire: IMF Conditionality and the Reinscription of the North/South Divide', *Leiden Journal of International Law* 13, no. 4 (2000): 749–813.

30. Hercus, *The Struggle over Human Rights*, 10.

31. Hercus, *The Struggle over Human Rights*, 128.

32. Daniel Moynihan, quoted in Slaughter, 'Hijacking Human Rights', 757.

33. Jessica Whyte, 'Powerless Companions or Fellow Travellers? Human Rights and the Neoliberal Assault on Post-Colonial Economic Justice', *Radical Philosophy* 2, no. 2 (2018): 13–29.

34. Rony Brauman, quoted in Whyte, 'Powerless Companions or Fellow Travellers?', 22.

35. Daniel Moynihan, quoted in Getachew, *Worldmaking after Empire*, 177.

36. Getachew, *Worldmaking after Empire*, 177.

37. Slaughter, 'Hijacking Human Rights', 757.

38. Whyte, 'Powerless Companions or Fellow Travellers?', 14.

39. Zachary Manfredi, 'Against "Ideological Neutrality": On the Limits of Liberal and Neoliberal Economic and Social Human Rights', *London Review of International Law* 8, no. 2 (2020): 296, 303.

40. Philip Alston and Gerard Quinn, 'The Nature and Scope of States Parties' Obligations under the International Covenant on Economic, Social and Cultural Rights', *Human Rights Quarterly* 9, no. 2 (1987): 156–229.
41. Manfredi, 'Against "Ideological Neutrality"', 303.
42. Alston and Quinn, 'The Nature and Scope of States Parties' Obligations', 158.
43. Alston and Quinn, 'The Nature and Scope of States Parties' Obligations', 160.
44. Alston and Quinn, 'The Nature and Scope of States Parties' Obligations', 219.
45. Alston and Quinn, 'The Nature and Scope of States Parties' Obligations', 182.
46. Alston and Quinn, 'The Nature and Scope of States Parties' Obligations', 182.
47. Alston and Quinn, 'The Nature and Scope of States Parties' Obligations', 221.
48. Manfredi, 'Against "Ideological Neutrality"', 306.
49. International Covenant on Economic, Social and Cultural Rights (ICESCR), New York, 16 December 1966, in force 3 January 1976, 993 UNTS 3.
50. Alston and Quinn, 'The Nature and Scope of States Parties' Obligations', 172.
51. Alston and Quinn, 'The Nature and Scope of States Parties' Obligations', 165.
52. Alston and Quinn, 'The Nature and Scope of States Parties' Obligations', 177.
53. Nicholas Snow, 'The Mont Pèlerin Quarterly Vol. 1 No. 1 April 1959', 5 October 2010, quoted in Whyte, 'Powerless Companions or Fellow Travellers?', 20. As Whyte notes, neoliberal development economists such as Peter Bauer followed Hayek in conceiving of the market as an information processor that alone could produce real material development.
54. Eitan Felner, 'Closing the "Escape Hatch": A Toolkit to Monitor the Progressive Realization of Economic, Social, and Cultural Rights', *Journal of Human Rights Practice* 1, no. 3 (2009): 402.
55. 'AI Seminar on Information Handling', DOC 15/01/78. Folder 132, Amnesty International. International Secretariat Archive. International Institute of Social History, Amsterdam.
56. Frances Stewart, 'Basic Needs Strategies, Human Rights, and the Right to Development', *Human Rights Quarterly* 11, no. 3 (1989): 347–74.
57. R. J. Goldstein, 'The Limitations of Using Quantitative Data in Studying Human Rights Abuses', *Human Rights Quarterly* 8, no. 4 (1986): 607–27.
58. Danilo Türk, *Progress Report on the Realization of Economic, Social and Cultural Rights* (E/CN.4/Sub.2/1990/19), 6 July 1990, 3–4.

59. *Report of the Seminar on Appropriate Indicators to Measure Achieve-ment in the Progressive Realization of Economic, Social and Cul-tural Rights*, UN World Conference on Human Rights, UN Doc. A/CONF.157/PC/73, 20 April 1993.
60. *Report of the Seminar on Appropriate Indicators*, 14.
61. Judith V. Welling, 'International Indicators and Economic, Social, and Cultural Rights', *Human Rights Quarterly* 30 (2008): 933–58.
62. Satterthwaite and Rosga, 'The Trust in Indicators'.
63. Manuel Mario Guzman, 'The Investigation and Documentation of Events as a Methodology in Monitoring Human Rights Violations', *Statistical Journal of the United Nations* 18 (2001): 249–57.
64. Welling, 'International Indicators', 944.
65. Todd Landman and Edzia Carvalho, *Measuring Human Rights* (London and New York: Routledge, 2009).
66. Satterthwaite and Rosga, 'The Trust in Indicators'.
67. *OHCHR Report on Indicators for Monitoring Compliance with International Human Rights Instruments*, UN Doc. HRI/MC/2006/7, 11 May 2006.
68. Satterthwaite and Rosga, 'The Trust in Indicators'.
69. OHCHR, *Human Rights Indicators: A Guide to Measurement and Implementation* (New York: United Nations, 2012).
70. Its methodology is in turn used by organisations like the Human Rights Measurement Initiative (HRMI). See <https://humanrightsmeasurement.org/methodology/measuring-economic-social-rights/> (last accessed 24 February 2022).
71. Allison Corkery, Sally-Anne Way and Victoria Wisniewski Otero, *The OPERA Framework: Assessing Compliance with the Obligation to Fulfill Economic, Social and Cultural Rights* (New York: CESCR, 2012).
72. Right to Education Project, *Right to Education Indicators* (2016), <https://www.right-to-education.org/monitoring/sites/right-to-education.org.monitoring/files/RTE_Right_to_Education_Indicators_List_2016_En.pdf> (last accessed 27 February 2022).
73. See <https://www.progressegypt.org/en/> (last accessed 24 February 2022).
74. Susan Leigh Star, 'The Structure of Ill-Structured Solutions: Boundary Objects and Heterogeneous Distributed Problem Solving', in *Boundary Objects and Beyond: Working With Leigh Star*, ed. Geoffrey C. Bowker, Stefan Timmermans, Adele E. Clarke and Ellen Balka (Cambridge, MA: MIT Press, 2015), 253.
75. Satterthwaite and Rosga, 'The Trust in Indicators'.
76. Bal Sokhi-Bulley, 'Governing (Through) Rights: Statistics as Technologies of Governmentality', *Social and Legal Studies* 20, no. 2 (2011): 139–55.
77. David McGrogan, 'Human Rights Indicators and the Sovereignty of Technique', *European Journal of International Law* 27, no. 2 (2016): 388.
78. OHCHR, *Human Rights Indicators*, 17.
79. Sally Engle Merry, 'Measuring the World: Indicators, Human Rights, and Global Governance', *Current Anthropology* 52, no. 3 (2011): 89.

80. Mary Poovey, *A History of the Modern Fact* (Chicago: University of Chicago Press, 1998).
81. Satterthwaite and Rosga, 'The Trust in Indicators', 305.
82. Landman and Carvalho, *Measuring Human Rights*.
83. Merry, 'Measuring the World', 88.
84. McGrogan, 'Human Rights Indicators', 395.
85. Wendy Brown, *Undoing the Demos: Neoliberalism's Stealth Revolution* (Cambridge, MA: Zone Books and MIT Press, 2015), 129.
86. Brown, *Undoing the Demos*, 130.
87. Siobhan McInerney-Lankford and Hans-Otto Sano, *Human Rights Indicators in Development: An Introduction* (Washington DC: World Bank, 2010), 14.
88. Judith Asher, *The Right to Health: A Resource Manual for NGOs* (London: Commonwealth Medical Trust, the AAAS Science and Human Rights Program and HURIDOCS, 2004), 89.
89. Donna Haraway, 'Situated Knowledges: The Science Question in Feminism and the Privilege of Partial Perspective', *Feminist Studies* 14, no. 3 (1988): 575.
90. Bruno Latour, *The Pasteurization of France* (Cambridge, MA: Harvard University Press, 1988).
91. Corkery et al., *The OPERA Framework*, 8.
92. McGrogan, 'Human Rights Indicators', 395.
93. Corkery et al., *The OPERA Framework*, 8. The SERF index, for example, uses a measure called Achievement Possibility Frontiers (APS) which uses an 'evidence-based' approach to 'what is feasible to achieve when a country allocates the maximum of available resources to fulfilling economic and social rights and uses those resources effectively as is evidenced by the experience of the best performing countries at different per capita GDP levels'. See Susan Randolph, John Stewart, Sakiko Fukuda-Parr and Terra Lawson-Remer, 'SERF Index Methodology 2019 Update Technical Note' (Economic and Social Rights Empowerment Initiative, 2019), <https://www.serfindex.org/overview/> (last accessed 24 February 2022); Sakiko Fukuda-Parr, Terra Lawson-Remer and Susan Randolph, 'Measuring the Progressive Realization of Human Rights Obligations: An Index of Economic and Social Rights Fulfillment', *Economic Rights Working Paper Series*, Working Paper 8 (Storrs, CT: The Human Rights Institute of the University of Connecticut, 2008), 4.
94. OHCHR, 'Human Rights Indicators – Main Features of OHCHR Conceptual and Methodological Framework' (2020), <https://www.ohchr.org/en/issues/indicators/pages/framework.aspx> (last accessed 24 February 2022).
95. For treatments of this issue, see Nick Dyer-Witheford, *Cyber-Proletariat: Global Labour in the Digital Vortex* (London: Pluto Press, 2015); Sandro Mezzarda and Brett Neilson, *The Politics of Operations: Excavating Contemporary Capitalism* (Durham, NC and London: Duke University Press, 2019).

96. William Davies, *The Limits of Neoliberalism: Authority, Sovereignty and the Logic of Competition* (Los Angeles: SAGE Publications, 2014), 36.

97. Susan Randolph, Sakiko Fukuda-Parr and Terra Lawson-Remer, 'Economic and Social Rights Fulfillment Index: Country Scores and Rankings', *Journal of Human Rights* 9, no. 3 (2010): 231.

98. As the authors of the index note, 'data constraints coupled with the different right challenges in high income countries versus other countries have led to our creation of two separate assessment standards: The "low and middle income" assessment standard holds countries to a basic level of rights fulfilment and is most relevant to low- and middle-income countries. The "high-income" assessment standard holds countries to a higher standard more relevant to the right challenges facing high-income countries.' Susan Randolph, John Stewart, Sakiko Fukuda-Parr and Terra Lawson-Remer, 'SERF Index Methodology 2020 Updated Technical Note' (Economic and Social Rights Empowerment Initiative, 2020), <https://www.serfindex.org/overview/> (last accessed 24 February 2022).

99. Audrey Chapman, 'A "Violations Approach" for Monitoring the International Covenant on Economic, Social and Cultural Rights', *Human Rights Quarterly* 18, no. 1 (1996): 33.

100. Snyder et al., 'A Global Monitoring System', 247.

101. Jonathan Beller, *The World Computer: Derivative Conditions of Racial Capitalism* (Durham, NC and London: Duke University Press, 2021), 24.

102. Snyder et al., 'A Global Monitoring System', 247.

103. Chapman, 'A "Violations Approach"', 38.

104. Chapman, 'A "Violations Approach"', 38.

105. Kenneth Roth, 'Defending Economic, Social and Cultural Rights: Practical Issues Faced by an International Human Rights Organization', *Human Rights Quarterly* 26, no. 1 (2004): 68.

106. Roth, 'Defending Economic, Social and Cultural Rights', 69.

107. Felner, 'Closing the "Escape Hatch"', 403.

108. Gillian MacNaughton, 'Equality Rights beyond Neoliberal Constraints', in *Economic and Social Rights in a Neoliberal World*, ed. Gillian MacNaughton and Diane Frey (Cambridge: Cambridge University Press, 2018), 105.

109. Whyte, 'Powerless Companions or Fellow Travellers?', 21.

110. Whyte, 'Powerless Companions or Fellow Travellers?', 69.

Chapter 4

When Violations Become Vectors: Human Rights Work in the Era of Big Data

Karl Marx spent 12 years in the British Library developing both carbuncles and the intellectual framework for Das Kapital. [. . .] It's doubtful, however, whether he would have foreseen an automaton one day being able to look through all of the sources that he used – and millions more – within a fraction of the time he spent, and being able to present its own models of history.

– Ian Steadman, 'Big Data and the Death of the Theorist'

Important questions in the social sciences and humanities about equality, power, voice, justice, fairness will always be around, will always require sustained and critical inquiry, and won't ever fully be answered by computers alone.

– Mark Graham, 'Big Data and the Death of the Theorist'

In the decades following the 'white heat' of the first information revolution, capitalism's computational reconfiguration of the world has only intensified. Enabled by both exponential increases in computational power and the infrastructure of the internet (another product of Cold War military research that was only ever briefly the libertarian playground of cyberpunks),[1] capital's processes of exploitation and dispossession are now iteratively figured and reconfigured, worked and reworked, across the index of national spaces through the dense meshing of the network. In this emerging order, data emerges as the lifeblood of cybernetic capitalism, pouring out from an ever increasing array of devices and platform interfaces and flowing through its reticular veins into vast server farms erroneously called 'the cloud'. Data has become a vital means of finding and capturing new value for all sectors of capital.[2] Data on human biology and sociality, on human and non-human relations, and much else besides now feeds commercial banks and supermarket chains as much as it does social media platforms and 'smart' appliance manufacturers. Corporate maxims like 'Data is everything, everything is data' reflect this new era of big data.[3]

Of course, it is not simply the vastness of data that makes it valuable but the new forms of data practice that, as David Beer puts it, make our data 'speak'.[4] Data analytics, algorithmic technologies, machine learning and artificial intelligence are overlapping terms that describe this increasingly automated set of practices which work over, order and arrange data so as to produce value. But more than value, they have also become knowledge-making tools which, integrated as they are in the infrastructures of both corporations and state institutions,[5] are beginning to greatly affect the way we see, understand and act upon the world. As data-led practices proliferate, they obviously pose important epistemological questions. Chiefly, how precisely do data-led practices make data speak, and furthermore, how does this transform, intensify or sediment our dominant modes of knowing?

In 2008, just as the 'data revolution' was beginning to take shape, Chris Anderson, then editor of *WIRED* magazine, wrote a now widely cited opinion piece enthusiastically endorsing some of its many possible consequences. Titled 'The End of Theory', Anderson's editorial argued that the sheer ubiquity of data emerging over the next decade would make traditional pillars of scientific work – hypothesising, modelling, testing – obsolete. Casting aside whole fields of knowledge – 'out with every theory of human behavior, from linguistics to sociology. Forget taxonomy, ontology, and psychology' – Anderson argued for the purity of data and the efficacy of the new data analytics. 'With enough data', Anderson concluded, 'the numbers speak for themselves.'[6] Undoubtedly, Anderson's enthusiasm rests on an understanding of data which is, in many senses, already inscribed into its very name. As Rob Kitchin reminds us, the etymological root of data is the Latin *dare* meaning 'to give', which readily conjures a substance that is already given; a trace or slice of the real.[7] The promise of big data, Anderson's editorial seems to suggest, is the possibility of working over enough slices for reality to finally reveal itself.

Anderson's manifesto for big data, if one can call it that, is by no means an outlier. What he celebrates as a 'better way' of doing science is increasingly acknowledged by critics as a dangerous paradigm shift in the process of knowledge production. In a recent article, for instance, the sociologist William Davies lamented the emergence of a new socio-political imaginary in which it is assumed that 'data can simply "speak for itself"'. Big data and automated analytics, Davies contends, propel the fantasy of a 'pure truth', one 'unpolluted by any deliberate human intervention'.[8] Similarly, Clemens Apprich et al.

argue that the socio-cultural expansion of data analytics has both extended and radicalised the epistemological positivism most associated with Karl Popper. For Apprich et al., the proposition of 'big data' is to radically repudiate if not entirely banish the hermeneutics of interpretation (of which theory is a central pillar) in the name of an analytics which largely treats all data as unbiased 'fact'. This, even if 'a priori choices and decisions as well as unacknowledged biases' inevitably do shape the production of data, meaning that 'hermeneutics creeps in through the backdoor of analytics'.[9]

Among the key stakes raised by big data and its practices, then, has been not only a reaffirmation but also a radicalisation of cybernetic capitalism's epistemological commitments. A new layer of informational logic emerges in the reification of the 'given' of data as signal and, conversely, the exclusion of interpretive and critical knowledges as suspicious forms of human intervention, intrusive framing and bias: noise. Accordingly, the human rights movement, with its own faith in the capacity of 'facts' to simply 'speak for themselves', seems like it would be primed to embrace new data-driven processes and to work enthusiastically within the data imaginary outlined by Anderson. It is certainly true that the movement is embracing new data practices and now relies not only on traditional forms of 'events-based data' but also on new and derivative 'forms of data made possible through machine learning and artificial intelligence (AI) applications'.[10] But as I aim to demonstrate, the ways in which new data practices are reconfiguring the informational logic of human rights are complex and fragmented. Across different kinds of human rights work, data practice collides and coheres with different forms of legal, pragmatic and probabilistic thinking. Understanding how human rights work functions in the data age thus depends on a sustained engagement with different data practices to understand this differential production of information.

With this in mind, this chapter explores three distinct data-led practices within the human rights field: the application of machine learning techniques to the estimation of political killings; the use of machine learning to piece together composite evidence of violations within large corpuses of video footage; and the practice of scraping social media to find new and emerging information about human rights violations.[11] With each practice, I carefully consider how the novel epistemic coordinates of data analytics affects human rights practice to explore how informational logic is being reshaped in the contemporary world. While the traversal of these examples demonstrates the uneven effects of data analytics, it also elucidates a common thread that weaves through all of them: sidestepping structural critique and transformative thinking, new data practices seem to promise access to greater analytic insights and, in doing so, buttress a belief that greater, cleaner, better information can support the fight for human rights. This belief, I conclude, is ultimately what the informational logic of human rights coheres around today.

The Datafication of Human Rights

The entry of new data practices into the world of human rights cannot be straightforwardly reduced to a blind technological optimism or a brute techno-determinism. For some time now, human rights scholars and practitioners have carefully considered how new digital technologies might be integrated into human rights. Authors like Jay Aronson and Sam Gregory have led efforts to explore both the opportunities and potential consequences of utilising new digital technologies in rights work, charting out 'when, where, and under what conditions technology can strengthen and protect rights'.[12] That said, even where scholars and practitioners are alive to the potential dangers of digital technologies, there remains a persistent feeling that new data-led practices, particularly forms of machine learning, have become increasingly necessary for human rights work to succeed.

There are several overlapping and mutually reinforcing reasons for this turn to increasingly complex data practices. On the one hand, the possibility of states misrecognising and thus dismissing certain forms of information as biased, political noise has had the effect of progressively tightening what counts as human rights information around numeric, quantitative forms; 'technologies of trust', as Theodore Porter has put it, whose methods at least appear to screen out issues of subjectivity and bias and can thus be more readily parsed as objective.[13] Thomas Marks, a former US military officer and counterinsurgency expert, has neatly articulated this predicament in his complaint that 'what [human rights groups] present now is like academic theory which attempts to impose itself on the data. If HR groups want to up their credibility', Marks warns, 'they must begin to ground their analyses in the realities of the situation, particularly numbers.'[14] Responding to this issue, human rights organisations have increasingly turned to statistical methods, data analytics and other quantitative data practices which appear more readily equipped to '[make] their cases valid in the eyes of the world'.[15] Through organisations like Human Rights Data Analysis Group (HRDAG), an NGO that deploys advanced statistical techniques for human rights causes, this has also meant integrating tools like machine learning to enable increasingly complex calculations.

Undoubtedly, this quantitative turn has been reinforced by the rise of juridical and quasi-juridical accountability practices within the human rights field. As human rights have been codified and incorporated into the institutions and legal frameworks of post-Cold War global governance, international criminal proceedings, truth commissions and other forms of 'transitional justice' have not only been enabled but also normalised as a response to periods of mass violence and atrocity. As members of HRDAG argue, 'these trends have forced human rights workers to adopt more rigorous methodology in counting the dead, the disappeared, and the damaged'.[16] In this way, the growing mobilisation of expertise in data science and analytics, with their attendant computational approaches to quantification, should also be seen partly as a response to a more juridical threshold for producing facts that now occupies a significant place within human rights practice.

At the same time, however, the movement's turn to big data practices has also been shaped by the broader set of social and economic developments that have accompanied the latest phase of cybernetic capitalism. The exponential growth of data both flowing from smart devices and through online platforms, and the transformation of so many social and economic practices to deal with this 'data deluge', can also be understood as a major dynamic now at work in the transformation of the human rights movement. The ubiquity of video, image and text-based information circulating on social media platforms has greatly expanded the potential evidence base for human rights groups, an issue that brings potentially monumental implications for their work. As Eyal Weizman has recently summarised, while historically 'human rights research was limited by the scarcity of sources and evidence, at present, there is such a large quantity of information that the problem becomes instead how to manage and generate insights from an overabundance of data'.[17] In this context, human rights organisations have turned not simply to quantification practices but also to new techniques in machine learning and AI that make it possible to navigate this emerging mass of data by: scraping relevant information from the vast archives of social media platforms; piecing together many fragments of video footage; or identifying evidence of violations across large corpuses of images.

Concomitantly, new forms of data practice have optimistically been mobilised as the potential solution to two intractable problems for human right organisations: time and (human) resources. The 'paper avalanche' of documents that Amnesty International first sought to address in the 1970s has only grown larger; with the proliferation of human rights groups and international legal institutions comes a growing mass of electronic and paper documents (case law, reports, resolutions, and so on) which need to be sorted, logged and rendered useable within organisational settings. In response, human rights organisations have turned to several kinds of data practice. On the one hand, machine learning and AI have been used to scrape documents for relevant metadata and input it into a database, or to automatically find, retrieve and upload relevant documents from international legal institutions, offering the potential to automate much tedious and time-consuming work.[18] In some ways this runs counter to existing debates about automation in contemporary capitalism, which tend to express concern about job losses and mass unemployment.[19] As a project manager at an organisation specialising in producing human rights databases once assured me, 'while automation can mean job losses in the broader social context, within the human rights context, where resources are overstretched, automation could free up time for more pressing tasks'.[20]

The time-resource problem has also been addressed through forms of highly distributed 'human computing' enabled by contemporary network technologies, particularly the advent of cloud computing. In these cases, large numbers of volunteers are connected to online repositories of human rights data and asked to tag and code it so that it can be rendered both legible and useable. An example of this kind of work is Amnesty International's Decoders programme, which organises large numbers of volunteers to do microtasks that add up to huge amounts of informational work; for example, AI's Strike Tracker project, which asked volunteers to help the organisation create a timeline of airstrikes in Syria by comparing satellite images and tagging when buildings had been destroyed. As Amnesty boasts, the project used 3,101 'decoders', who made 138,557 contributions, and identified the timelines of 11,218 buildings.[21] Importantly, volunteer-based microtasking is not entirely unrelated to the use of machine learning in human rights. Through tagging, labelling and other disambiguation processes, volunteers on programmes like Decoders make data ready for further rounds of data analysis, including those that make use of machine learning algorithms.

The above points towards the sheer breadth of novel data practices that are now working over human rights information, reflecting many possible sites of enquiry that may unlock interesting connections between cybernetic capitalism, human rights and informational logic. The distributed human computation of projects like Amnesty's Decoders is interesting insofar as it mirrors the hyper-precarious forms of informational labour that are developing at the new frontier of contemporary capitalism. Strike Tracker simulates the kinds of 'crowdwork' epitomised by Amazon's Mechanical Turk service, which outsources processes that are not yet computable as small and discrete 'human intelligence tasks' to an online, 'hyperflexible, [and] on-demand workforce which can be accessed and let go in seconds'.[22] Moreover, insofar as the crowdwork of volunteers renders data useable for further analytics including machine learning, it also affirms Gemma Newlands's point that the time saved by apparently 'automated' machine intelligence often leans heavily on forms of human labour that are simply shunted into more infrastructural and therefore less visible parts of the process.[23] From this perspective, programmes like Decoders might readily provide glimpses of how broader trends in capitalism's transformation of informational labour continue to reshape and configure the practice of human rights.

At the same time, however, a 'human computation' project like Decoders might tell us less about the operations of novel computational techniques on human rights data. Accordingly, the chosen examples focus on practices which, to varying degrees, utilise machine learning and related data processing techniques. I take this direction precisely because understanding how these techniques operate on data is crucial to grasping the complex set of epistemic and technical shifts at stake in the contemporary informational logic of human rights. Indeed, I would go so far as to argue that each of the practices explored below can be read as a material manifestation of contemporary informational logic as it works through human rights organisations and their infrastructures. Given that machine learning is mobilised in each of the examples, it is perhaps best to begin by outlining what is invoked by this term by setting out a conceptual history and technical overview, which sketches out the key practical and epistemic stakes of machine learning in ways that inform the later analysis of the examples.

Machine Learning: Something Old, Something New

Though machine learning techniques have now come to signify the bleeding edge of our emergent data society, it is perhaps surprising to note that they are not entirely new, based as they are on a set of intellectual trajectories and computational techniques stretching back around seventy years. As Bernhard Rieder has recently shown, many machine learning techniques are rooted in information science and particularly in its efforts, beginning in the 1950s, to apply statistical techniques to the identification and retrieval of information such as documents in libraries.[24] Pioneered by a wave of information scientists such as Hans Peter Luhn, Gerard Salton and Karen Spärck Jones, the statistical approach to information retrieval used various probabilistic techniques to identify relevant material based on user query terms. This array of techniques, as Rieder demonstrates, laid the groundwork for a number of contemporary practices that have folded into machine learning. Processes that underpin what is now commonly known as 'text mining', statistical methods that operate on data such as 'clustering' and 'classification' (which, simply put, are probabilistic ways of grouping data), and the arrangement of data into 'vectors', a commonly used way of organising data in machine learning processes that I will return to later, are all rooted in these developments.

However, one of the most recognisable beginnings of machine learning is the perceptron developed by Frank Rosenblatt in 1957.[25] A first attempt at operationalising Warren McCulloch and Walter Pitts's cybernetic model of the neuron, the perceptron provided the basic blueprint for a family of machine learning algorithms known as neural nets. The perceptron was a 'single-layered' neural net, a network of weighted nodes, initially designed to learn how to recognise and distinguish between two classes of images, though it could also be put to other tasks where distinguishing between two different classes was a desirable outcome (for this reason it is renowned as the first binary classifier). Though the promise of the perceptron initially seemed great, it was soon discovered that it struggled to recognise many complex classifications, leading to a loss of interest in the field. Neural nets only began to gain traction once again in the 1980s–90s when more complex and multi-layered nets, capable of moving forward and backward through different weighted nodes, came to be seen as incredibly effective classifiers.[26] This sparked a new wave of research and an expanding set of possible applications that would only fully flourish in the early twenty-first century.

The return of techniques developed in the mid-twentieth century as a ubiquitous if not entirely visible part of everyday life demonstrates that cybernetic capitalism's increasingly algorithmic articulation is reducible neither to the emergence of a new philosophy of artificial intelligence nor to the emergence of novel techniques (though there has inevitably been a bit of both).[27] Rather, as software studies scholars like Adrian Mackenzie and Rieder argue, the very recent proliferation of machine learning is at least partly rooted in new developments in computational infrastructure and concomitant increases in computational power.[28] Drawing attention to some of the most immediately relevant technical innovations provides a sense of how deeply machine learning is entwined with its infrastructure.

The displacement of the ordinary central processing unit (CPU) by the graphical processing unit (GPU), first developed for computer gaming in the late 1990s, as a technology for processing machine learning computations was particularly crucial. Because GPUs were already primed for the kinds of vector-based computations that are central in machine learning, they significantly improved the speed of data processing, enabling vast increases in the amount of data on which machine learning algorithms could feasibly work. The 'parallel computing' enabled by GPUs has also been enhanced by the distributed computing made possible by the cloud. Itself reliant on the network infrastructures of the internet, cloud computing provides access to large amounts of computational power distributed across network servers.[29] For this reason, large tech companies have been able to leverage the vast amounts of computational power available to them to provide platform data services, such as Amazon Web Services, that are now part of the everyday fabric of machine learning.

Of course, these infrastructural innovations, and machine learning in general, are inextricably entwined with the broader socio-technical developments undergirding the era of big data. The exponential increase of data not only through the flow from networked devices and social media platforms but also in the areas of logistics, health, migration, genomics, and so on, have required new and automated techniques to process the vast quantities of information produced today. But, as Dyer-Witheford et al. have recently argued, 'machine intelligence is the product not just of a technological logic but simultaneously of a social logic, the logic of producing surplus value'.[30] In doing so, they call attention to the fact that the necessary investments in infrastructures for machine learning have also occurred because the possibility of working on this data, of making it speak, across many of these areas has become densely enmeshed in the capitalist process of valorisation. As a central aspect of the data analytics industry that is at the new frontier of value extraction, in other words, machine learning has increasingly become worthy of investment.[31]

What Do Machine Learners Learn?

The wide array of applications for machine learning mentioned in the section above, from health research and genomics to Facebook (military and financial applications could also be added to this list), says something important about the dynamics of machine learning itself. Harbouring its own version of the mania that characterised cybernetics, machine learning does not appear to have any predefined limits on its possible applications, nor can it be narrowly defined as a 'discipline', operating as it does at the intersections between mathematics, statistics and computer science. Instead, machine learning primarily exists as an abstracted set of techniques that can be utilised to work over anything that could possibly be read as data. These techniques are often mathematical operations, functions, that are translated into and thus crystallised in programming languages such as R and Python. In turn, as Rieder suggests, functions agglomerate in 'code libraries' or 'packages' where they become 'an ever-growing archive of techniques, ready to hand for those skilled to apply them'.[32] The combined efforts of skilled human operators and computer-based algorithmic processes that populate libraries and packages, as Mackenzie has argued, are perhaps best understood as entanglements of human and non-human agency that he refers to as machine learners.[33]

The epistemic and socio-political stakes of machine learning become apparent through a closer reading of how these techniques both see and operate on data. In terms of seeing data, it is important to understand that machine learners 'inhabit a vector space' and thus 'encounter data in specific vectorized shapes'.[34] Vectors are lines of data that express both relationality and difference across the objects they map. The ages of victims or their gender, for instance, could each constitute a vector that express differences (in age or gender) between related 'objects' (in this case, victims). Hence, a vector often appears to have some similarity to the 'column' in data's traditional container, the table. But there are also some extremely important differences. As both Rieder and Mackenzie point out, vectorisation treats data as 'spatialised' coordinates in a vector space, which enables algorithms to see and operate upon the data as if it had a kind of 'geometric' form.[35] Here, vectors – which can be arrayed together even from across multiple datasets – each become a dimension of a vector space that machine learning algorithms traverse by examining the relations that emerge within its spatial configurations. Importantly, insofar as each vector becomes one dimension, vector spaces can rapidly expand into very high dimensions, providing a potentially vast and morphological topography for machine learners to explore.

The expansive vision enabled by the vector space is reinforced by an enhanced miscibility of data embedded within the logic of vectors. The 'vectorisation' of data can, and commonly does, involve the transformation of the different datatypes into the same numeric form. Qualitative data, such as a row of categorical data (divided into categories like true/false, yes/no), can be rendered into numeric form (so that 0=False and 1=True, and so on).[36] As Mackenzie notes, this provides contemporary data practice with a remarkable capacity to '[smooth] over important fault lines of difference that vertically divided the tabular data', so that it can be handled through the same statistical operations as other data that might already be arrayed in the vector space.[37] To use human rights data as an example, machine learning would transform the distinct tables of the Events Model (Event, Act, Victim, etc.) into a series of vectors that can be arrayed in multiple different combinations, depending on the task at hand. The ages and genders of victims might be thus arrayed with the genders of perpetrators, and the types of act committed, which are all now vectorised in numeric forms. Machine learning algorithms are designed to see within these quantitative vector spaces, 'feeling' for patterns, segmenting them with lines that cluster and partition.

The process of distinction-making within a vector space is precisely what machine learners learn. In the case of supervised learning, by far the most common form of machine learning in human rights applications, models are 'trained' to categorise, classify or rank a small subset of 'training data', a sample of the data that has been (often laboriously) pre-labelled by human supervisors, before being mobilised on the full and as yet unseen dataset to find its partitions and segmentations. To 'feel' for patterns, supervised learners operate recursively on the training data with a set of weights or parameters that iteratively adjust until the learner has found the parameters which most accurately classify, predict or order the pre-labelled data. At this point, the algorithm may present a number of classified outputs for a human supervisor to check the accuracy of the classifier's outputs and identify any wrongly classified, ranked or predicted data points. This feedback folds into the algorithm which adjusts its weights accordingly in a new round of recursive movement over the data. Unsupervised learners, by contrast, are immediately mobilised on a dataset, exploring the vector space without having been previously trained. Unsupervised learners divide and cluster data into new and unforeseen partitions through algorithms such as k-means clustering or anomaly detection.[38]

Importantly, the outputs provided by machine learning algorithms are seldom given to human operators as certain. Machine learning algorithms, as Matteo Pasquinelli points out, function through techniques 'that always take the form of statistical inferences' about the vast sets of data which learners work over.[39] As Pasquinelli demonstrates, machine learners treat all problems as statistical problems even where questions of recognition or parsing semantic meaning are concerned. Their classifications, categorisations and predictions of data points (or 'observations' as they are usually called in machine learning) are thus made on the basis of statistical probabilities and degrees of likelihood, so that each output is assigned a probability score. In machine learning, probability is usually parsed as a figure between 0 and 1, where 0.69, for instance, is more probable than 0.3. The classification or prediction of an output will usually be set at a specific parameter so that, for example, the line of inclusion and exclusion might be a probability of 0.5. The probabilistic nature of outputs is indicative of the broader way probability suffuses machine learning as its central epistemological premise. In a very real sense, machine learning techniques only know the world insofar as they can probabilise it.

Consequently, as machine learning techniques have entered the field of human rights they have begun to precipitate a crucial shift in the movement's own epistemic foundations. In the past, human rights information has largely been underpinned by a desire to eliminate chance. Striving for certainty was important for organisations that needed to keep a grip on their claims to having (only) the facts and representing the real of violence. But, as we will soon see, when machine learning techniques enter the picture, chance, probability and intuitions pervade human rights practice. Probability comes to be embraced by human rights groups as a kind of material that can be worked with, that can be weighted, balanced and teased in order to produce desired outcomes. This means, as Weizman puts it, human rights has now been sutured to a scientific paradigm in which findings are 'qualified by indeterminacies, contradictions, margins of error, and probability calculations'.[40] What does this epistemological shift mean for the informational logic of human rights when violations, and their victims, become vectors; or, perhaps more precisely, when they become a vector space? With a better grip on what should be understood by machine learning, it is now possible to explore these questions through a reading of some of the human rights applications.

Counting the Dead: Statistical Estimation in Human Rights

'When human rights fact-finding looks to quantitative approaches, it may be tempted by the buzzwords of the day: "big data," "evidence based," and "analytics".' But, as the Research Director of HRDAG Patrick Ball warns, while the 'big' in 'big data' often connotes its vastness, and this in turn can stand in for its completeness, this is often not true of human rights data. 'In the context of human rights', Ball reminds us, 'much of the information about the universe of violence is hidden, sometimes intentionally, and sometimes by complicated patterns of social visibility.'[41] I will soon return to these patterns of (in)visibility, but for now I want to highlight the broader point, namely that the kinds of data produced by the Events Model, which Ball himself contributed to developing, provide truths that are, in important ways, always partial. The data in human rights databases captures only a portion of the total number of violations in any given context.

For HRDAG this is a complex ethical problem as much as it is a scientific one. On the one hand, 'ignoring the unrecorded violations, [does] a disservice to victims whose stories have not yet been told'.[42] But at the same time, incomplete data carries the significant risk of misrepresenting patterns of mass violence by over-emphasising the significance of some (observed) events. This opens up human rights claims to accusations of politicisation and bias, which can also serve to undermine the movement. In order to address this problem, the organisation has developed advanced statistical techniques that can be used to estimate the real total number of killings from these incomplete datasets. These methods promise 'a scientifically rigorous, transparent method to "count the uncounted"', one which produces results that 'are less vulnerable to claims of partiality or bias'.[43] Such claims are backed up by the legal applicability of HRDAG's work. Over the last twenty-five years, the organisation's findings have been used in many human rights prosecutions, including high-profile cases like the trial of Slobodan Milošević and the successful conviction of General José Efraín Ríos Montt for his role in the genocide of Ixil Mayan communities in Guatemala.[44]

It is already possible to detect, here, a variation of the informational logic of human rights. The enrolment of science, and data science in particular, within HRDAG's work is intended to undergird the objectivity of numbers and distance them from politics. There is a belief, in other words, that better, cleaner information provides a proper basis for disentangling signal from noise. As I will demonstrate, the more objective basis for number that HRDAG insists upon is delivered through a statistical data practice that incorporates the same kind of machine learning techniques, infrastructures and forms of data processing that are found within the broader milieu of big data. Indeed, programming languages like R and Python as well as the necessity of cloud-based computation run through the technical notes and blog posts that accumulate on the organisation's website.[45] Nevertheless, what makes statistical estimation a particularly intriguing example is the ways it crucially differs from the other examples chosen in this chapter, which all deal with human right contexts where the problem is successfully wading through the overabundance of data. In contrast, HRDAG's process foregrounds a keen awareness of, and attentiveness to, the incompleteness of data which it attempts to account for in its statistical operations. The result, I will suggest, is a thoughtful and reflective set of data-led practices that paint a complex, multifaceted picture of the informational logic of human rights today.

The starting point for HRDAG's work is a conviction that statistical tools which embrace prediction and probability can be used to successfully extrapolate from incomplete data. There are, however, specific conditions under which this kind of work is possible. Perhaps most of all, estimating the total number of deaths requires working with two or more datasets that have recorded events within the same conflict, and which have some degree of overlap such that at least some of the events can be identified across multiple databases. Fortunately, this is quite common in human rights situations where there are often several organisations working to document violations and, additionally, where state bureaucracy can leave at least some 'official' trace of violations. But all of the data also has to be of a good enough quality, with enough unique information for particular victims and events to be identified across the datasets. This requires additional work to process or 'clean' the data, a painstaking procedure that involves removing anonymous, unidentifiable records as well as ensuring that variables are all coded accurately and that obvious spelling errors are corrected.[46] Finally, HRDAG is largely confined to examining the issue of lethal violence. This is because one person can be killed only once whereas one person could be the victim of multiple incidents of non-lethal violations. In the latter case, finding the overlaps in datasets becomes far too complex, even for machines.

When these conditions are met, HRDAG can use a family of techniques called multiple systems estimation (MSE), sometimes known as capture–recapture, to make its estimates. MSE is a set of statistical methods that has its origins in ecology at the turn of the twentieth century, where it was primarily developed to predict the size of animal populations based on multiple overlapping samples.[47] It has subsequently found applications in epidemiology and demography.[48] Within the human rights context, the basic premise of MSE is that patterns of overlap between different human rights datasets can be used to infer the total size of lethal violence. The most important measure is the magnitude of the overlap, the number of incidents appearing in more than one database, which has direct implications for the estimate. As HRDAG puts it,

> if the overlap is small, this implies that the population from which the lists were drawn is much larger than the lists. If, on the other

hand, most of the cases on the lists overlap, this implies that the over-all population is not much larger than the number of cases listed.[49]

MSE can also be used to identify patterns of violence within the total population of violations, furnishing the movement with finer grained information. In Colombia, for example, HRDAG estimated 'patterns and magnitude of killings and disappearances side by side', which helped to 'reveal strategies of perpetrators and conflict dynamics'.[50]

Probability, Uncertainty and the Body Count

For HRDAG, the probabilistic vision inherent in machine learning is a central means through which different forms of uncertainty about the world of violence in which the organisation is interested can be embedded into practice. Probability here becomes central not only to thinking about possible lacunae in the data, missing connections or numeric absences, but also to the process of accounting for them. One crucial arena for this probabilising strategy comes in the record-linkage stage, where the incidents appearing in more than one dataset are identified and linked together in order to measure the overlaps. Uncertainty pervades the matching process: some names might be spelled or translated differently in different datasets; the same name might refer to different people; there might be slight discrepancies with incident dates; or the ages of victims might be slightly different. At the same time, the number of possible matches generated by even a collection of reasonably small datasets means that it is impossible for a human to make matching decisions about these uncertainties in a reasonable amount of time.[51]

Machine learning responds to both of these problems by statistically inferring probable correlations in the data to navigate this uncertainty at speed and with a high degree of consistency. A semi-supervised model runs over human-labelled training data, learning 'how to weight the various measures of similarity between a pair of records to estimate the probability that the two records refer to the same person or to two different people'.[52] It should be noted here, then, that no match is a certainty but based on a threshold of probability as a form of measurement that can be worked through and over. Indeed, once the machine learner has matched the training data it outputs a small number of matches for the human analyst to assess. As in other supervised learning processes, the human input is then enrolled into the model, which adjusts its weights and generates new probable matches and non-matches.[53] In this sense, uncertainty is not overcome but, via the process of weighting and reweighting, adjusted and remobilised in productive ways. Once the learner is deemed accurate enough, it works over the unlabelled data where it clusters together matched pairs, mapping the degree of overlaps between datasets as it does so.

At the next stage of the process, uncertainty and probability expand into broader questions about the 'social patterns of invisibility' that were emphasised above by Ball. Accurate estimations, as it turns out, require careful thinking about the uncertainties inherent within the existing datasets, particularly the kinds of patterns of bias that may make some deaths more likely to be recorded and others to be missed. Some of this requires expert intuitions about broader issues of social structure, for instance the likely underreporting of incidents by already marginalised groups. Other forms of uncertainty are tied to the kinds of bias that shape the data collection processes of human rights groups such as having greater documentation capacities in urban centres over rural areas.[54] To account for these myriad possibilities, MSE requires a process of stratification, where the data is partitioned according to certain 'features' of the incidents: place, time, perpetrator, and victim characteristics such as gender and ethnicity. Stratification means that when the MSE process runs, it computes each stratum separately. Consequently, these uncertainties become discernible in the patterns of difference emerging within each stratum: lower rates of overlap for marginalised groups than others, for example. Expert judgements regarding bias are thus tested through stratification and clarified through an exercise in pattern discrimination.

In the final stage of the MSE process, probabilisation turns to the production of a numerical estimate of lethal killings. In this stage, HRDAG models the different possible overlaps between datasets to calculate a total of the observed and unobserved deaths. Each different possible combination of overlaps is a model for the data, and from each model an estimate of the total is provided. The difficulty comes when several plausible models produce very different estimates. How to choose the right model? In most cases, HRDAG 'fully incorporate[s] uncertainty about the model itself' by applying a probabilistic Bayesian approach to the models.[55] Treating the models not as singular numeric estimates but as probability distributions, one advantage of this approach is the ability to weight and combine the models – rather than choosing only one – into a singular probability distribution for the total number of estimated deaths. From there one can simply derive the median and an accompanying 'credibility interval', which measures the degree of uncertainty about where the most accurate estimate lies (the larger the credibility interval, the less certainty there is about the estimate and vice versa). In this sense, uncertainty becomes the texture and grain of statistical estimation, even its final outputs.

The forms of probabilisation that suffuse the MSE process initially seem at odds with the traditional informational logic of human rights and its preference for bare facts whose objectivity is rooted, at least partly, in a sense of certainty. But I want to suggest that probabilisation is not the end of objectivity but its transposition into a different form. As Lorraine Daston and Peter Galison note in their careful historical work, objectivity is not a monolithic concept but has multiple meanings that differ and entangle across distinct scientific milieus and communities of practice.[56] For instance, traditional human rights data reflects a kind of 'mechanical objectivity' which emerged alongside the invention of the camera in the nineteenth century and was underpinned by the possibility of unproblematically capturing the real. As with this form of mechanical objectivity, traditional human rights data 'aimed for [the] purity of observation'.[57] But the statistical approach of HRDAG is closer to what Daston and Galison call 'structural objectivity', where uncertainty is dealt with by 'the objectivity of mathematics and logic' and 'the seamlessness of the chain of inferences'.[58] Even if some uncertainties about the incompleteness of data are intuited by 'trained judgement', understood here as 'cultivated perception and cognition', this judgement is objective insofar as it can be formalised in reproducible mathematical operations and subjected to the tight control of the chain of statistical inference.[59]

Importantly, the formalism of the structural objectivity shaping HRDAG's vectoring and arraying of violations also aims at an even 'purer' picture of the real than the empirical data. By reverse engineering the possible biases in datasets, MSE seeks to capture what a 'snapshot of the real' might look like if it had not been fallibly collected by human actors. In identifying possible lacunae and estimating their size, the objective is to point, with ever more clarity, to an even 'purer' rendering of the real whose reality appears – paradoxically – entirely cleaved from the frailties of human intervention. As Ball puts it, 'data on homicides in the context of conflict are partial', but 'in some cases data can be adjusted with statistical models to get less biased estimates'.[60] In this sense, the structural objectivity carefully constructed by HRDAG shares in mechanical objectivity's aim to 'represent things as they are or as they would be supposing I did not exist'.[61]

In some ways it is impossible not to admire a practice that tries to embrace uncertainty so transparently. But in the commitment to 'reducing bias', this 'structural' configuration of objectivity maintains the ongoing bifurcation of information between signal and political noise: ever more defensible facts that can be cleaved from politics. Even as statistical estimation mobilises probability and prediction to pin down and 'purify' the real, the scientism of the project and the desire for credibility means that more radical mobilisations of uncertainty are, at least implicitly, excluded. The predominance of probability and prediction leaves little room for broader notions of 'possibility' and 'speculation' that might serve more transformative political projects. As Terranova might suggest, probabilisation acts to contain uncertainty, including the possibilities and 'virtualities' within a given situation, by eliminating '(im)probable alternatives [. . .] such as other modes of knowledge or methods of analysis'.[62] Indeed, more open-ended valences of uncertainty such as possibility are more readily perceived as a potentially deleterious contravention of the epistemological foundations of human rights.

Fitting the Footage: Processing Video Material

If HRDAG demonstrates what can be done when there is not enough data, what happens when there is too much of it? In recent years, the proliferation of documents, social media evidence and citizen-made video footage has led to swelling human rights databases. As an example, the database of the International, Impartial and Independent Mechanism (IIIM) for Syria, a UN body set up to investigate human rights violations related to the country's decade-long civil war, now has a database of documents, images and video material standing at tens of millions of records.[63] Among these growing bodies of human rights data, the video evidence made by ordinary people on their smartphones and uploaded to social media platforms has become a particularly fruitful terrain for human rights investigations. Eye-witness footage is 'undoubtedly persuasive and compelling in a world where "seeing is believing"',[64] and its proliferation in online public spaces like YouTube has provided more direct visual access to human rights violations than has previously been available.

But when these videos need to be found among the terabytes of irrelevant, noisy data that circulates across various social media platforms and, moreover, when the corpus of relevant footage can reach hundreds if not thousands of videos, the tasks of finding, ordering and using the data become challenging. Activists and practitioners have begun using machine learning to respond to these difficulties in several different ways. In the case of finding relevant video material within the vast sea of social media content, supervised learners have been developed and trained to successfully identify videos containing evidence of human rights violations. These classifiers are often trained on existing corpuses of video material, and sometimes on synthetic images,[65] learning to recognise objects such as tanks and weapons; actions such as explosions or weapons firing; human behaviour such as running, crying or screaming; as well as specific locations where violence is taking place. Once trained, machine learners identify relevant footage by assigning individual videos with a probability score. If the score is above a designated threshold for relevance, the video will be automatically collected.[66]

Certainly, the capacities of machine learning techniques in regard to scraping the archive of social media is an important example of how new data-led practices are reshaping human rights work. But I want to leave a more extensive exploration of such techniques for the next section where I examine the use of classifiers to identify emerging patterns of violations through Twitter content. For now, I am more interested in the ways that machine learning is also being applied to video analytics, particularly in the areas of synchronisation and localisation for specific human rights events. In this context, novel data techniques are used to piece together the fragments of footage recorded by witnesses to human rights violations into a composite for the purpose of event reconstruction: constructing 'a visual and spatial narrative of an event that is as comprehensive as possible'.[67] Such practices are very directly embedded in, and come to bear upon, the process of knowledge production within human rights documentation practices and can thus say much about how informational logic operates today.

Video synchronisation for event reconstruction has its origins in well-established forensic techniques such as crime scene reconstruction. However, traditional, manual processes for video synchronisation are incredibly time-consuming because footage can be fragmented across very different perspectives of the event and visual disturbances like smoke, pixelation and blurriness can make it difficult to place videos in similar or distinctive locations. Under these conditions, it can take a human worker months to stitch together only a small amount of video into a composite. Such timescales are problematic when the amount of footage can stretch into tens, even hundreds, of hours. Over the last decade, machine learning techniques have begun to respond to this time-resource problem by automating key aspects of the processes involved in producing composites. Pioneered by organisations like Forensic Architecture in the context of the Israel–Palestine conflict, automated data practices to support event reconstruction from video footage are novel and remain somewhat experimental.[68] In recent years, the Center for Human Rights Science (CHRS) at Carnegie Mellon University has built on this work to develop tools for lawyers seeking accountability for human rights violations during the 2013–14 'Euromaidan' protests in Ukraine.[69]

What is particularly interesting about the latter approach is its unique response to the issues of reading visual distortions and disturbances mentioned above. Since noises from incidents – gunfire, screams, explosions – are more likely to be detected across several videos than visual clues, especially when the footage is shot from very different perspectives, the CHRS instead relies on the audio content of the footage to make matches. Doing so first requires unsupervised learning techniques to assign each video clip a unique 'sound print' made up of a recognisable sequence of 'features', which are then automatically compared across the videos and output as a list of pairwise matches.[70] Through this process the machine learner feels through the audio data and 'assign[s] probabilities that two or more videos were filmed at the same time'.[71] The potential matches are then reviewed by a human analyst to make a final determination about a match. Through the interactions between human and machine learners, then, uncertainty is navigated such that the clips gradually form into composites of distinct events.

Once videos have been synchronised, they can be localised or mapped onto specific geographic spaces. Given that the infrastructures of social media platforms often strip videos of their metadata (date, geographic location, author), making the question of what one is actually seeing much more uncertain, the localisation process is crucial insofar as it serves to authenticate the video by furnishing it with a sense of place. The localisation process relies on another set of semi-automated techniques. First, the system asks its users to select an area that covers possible locations for the event(s): the 'localization system starts downloads [sic] images from Google Street View and Flickr near the location'. Low-level or elementary visual features are then 'extracted from the images and matched to each of the video [sic]. The GPS of the closest matched image is assigned to the corresponding video.'[72] In doing so, localisation inscribes the composite on a specific geographic terrain, often quite literally since the archive of composites outputted through the process is pinned to a graphical map of the world.

Interestingly, the synchronised and localised composites are not ends in themselves and are often subjected to further analysis in order to identify a number of different features. Additional analytic tools might identify the source of gunshots, estimate the size of crowds, or track persons of interest.[73] Video synchronisation, in other words, provides new opportunities to probe, measure and evaluate human rights events in any number of ways. For this reason, I suggest that, in its stitching together of aural and visual information, the synchronisation and localisation of video material might be understood as the construction of a window through which human rights organisations seem to peer directly at violent events. The outputted composites thus become the basis upon which narratives about violations can emerge or dominant narratives can be affirmed or challenged.

But even if composite videos enabled by machine learning techniques really do open up novel windows of observation, it is important to remain attentive to the fact that such practices remain grounded in a much older epistemological ideal that, as I noted earlier, Daston and Galison call mechanical objectivity. Taking the camera as its signature dispositif, mechanical objectivity valorised the photographic image as uniquely capable of capturing an objective real 'uncontaminated by interpretation', and, conversely, dispelling the subjective tendency to 'aestheticize or theorize the seen'.[74] Synchronisation and localisation techniques work in a similar way as mutually reinforcing epistemic devices that are intended to provide human rights work with legitimate purchase on claims of objectivity. While video synchronisation stitches together many sites of capture into a multi-perspectival snapshot of a human rights violation that is understood to tightly mirror its reality, localisation underpins and authenticates the observation by assigning it a particular geographic terrain.

This is not to say that human rights organisations and practitioners lack awareness of the camera's 'sociality' and long-standing questions regarding its capacity – or not – to produce neutral or seemingly unmediated representations of the world. As Aronson has suggested, footage of human rights violations needs to be considered carefully in terms of how socio-cultural issues condition the making and interpretation of images.[75] Human rights, Aronson suggests, must be alert to the fact that although the images produced by video technologies have a naturalistic quality, they are always shaped and framed by the person holding the camera, their social position and their interests. This is particularly important when video footage becomes evidence in legal proceedings because its naturalistic qualities can mislead audiences into the belief that they are direct witnesses to the event in question, even though their vision is limited by the camera's lens (and, moreover, its direction by the aforementioned issues of the videographer's social position).

Nonetheless, there is also the sense that machine learning techniques have emerged as a possible means of overcoming the problems of representation and mediation:

> One advantage of citizen media is that a given event is often filmed from multiple locations, allowing for its multi-perspectival reconstruction. The availability of numerous accounts of an event can hopefully shed light on the limitations of any one view. It can also provide a richer accounting of what happened by expanding the amount of information that can be gathered about an event, as well as what happened immediately before and after it.[76]

One of the crucial interventions of machine learning is to enact a multiplication of perspectives, which is understood to help nullify, even if not completely, the particularity of any one lens. Machine learning becomes a means of surmounting thorny issues such as the social positionality of the observing subject in order to realise the mimetic ideal of mechanical objectivity. Much more than the other examples explored in this chapter, then, the synchronisation of video footage is coupled to the broader contemporary data imaginary sketched out earlier, one where, if there is enough of it, the data can simply 'speak for itself'.

Of course, what is at issue is not so much whether this family of machine learning techniques can actually realise the promise of complete and objective observations of violence (though it may well be worth asking the degree to which shared social and cultural norms do inherently shape and frame large collections of footage in ways that cannot be overcome by splicing enough of it together). Rather, the critical issue is the way that this promise of complete observation fuels the informational logic of human rights by forging new possibilities for knowledge production within existing and tightly delimited epistemological boundaries. Fitting video footage contributes to an imaginary of ever 'better' and more 'complete' information that takes centre stage in human rights work, whilst making no demands upon us to think and theorise structurally or transformatively about the contexts that shape violations. In this sense, machine learning opens a new frontier for human rights practices whose considerable techno-futuristic allure binds the contemporary movement even more tightly to its informational project.

Scraping the Real-Time Archive, Predicting the Future?

As machine learning has insinuated itself into the infrastructures of daily life, one of its most valued capacities has been in the area of

social prediction. The anticipation of stock values, consumer prefer-
ences and social trends is just one aspect of the new terrain of value
extraction unlocked by machine learning in cybernetic capitalism's
data age.[77] But these powers of prediction have also become another
promising avenue within human rights where new techniques have
been developed to scrape the archive of Twitter in order to identify
emerging patterns of violations. These developments appear to be
driven by a tension between the difficulty of dealing with information deluge and the new possibilities that become available if only
the information could be taken under control and navigated. More
precisely, 'social media monitoring poses major technical challenges
for human rights NGOs, most critically the huge amount of effort
that would be needed to manually identify human rights events from
the massive amount of data'.[78] But 'thanks to the relative anonym-
ity of users, the rapid spread of information, and the use of infor-
mal, dynamic language [that can evade censorship]', social media
holds 'great potential for monitoring emerging human rights emergencies [. . .] and calling attention to specific events or patterns that
might otherwise escape notice'.[79] The possibilities inherent in social
media as a real-time archive of social interactions are therefore being
unlocked through a bundle of text-based machine learning processes.

Such techniques are central to an online human rights platform
called Ceasefire, set up through a partnership between academic
researchers and the organisation Minority Rights Group International (MRGI) in order to monitor human rights violations in Iraq (it
will soon cover the broader Middle East and North African region).
As well as a crowdsourcing platform, which allows the public to log
violations online, Ceasefire features a 'continuous stream of [Twitter]
data that have been classified as signals of potential human rights violations within the same region'.[80] This work is performed by binary
classifiers that divide tweets into two categories: 'human rights abuse'
and 'not human rights abuse'. Those which are classified as human
rights abuse then obviously become the throughput of the signal
stream where they can be subjected to further analysis by MRGI.

As we have already witnessed, the development of binary classification systems requires intensive articulation work by human
actors in the data processing stage. But the work involved is even
more taxing in this case because the relevant social media dataset
is not available pre-packaged to pick 'off the shelf', so to speak. To
solve this problem the Ceasefire project crowdsourced a selection
of 20,151 pre-labelled Arabic language tweets 'covering violent acts
such as killing, raping, kidnapping, terrorism, invasion, explosion,
or execution'.[81] The resulting data, the Arabic Violence on Twitter
(AVT) dataset, was then divided into violent acts that constituted

human rights abuse and those which did not by five human classifiers. After this process tweets were subjected to a process of regularisation, removing unnecessary characters, hyperlinks, and so on. Tweets were arrayed into a set of feature vectors according to their morphological and lexical features and weighted so that terms of more relevance were given more attention by the learners. Once arrayed in the vector space, the AVT dataset could be used for the development and training of the machine learners.

But even at this stage much articulation work remains. Selecting the right classifier requires the careful process of testing various learners, each of which cuts the data in different ways. More basic learners such as M. E. Maron's Naive Bayes classifier and newer more complicated techniques such as convolutional neural networks (CNNs) and long short-term memory (LSTM) networks were all given opportunities to traverse the vector space and evaluated according to their performance. As is standard practice, the Ceasefire project measured these different learners not by a single criterion but by striking a balance between 'precision', the rate at which the learner correctly selects relevant tweets, and 'recall', the rate of violation-related tweets that are discarded as (false) negatives. As the issue of balance implies, the aim is not to find learners with 'decision boundaries' that are completely accurate, a feat that rarely – if ever – happens, but to find those which operate at workable levels of accuracy. For the Ceasefire project, a precision rate of 85 per cent and recall of 65 per cent achieved by the LSTM was deemed a good enough balance to '[make] this approach viable for practical use'.[82] A necessary consequence is that what flows through Ceasefire's signal stream is not certain to be violation-related content but only that which is likely to be so, meaning that the stream itself may be reasonably noisy.

Other machine learning techniques tackle the problem of scraping social media platforms very differently. The non-parametric heterogeneous graph scan (NPHGS) method, for instance, offers a very distinctive approach. As the invocation of a 'heterogeneous graph' indicates, the process centres on mapping relevant information into a reticular diagram composed of nodes and edges. Unlike earlier processes, which focused on sorting and classifying one kind of data (locations, hashtags, text), the novelty of NPHGS is its 'heterogeneity', which brings together six types of data (User, Tweet, Location, Term, Hashtag and Link) and treats them as differentiated nodes. Each node then has numerous features 'such as the numbers of tweets and users for a given geographic location', or 'the klout (a measure of influence) and sentiment score for a given tweet'.[83] The nodes and their features cohere into an unusually 'massive' and 'complex' network structure through which the machine learner has to sift – a reminder, if any was needed, of the present ubiquity of the network form within the infrastructures of our digital world.

To identify human rights events in the graph, the learner is trained to find clusters of nodes (also called sub-graphs) where activities are particularly anomalous. Anomalies here could mean a user has been mentioned an unusually large number of times or that particular locations have very high levels of activity in comparison with previous days. The learner identifies anomalies by measuring present activity against a baseline of the historical activity of each node in the cluster, producing a score by which clusters can be ranked. In the testing phase, the designers of this learner demonstrated that 78 per cent of the top 50 ranked clusters and 87 per cent of the top 30 clusters referred to human rights events. Moreover, the learner was 'able to identify clusters of tweets related to events of interest prior to international news sources, and in some cases, prior to local news reports'.[84] It is hoped, therefore, that this machine learner 'could be used to provide human rights NGOs with timely information about current events of interest, enabling them to respond quickly and appropriately'.[85]

In seeking to identify the most anomalous events, the NPHGS engenders an operational logic that runs completely counter to other practices mentioned in this chapter such as those developed by HRDAG. Where the practice of statistical estimation seeks to identify the most probable scenario within a situation of uncertainty, this particular form of social media scraping attempts to identify 'outliers' within patterns of communication and information flow that are otherwise understood to be normal. In this way, the NPHGS engages with probability not in terms of what is most likely but in terms of what is least probable in order to find events that might otherwise remain unseen. The NPHGS technique is thus an important reminder that the probabilising processes that suffuse machine learning techniques are far from monolithic and instead show a high degree of adaptability and variation. For machine learning, and thus for human rights, probability is a complex and multiplicitous epistemological device that morphs as it moves across efforts to solve different kinds of problems.

More broadly, this set of social media classifiers share a sense of purpose that is quite different from the other examples explored in this chapter. Within this context, machine learning becomes the technical substrate for a kind of 'sensory system' that is intended to make advanced forms of detection, and even prediction, possible. With the emphasis placed on harnessing the speed and scope of social media, the promise is of a kind of 'early warning' that, in identifying human rights violations as they emerge, can draw attention to new possible patterns which may require the movement to mobilise its resources. In this respect, the objective of social media scraping shares an important resonance with the network optimisms that shaped the movement as an information politics. As Chapters 1 and 2 demonstrated, organisations such as HURIDOCS saw the opportunity of utilising well-configured human rights networks to create fast information flows, arguing that 'quick dissemination of information to alert the international community had [already] prevented human rights violations'.[86] Social media scraping realises something of this anticipated potential of network velocity, even if the infrastructures of the internet have ended up providing larger, denser and more readily accessible social networks through which this kind of work might take place than HURIDOCS could have imagined.

As mechanisms for sensing, even anticipating, violations, this family of machine learners pose a familiar promise: faster, cleaner and better information which, it is supposed, can make all the difference. But, as ever, it is important to think carefully about what kinds of information fold into machine learning practice and what is excluded and rendered invisible. Across both the introductory and more technical literature, it is curious, if telling, that the capacity to find and/ or anticipate violations does not turn on any structural arguments or theoretical engagement with their causes. All that is required is the capacity to feel around for any positivistic traces of violence left in the real-time archives of social media platforms. Consequently, more information does not mean a broader engagement with knowledge, nor does it mark a point of departure from the ways of knowing that have traditionally underpinned human rights work. Rather, social media scraping simply funnels human rights into its existing work of finding, building and circulating information, only now at a velocity previously unthinkable. Attached to the bounded rationality of early warning, machine learning becomes part of a technical architecture that simply circumscribes human rights within its existing limits. In providing an impetus to more of the same, social media scraping thus operates as another socio-technical appendage of an increasingly multifaceted informational logic.

Embracing the Data Age

When taken together, the examples traced in this chapter demonstrate the degree to which the contemporary human rights movement embodies the contemporary data age, even if they sketch out only some of the many ways contemporary data practices are being applied in the field. A careful reading of these practices elucidates some of the real transformations to the movement's informational project precipitated by the embedding of new data-led practices. Perhaps most of all, a subterranean shift within the movement's epistemological grounding has begun to entrench a thoroughgoing engagement with uncertainty and probability as the norm. Subterranean, here, in the sense that the source of this epistemic transformation is the integration of new information infrastructures which, as sociologists have long understood, remain largely invisible – at least until the moment they break down.[87] To speak of subterranean epistemological shifts is thus to acknowledge their location within this obfuscated substrate of practice, in the spaces sitting behind human rights reports, media coverage and legal evidence.

At the same time, emphasising the subterraneity of these transformations also acknowledges that the epistemic turn towards uncertainty and probabilisation bubbles under the surface of informational forms that continue to bear resemblance to those that have always been central to the contemporary human rights movement. Whether the output is a composite video or a statistical estimation, new forms of data practice continue to harbour faith in an objective reality that can be presented through brute facts that appear deracinated from systemic forms of thought and theorisation. As HRDAG might put it, data practices work best when 'the debate hinges on a question of fact [. . .] if the question is one of quantity or patterns' but not 'if the question is one of ideology'.[88] The movement's data-led orientation thus reinscribes an informational logic that is invested in witnessing the 'real' of violence, while remaining resistant to critical and political forms of knowledge-making that subject norms and values, as well as the power relations and ideological frames that structure the social, to interrogation. It is in this sense that human rights facts still appear to 'speak for themselves', and, accordingly, fit within cybernetic capitalism's data imaginary and its similar ideological and epistemological investments in the idea that data just speaks for itself.

This is not to say that the outputs of human rights data practices are 'unpolluted by any deliberate human intervention', as popular discourses about data would have us believe.[89] The cases explored in this chapter attest to the fact that even the most automated of data practices requires careful human intervention to process the data, interact with uncertainty, and, in some cases, think quite carefully about how data might be folded and compartmentalised in vector space. Getting the data to talk, as it happens, is a rather tricky business involving knowledge apparatuses distributed across human and non-human agencies – cybernetic machines. But the cases do also seem to indicate that the movement's contemporary informational logic coils ever more tightly around a limited repertoire of facts which, more and more, are synonymous with the outputs of new 'automated' techniques. In this sense, embracing the data age takes human rights further away from, and not closer to, a more radical, consciously political project.

The crucial question is whether this new instantiation of the movement's informational project is, and will continue to be, enough for the challenges facing the world today. In the long decade since the financial crash, cybernetic capitalism has undergone an accelerated dissolution of human rights with the emergence of a reinvigorated far right, new rounds of structural adjustment, and intensification of the forms of precarity, suffering and, as Saskia Sassen has put it, 'expulsion'.[90] In the coming years, this dissolution of rights is likely to accelerate as the resource extraction and energy consumption necessary to maintain the growing digital infrastructures of cybernetic capitalism drive the potentially existential emergency of climate breakdown.[91] While this suggests that human rights organisations need to think about how their technologies contribute to the problems they seek to address, more importantly it also signals that the fight for human rights may now necessitate a sustained engagement with social and political critiques that bring the logics, procedures and infrastructures of capitalism into question and, consequently, a new epistemological model. This will of course require divesting from the modes of activism that have prevailed since the late 1970s, which, in their emphasis on signal recognition and the exclusion of political noise, are inadequate for this task. But such a disinvestment also leaves open a space for creative and imaginative thinking, for speculating in the uncertainty of the present, about what human rights might look like after information politics. It is this space I occupy next.

Notes

1. Indeed, McKenzie Wark has recently reflected on her optimism at the turn of the millennium that the internet was the basis of a new information commons. 'What I did not anticipate', she argues, 'was the emergence of a whole other technique for the capture of creation.' Wark did not foresee, in other words, that the commons of the internet would become the vast data mine of late capitalism. See McKenzie Wark, *Capital Is Dead: Is This Something Worse?* (London and New York: Verso, 2019), 54–5.

2. See Marion Fourcade and Kieran Healy, 'Seeing Like a Market', *Socio-Economic Review* 15, no. 1 (2017): 9–29; Jathan Sadowski, 'When Data Is Capital: Datafication, Accumulation, and Extraction', *Big Data & Society* 6, no. 1 (2019): 1–12.

3. IPC, <https://www.ipc.com/insights/blog/data-is-everything-everything-is-data/> (last accessed 24 February 2022).

4. David Beer, *The Data Gaze: Capitalism, Power and Perception* (London: SAGE Publications, 2018).

5. Examples in the US, such as the use of algorithms for predictive policing and to assist judges with bail decisions, show the ways in which new data practices are being bound into the criminal justice system. But as Jackie Wang has argued, while these algorithmic practices have been seen as a way of making policing and justice 'fairer' and 'unbiased', they have actually automated racialised decision-making, compounding existing problems. See Jackie Wang, *Carceral Capitalism* (South Pasadena, CA: Semiotext(e), 2018).

6. Chris Anderson, 'The End of Theory: The Data Deluge Makes the Scientific Method Obsolete', *WIRED*, 23 June 2008, <https://www.wired.com/2008/06/pb-theory/> (last accessed 24 February 2022).

7. Rob Kitchin, *The Data Revolution* (London: SAGE Publications, 2014), 2.

8. William Davies, 'Why Can't We Agree on What's True Any More?', *Guardian*, 19 September 2019, <https://www.theguardian.com/media/2019/sep/19/why-cant-we-agree-on-whats-true-anymore> (last accessed 24 February 2022).

9. Clemens Apprich, Wendy Hui Kyong Chun, Florian Cramer and Hito Steyerl, *Pattern Discrimination* (Minneapolis and London: University of Minnesota Press, 2019), 33–5.

10. Todd Landman, 'Measuring Modern Slavery: Law, Human Rights, and New Forms of Data', *Human Rights Quarterly* 42, no. 2 (2020): 303–31.

11. Jay D. Aronson, 'Computer Vision and Machine Learning for Human Rights Video Analysis: Case Studies, Possibilities, Concerns, and Limitations', *Law and Social Inquiry* 43, no. 4 (2018): 1188–209; Jay D. Aronson, McKenna Cole, Alex Hauptmann, Dan Miller and Bradley Samuels, 'Reconstructing Human Rights Violations Using Large Eyewitness Video Collections: The Case of Euromaidan Protester Deaths', *Journal of Human Rights Practice* 10, no. 1 (February 2018): 159–78; Patrick Ball and Megan Price, 'Using Statistics to Assess Lethal Violence in Civil and Inter-State War', *Annual Review of Statistics and Its Application* 6, no. 1 (2019): 63–84; Christopher J. Fariss, Fridolin J. Linder, Zachary M. Jones, Charles D. Crabtree, Megan A. Biek, Ana-Sophia M. Ross, Taranamol Kaur and Michael Tsai, 'Human Rights Texts: Converting Human Rights Primary Source Documents into Data', *PLoS ONE* 10, no. 9 (2015): 1–19.

12. Molly K. Land and Jay D. Aronson (eds), *New Technologies for Human Rights Law and Practice* (Cambridge: Cambridge University

Press, 2018), 5; Sam Gregory, 'Cameras Everywhere: Ubiquitous Video Documentation of Human Rights, New Forms of Video Advocacy, and Considerations of Safety, Security, Dignity and Consent', *Journal of Human Rights Practice* 2, no. 2 (2010): 191–207.

13. Theodore M. Porter, *Trust in Numbers: The Pursuit of Objectivity in Science and Public Life* (Princeton, NJ: Princeton University Press, 1995), 15, 75.
14. Thomas Marks, quoted in Winifred Tate, *Counting the Dead: The Culture and Politics of Human Rights Activism in Colombia* (Berkeley: University of California Press, 2007), 15.
15. Jana Asher, David Banks and Fritz Scheuren (eds), *Statistical Methods for Human Rights* (New York: Springer, 2008), 17–18.
16. Kristian Lum, Megan Price and David Banks, 'Applications of Multiple Systems Estimation in Human Rights Research', *American Statistician* 67, no. 4 (2013): 191.
17. Eyal Weizman, *Forensic Architecture: Violence at the Threshold of Detectability* (Cambridge, MA: Zone Books, 2017), 115.
18. Some of these machine learning applications have become a preoccupation for organisations like HURIDOCS, which have implemented processes like document scraping in their Uwazi software. See Natalie Widmann, 'Making Uwazi Smarter: Our Vision for Integrating Machine Learning into Uwazi', HURIDOCS, 13 September 2017, <huridocs. org/2017/09/making-uwazi-smarter-our-vision-for-integrating-machine-learning-into-uwazi/>; Lauren L. Finch, 'How Machine Learning Is Helping Plan International Put Girls' Rights at the Forefront of the International Agenda', HURIDOCS, 4 May 2020, <huridocs.org/2020/05/how-machine-learning-is-helping-plan-international-put-girls-rights-at-the-forefront-of-the-international-agenda/> (both last accessed 24 February 2022).
19. For an introduction to these concerns, see Nick Srnicek and Alex Williams, *Inventing the Future: Postcapitalism and a World Without Work* (London and New York: Verso, 2015).
20. Paraphrased, taken from author's field notes, June 2019.
21. Amnesty International, 'Strike Tracker', <decoders.amnesty.org/projects/strike-tracker> (last accessed 24 February 2022).
22. Moritz Altenried, 'The Platform as Factory: Crowdwork and the Hidden Labour behind Artificial Intelligence', *Capital and Class* 44, no. 2 (2020): 146.
23. Gemma Newlands, 'Lifting the Curtain: Strategic Visibility of Human Labour in AI-as-a-Service', *Big Data & Society* 8, no. 1 (2021): 1–14.
24. Bernhard Rieder, *Engines of Order: A Mechanology of Algorithmic Techniques* (Amsterdam: University of Amsterdam Press, 2020).
25. F. Rosenblatt, 'The Perceptron: A Probabilistic Model for Information Storage and Organization in the Brain', *Psychological Review* 65, no. 6 (1957): 386–408.
26. A history of neural nets from Rosenblatt's perceptron to the present day is given in Matteo Pasquinelli, 'Machines that Morph Logic: Neural

Networks and the Distorted Automation of Intelligence as Statistical Inference', *Glass Bead* 1, no. 1 (2017): 1–17.

27. Speaking with Matthew Fuller and Andrew Goffey, one might argue that machine learning techniques are part of the 'grey media' that characterise contemporary society. Grey media, as they suggest, are those unobtrusive infrastructural technologies in which 'a certain recessiveness is often a crucial aspect of their efficacy'. See Matthew Fuller and Andrew Goffey, *Evil Media* (Cambridge, MA: MIT Press, 2012), 12.

28. Adrian Mackenzie, *Machine Learners: Archaeology of a Data Practice* (Cambridge, MA: MIT Press, 2017); Rieder, *Engines of Order*.

29. Alexander L. Fradkov, 'Early History of Machine Learning', *IFAC-PapersOnLine* 53, no. 2 (2020): 1385–90.

30. Nick Dyer-Witheford, Atle Mikkola Kjøsen and James Steinhoff, *Inhuman Power: Artificial Intelligence and the Future of Capitalism* (London: Pluto Press, 2019), 3.

31. David Beer's *The Data Gaze* provides an interesting overview of this new analytics industry.

32. Bernhard Rieder, 'Scrutinizing an Algorithmic Technique: The Bayes Classifier as Interested Reading of Reality', *Information Communication and Society* 20, no. 1 (2017): 102.

33. Mackenzie, *Machine Learners*.

34. Mackenzie, *Machine Learners*, 51.

35. As Rieder points out, the vectorised shape enables machine learners to operate as if the data were a geometric space and thus authorises 'the application of linear algebra'. See Rieder, *Engines of Order*, 219.

36. Though this example is of binary classifications, as one of the most popular manuals on machine learning points out, 'when there are more than two categories, several alternatives are available'. See Trevor Hastie, Robert Tibshirani and Jerome Friedman, *The Elements of Statistical Learning: Data Mining, Inference, and Prediction* (Berlin: Springer Science and Business, 2009), 12.

37. Mackenzie, *Machine Learners*, 63.

38. Though unsupervised learners are less common in a human rights context, institutions like the International, Impartial and Independent Mechanism (IIIM), which documents evidence of human rights violations in Syria, have used unsupervised learners to 'cluster' documents and images that might refer to similar violations. See Elena Radeva, 'The Potential for Computer Vision to Advance Accountability in the Syrian Crisis', *Journal of International Criminal Justice* 19, no. 1 (2021): 131–46.

39. Matteo Pasquinelli, 'How a Machine Learns and Fails – A Grammar of Error for Artificial Intelligence', *Spheres* 5, no. 1 (2019): 10. See also Mercedes Bunz, 'The Calculation of Meaning: On the Misunderstanding of New Artificial Intelligence as Culture', *Culture, Theory and Critique* 60, no. 3–4 (2019): 264–78.

40. Weizman, *Forensic Architecture*, 83.

41. Patrick Ball, 'The Bigness of Big Data: Samples, Models, and the Facts We Might Find When Looking at Data', in *The Transformation of*

Human Rights Fact-Finding, ed. Philip Alston and Sarah Knuckey (Oxford: Oxford University Press, 2016), 427.

42. Megan Price and Patrick Ball, 'The Limits of Observation for Understanding Mass Violence', *Canadian Journal of Law and Society* 30, no. 2 (2015): 239.

43. Tamy Guberek, Daniel Guzmán, Megan Price, Kristian Lum and Patrick Ball, *To Count the Uncounted: An Estimation of Lethal Violence in Casanare* (Palo Alto: Benetech Human Rights Program, 2010), 2.

44. More details on HRDAG's contribution to these cases is available on its website at <https://hrdag.org/> (last accessed 25 February 2022).

45. Much of this is collated in what HRDAG calls its 'tech corner', a section on its website where information about R packages (RCapture and their own DGA package being two) mingles with mathematical formalisations and the issues with computation at scale.

46. For more on the process of cleaning, see Amelia Hoover Green, 'Multiple Systems Estimation: Collection, Cleaning and Canonicalization of Data', HRDAG, 13 March 2013, <https://hrdag.org/2013/03/13/mse-collection-cleaning-canonicalization-data/> (last accessed 25 February 2022). It might also be noted that the process of cleaning here is a reminder of the point made by critics such as Gitelman and Apprich et al. that raw data is never simply given but always subject to human (and therefore) social adjustment throughout its processing and preparation. See Lisa Gitelman (ed.), *'Raw Data' Is an Oxymoron* (Cambridge, MA and London: MIT Press, 2013); Apprich et al., *Pattern Discrimination*.

47. Price and Ball, 'The Limits of Observation for Understanding Mass Violence', 253–4.

48. Anne Chao, 'Capture–Recapture for Human Populations', *Wiley StatsRef: Statistics Reference Online*, 2015, 1–16, DOI: 10.1002/9781118445112. stat04855.pub2.

49. Amelia Hoover Green, 'Multiple Systems Estimation: Stratification and Estimation', HRDAG, 20 March 2013, <hrdag.org/2013/03/20/mse-stratification-estimation/> (last accessed 25 February 2022).

50. Kristian Lum, Megan Price, Tamy Guberek and Patrick Ball, 'Measuring Elusive Populations with Bayesian Model Averaging for Multiple Systems Estimation: A Case Study on Lethal Violations in Casanare, 1998–2007', *Statistics, Politics, and Policy* 1, no. 1 (2010): 1998–2007.

51. As HRDAG notes, its project on Syria used around '360,000 records, including many duplicates. That means that there are around 65 billion possible comparisons between pairs of records.' See Patrick Ball, 'How Do We Find Duplicates among Multiple, Giant Datasets?', HRDAG, <https://hrdag.org/tech-notes/adaptive-blocking-writeup-1.html> (last accessed 25 February 2022).

52. Ball and Price, 'Using Statistics to Assess Lethal Violence', 7.

53. Amelia Hoover Green, 'Multiple Systems Estimation: The Matching Process', HRDAG, 15 March 2013, <https://hrdag.org/2013/03/15/mse-matching-process/> (last accessed 25 February 2022).

54. Megan Price and Patrick Ball, 'Selection Bias and the Statistical Patterns of Mortality in Conflict', *Statistical Journal of the IAOS* 31, no. 2 (2015): 263–4; Green, 'Multiple Systems Estimation: Stratification and Estimation'.
55. Lum et al., 'Measuring Elusive Populations', 6.
56. Lorraine Daston and Peter Galison, *Objectivity* (New York: Zone Books, 2010).
57. Daston and Galison, *Objectivity*, 161. Of course, the faith in cameras to mimetically reproduce the real has been disturbed by a number of scholars working in photography and culture studies, who readily demonstrate that the camera and the photograph are shaped by social and cultural perspectives in quite complicated ways.
58. Daston and Galison, *Objectivity*, 265, 271.
59. Daston and Galison, *Objectivity*, 331.
60. Ball, 'The Bigness of Big Data', 425–6.
61. Charles Baudelaire, quoted in Daston and Galison, *Objectivity*, 187–8.
62. Tiziana Terranova, *Network Culture: Politics for the Information Age* (London: Pluto Press, 2004), 24.
63. Radeva, 'The Potential for Computer Vision to Advance Accountability'.
64. Aronson et al., 'Reconstructing Human Rights Violations', 161.
65. For example, Forensic Architecture recently worked with ElementAI in order to artificially render images of Triple-Chaser tear gas cannisters because there was not enough 'organic' data to train the classifier on. See Lachlan Kermode, Jan Freyberg, Alican Akturk, Robert Trafford, Denis Kochetkov, Rafael Pardinas, Eyal Weizman and Julien Cornebise, 'Objects of Violence: Synthetic Data for Practical ML in Human Rights Investigations', *ArXiv*, 2020, <https://arxiv.org/abs/2004.01030> (last accessed 25 February 2022).
66. Insofar as the identification of relevant objects, actions and behaviours might be achieved by using the visual, audio or semantic aspects of the footage, this family of techniques readily demonstrate the potency of machine learning. The capacity to fold radically different data types within the vector space is evidence of its decidedly omnivorous quality. With that said, it is also worth noting that automated content retrieval may not be enough on its own, especially when found footage becomes evidence in legal proceedings. In these circumstances, any found videos will need to have chain of custody assurances such as permanent and inalterable timestamping. For this reason, machine learning techniques for identifying video content are usually integrated into larger, complex infrastructural assemblages which bring together careful human work and technical processes such as hashing – the same cryptographic technique that maintains the integrity of blockchain technologies – which can preserve metadata that authenticates and verifies the video evidence. The necessity of metadata that authenticates video evidence was hammered home during in the short time I spent with Global Legal Action Network (GLAN), an organisation using eye-witness footage in its attempts to prosecute those responsible for human rights violations

in Yemen. For GLAN, the issue of preserving verifiable video evidence was of paramount importance. As one member of the team described it, 'To ensure its chain of custody' GLAN's database integrates the Uwazi platform developed by HURIDOCS with Digital Evidence Vault (DEV), software developed by the Center for Human Rights Science at Carnegie Mellon University. DEV uses hashing protocols to preserve information about the video, including the publicly available metadata and a screenshot of the page in which it was found.

67. Aronson et al., 'Reconstructing Human Rights Violations', 162.
68. See, for example, Forensic Architecture, *The Killing of Bassem Abu Rahman* (2014), <https://forensic-architecture.org/investigation/the-killing-of-bassem-abu-rahma> (last accessed 25 February 2022).
69. Aronson et al., 'Reconstructing Human Rights Violations'.
70. Junwei Liang, Desai Fan, Han Lu, Poyao Huang, Jia Chen, Lu Jiang and Alexander Hauptmann, 'An Event Reconstruction Tool for Conflict Monitoring Using Social Media', *Proceedings of the AAAI Conference on Artificial Intelligence* 31, no. 1 (2017), 5098.
71. Aronson et al., 'Reconstructing Human Rights Violations', 168.
72. Liang et al., 'An Event Reconstruction Tool', 5098 .
73. See, for example, Junwei Liang, Jay D. Aronson and Alexander Hauptmann, 'Technical Report of the Video Event Reconstruction and Analysis (VERA) System – Shooter Localization, Models, Interface, and Beyond', *ArXiv*, 2019, <https://arxiv.org/abs/1905.13313> (last accessed 25 February 2022).
74. Daston and Galison, *Objectivity*, 135, 139.
75. Aronson, 'Computer Vision and Machine Learning'.
76. Jay D. Aronson, 'Preserving Human Rights Media for Justice, Accountability, and Historical Clarification', *Genocide Studies and Prevention* 11, no. 1 (2017): 84.
77. See Adrian Mackenzie, 'The Production of Prediction: What Does Machine Learning Want?', *European Journal of Cultural Studies* 18, no. 4–5 (2015): 429–45.
78. Feng Chen and Daniel B. Neill, 'Human Rights Event Detection from Heterogeneous Social Media Graphs', *Big Data* 3, no. 1 (2015): 35.
79. Chen and Neill, 'Human Rights Event Detection', 34–5.
80. Ayman Alhelbawy, Mark Lattimer, Udo Kruschwitz, Chris Fox and Massimo Poesio, 'An NLP-Powered Human Rights Monitoring Platform', *Expert Systems with Applications* 153 (2020): 2.
81. Alhelbawy et al., 'An NLP-Powered Human Rights Monitoring Platform', 9.
82. Alhelbawy et al., 'An NLP-Powered Human Rights Monitoring Platform', 11.
83. Chen and Neill, 'Human Rights Event Detection', 35.
84. Chen and Neill, 'Human Rights Event Detection', 37.
85. Chen and Neill, 'Human Rights Event Detection', 35.
86. Lapham and Verstappen, 'Human Rights Violations and Standard Formats', 18.

87. Susan Leigh Star and Geoffrey C. Bowker, 'How to Infrastructure', in *The Handbook of New Media: Social Shaping and Consequences of ICTs*, ed. Leah A. Lievrow and Sonia Livingston (London: SAGE Publications, 2006), 230–45.
88. HRDAG, 'How We Choose Projects', <https://hrdag.org/how-we-choose-projects/> (last accessed 25 February 2022).
89. Davies, 'Why Can't We Agree on What's True Any More?'
90. Saskia Sassen, *Expulsions: Brutality and Complexity in the Global Economy* (Cambridge: The Belknap Press of Harvard University Press, 2014).
91. Sean Cubitt, *Finite Media: Environmental Implications of Digital Technologies* (Durham, NC and London: Duke University Press, 2017); Kate Crawford, *Atlas of AI* (New Haven, CT and London: Yale University Press, 2021). For some thoughts on the specific impacts of climate breakdown on human rights, see IBA Climate Change Justice and Human Rights Task Force Report, *Achieving Justice and Human Rights in an Era of Climate Disruption* (London: IBA, 2014).

Chapter 5

After Informational Logic: Rethinking Information/ Rethinking Rights

The fact that the terms politicize and politics themselves have been put under erasure by the world-media system that is computational racial capital requires another discussion [. . .] Ultimately it will entail the wholesale detournement of information.

– Jonathan Beller, *The World Computer*

In his 2017 book, Eyal Weizman provides a window into the kinds of digital human rights work that his organisation, Forensic Architecture, has pioneered since its formation in 2010.[1] From modelling the shooting of unarmed Palestinians to analysing bomb clouds and craters in Rafah, Weizman offers an overview of the innovative techniques that have enabled the organisation to uncover evidence of human rights abuses. Such an overview is particularly important given the growing contribution that techniques deployed by Forensic Architecture are making to the contemporary human rights movement. For instance, the organisation's use of digital technologies to recover traces of violence that would otherwise remain undetected has become evidence in a growing number of legal cases, notably in proceedings against the state heard at the Israeli High Court and evidentiary submissions to the International Criminal Court.

From my own perspective, however, what is most interesting is the book's engagement with the epistemologies of human rights, which simultaneously shape and constrain Forensic Architecture's work, and the socio-political dilemmas that emerge as the organisation attempts to produce knowledge about violations. As Weizman argues, a key difficulty lies in the gap between the expectations placed upon expertise, which is 'often understood to be preconditioned on a position of neutrality', and the reality that, in his experience at least, political commitments inevitably shape the position of the expert: 'no uninvolved investigator would have bothered to go to the lengths we have without being in solidarity with the victims'.[2] The dilemma for Weizman is that political motivations can be both a source of strength and a critical weakness. On the one hand, the political and ideological commitments of activists inform all practices that aim at 'fighting for and defending claims' and can help 'sharpen the quality of [their] research'. Nevertheless, 'wearing one's political passions too openly [. . .] can make one vulnerable'.[3] As Weizman points out, the ways his past statements and publications have been mobilised against Forensic Architecture's investigations attests to the fact that a too full-blooded embrace of politics can make organisations open to accusations of bias.

How to manage this dilemma? For Weizman the answer is to try to straddle the contradiction through a form of 'engaged objectivity', knowledge production which is cognisant of both the political commitments and labour involved in constructing 'the most simple of facts', whilst also acknowledging the importance of 'referring to the truth as something much more obvious, already simply there'.[4] Weizman's laudable aim is thus to try to find a space for politics whilst also appreciating that being heard by the legal, state and international institutions that Forensic Architecture's work intends to address requires the adoption of a strategic objectivity that can navigate an environment which takes for granted notions of neutrality and the existence of 'bare facts'. In this respect, Weizman's overview of Forensic Architecture's work also constitutes an honest reckoning with some of the knotty problems that inhabit much of the contemporary human rights project and its paradoxically apolitical information 'politics'. His epistemological reflections thus provide something of an antidote to the often-unquestioned assumption that politics can be entirely expunged from the informational work of human rights.

And yet, Weizman's notion of engaged objectivity also leaves me feeling uneasy. While his account tries to find both space and a place for politics, his proposal ultimately makes the political operational only in the background of Forensic Architecture's work, whilst also maintaining a commitment to producing information aligned to the kinds of mechanical objectivity that have always characterised the contemporary human rights movement. Ultimately, then, Weizman leaves the epistemological foundations of the contemporary human rights project largely untroubled. Even if only for strategic reasons, the adoption of the neutral(ising) and apolitical epistemology of human rights remains grounded in the apparent necessity of recognition, of the desire for information to be parsed as signal, by the institutions they address – that is, from the perspectives of the powerful. If, as I have argued throughout this book, concerns with recognition are at the heart of an informational logic which has limited the questions and the demands that can be articulated in the name of human rights, then engaged objectivity does not appear to offer a route beyond this problem.

In this final chapter of the book, I want to suggest that charting an escape route from the informational logic of human rights requires a more fundamental rethink of the informational model upon which the contemporary human rights movement is built. My proposal, however, is not premised on abandoning informational politics altogether. In the era of cybernetic capitalism, information has become an inescapable feature of contemporary thought and action, which requires engagement rather than retreat. Following Yoshimi, I contend that information is a space of contestation – 'a field of struggle' – for human rights, where 'different definitions confront each other leading to the creation of new practices and alternative concepts' of both information and human rights.[5] Consequently, reconfiguring the epistemological assumptions underpinning the movement's current conception of information can provide a crucial foundation for renewed attempts to realize the radical potential of human rights.

Pursuing this trajectory, the chapter draws together epistemological insights from Donna Haraway's concept of situated knowledges, Maurizio Lazzarato's theories of counter-expertise and battle truths, as well as Pooja Parmar's Third World Approaches to International Law (TWAIL) in order to develop an alternative model of information for human rights.[6] Against traditional, positivistic conceptions of objectivity and their dominant ways of 'seeing' and 'doing', the chapter first develops an alternative epistemology for human rights, which takes the point of view of exploited and marginalised groups – in short, all those who live without rights – as the starting point from which knowledges are made. As the chapter progresses, I consider the implications of the perspectival epistemology I am advancing not only for conceptions of 'information' and 'information politics' but, in turn, the digital technologies and socio-technical practices of human rights. As will become clear, the shift to knowledge-making processes based on situated 'counter-knowledges' does not call for an end to information politics nor its practices and technologies but, rather, their radical transformation. In thinking through some of these transformations, the chapter sketches out some contours for a more transformative vision of human rights politics.

What Future for Human Rights?

Before staging my intervention, however, it is first worth taking time to clarify an important issue which was sidestepped in the introductory paragraphs above, namely, if the contemporary human rights project has been deleteriously shaped by its emergence both alongside and within cybernetic capitalism, then what can be salvaged from it for the purposes of radical politics; why persist with human rights at all? There are, in fact, good reasons for believing not only that human rights can provide a fertile terrain for the development of radical political projects but also that it has become a particularly important space for making and realising transformative demands today. First, it bears repeating that history shows that human rights is not a monolithic discourse and is not reducible to the informational project that occupies a hegemonic position today. To recall Slaughter's argument: human rights have always been 'an uncertain and unstable discourse that covered a hugely varied collection (or better, dispersion) of principles and promises'.[7] From the Diggers and Levellers to the Third Worldists fighting for a New International Economic Order, the previous chapters of this book have paid testament to the fact that alternative ways of thinking about human rights have crystallised into a number of politically potent projects.

It is not mere coincidence that such radical instantiations of rights have emerged in times gone by. Drawing on the work of Jacques Rancière and Costas Douzinas, Illan Rua Wall has argued that human rights discourse is indelibly marked by a bifurcation of its sociopolitical functions.[8] On the one hand, the colonial, capitalist tradition which predominates today has solidified human rights as a particular legal order, one that emphasises state authority, norm building and consensus. This is, as I described in Chapter 1, human rights as informational law, 'the ethical control applied to communication [. . .] orderly and repeatable control of critical situations'.[9] Nevertheless, as Wall suggests, human rights are never entirely contained by this consensus. What escapes – the excess – is all the virtualities of human rights that harbour the socio-political potential of extending beyond any particular version of 'ethical control'. The constant availability of this excess provides groups with the grounding to make 'antagonistic right-claims' and to '[exceed] the rights that are given to them in order to reconstruct the social bond'.[10] It is not that human rights is a sliding or empty discourse, then; rather, 'it is a language of hegemony and counter-hegemony [. . .] of both power and resistance'.[11] With this being the case, there ought to be no intractable reasons why human rights cannot similarly be put towards radical ends today.

In fact, there is a growing sense that unlocking the radical potential of human rights has never been more pressing. As I have suggested at various points across the course of this book, the era of cybernetic capitalism is also an era of crisis. Indivisible crises of capitalism and climate engender not only a proliferation of human suffering (through forced migrations and authoritarian borders, drought, famine and growing inequalities, to name only a few of the baleful conditions some are already experiencing) but an existential threat to life on earth. The present historical juncture is thus one in which the spectre of an unin-habitable planet raises the stakes of finding tools that provide emanci-patory pathways from the present. But as Paul O'Connell has recently suggested, there is 'no reference point outside of capitalism from which we can begin to construct alternatives to it', and, consequently, there are no 'tools' we could find that would not be 'compromised and lim-ited by dint of the conditions under which [they] must be deployed'. With this in mind, I follow O'Connell in suggesting that 'human rights are one of the key "inadequate tools" we have at our disposal today', offering at least some promise in enabling us to move beyond the pres-ent conjuncture.[12]

I do so in the knowledge that important strands of the radical Black and postcolonial tradition, moving through figures like W. E. B. Du Bois, Frantz Fanon and Aimé Césaire, have seen the figure of the human as itself an important terrain of struggle. As both Sylvia Wynter and Alexander Weheliye point out, the Enlightenment figure of 'Man', which the 'Rights of Man' tradition of human rights has played a key role in articulating, has been a technology that config-ures the category of the human around the Western, bourgeois body by excluding the racialised and colonial subjects, which represent its other.[13] But by insisting on 'the historicity and mutability of the "human" itself', Black radicals have developed a politics aimed at creating a new figure of humanity that 'neither begins nor ends with the white masculine liberal subject'.[14] With this in mind, I would suggest that if the 'inadequate tools' of human rights are important today, it is not only because they might help to reconstruct the social bond, as Wall puts it, but also because they might simultaneously build new and emancipatory figures of the human.

Making the case for this radical, generative potential of human rights also takes shape in the context of a growing body of scholarship that has started grappling with what Kathryn McNeilly has succinctly called the 'human rights to come'.[15] Indeed, McNeilly's own work sits alongside that of scholars such as O'Connell, Douzinas, Wall and Manfredi, all of whom explore the potential for an egalitarian rewriting of human rights which is oppositional to the logic and function of late capitalism.[16] Much of this literature shares a conviction that the capacity to overwrite human rights in this way is also dependent on a shift towards a more confrontational and transgressive strategy. As McNeilly puts it, a more radical rights project involves 'visibilising the integral part of conflict [. . .] and embracing it as a driving force'. In emphasising conflict, 'the purpose of rights politics comes into view as being to challenge the existing consensus, to expose its limits based upon the conflictual claims of those on the margins'.[17]

My own thinking about human rights has been greatly informed by these contributions, and in particular their emphasis on moving away from the informational logic of signal recognition and consensus I have traced through the course of this book. In what follows, however, I intend to move these debates onto a terrain that I would suggest is crucial for reimagining human rights but which remains underexplored in current thinking: the reconfiguration of what Karin Knorr Cetina has called 'the machineries of knowing', attached to the movement's current conception of information.[18] For human rights, this machinery includes not only more conceptual components such as the epistemological and methodological approaches that orient the current ways of 'seeing' and 'doing' rights but also the material practices and socio-technical devices within which they are inevitably embedded. The reconsideration of human rights information which I pursue in the following sections considers how this machinery might be transformed by first reconstructing its conceptual components before reflecting on what this might mean for both seeing and doing rights in practice. In developing this set of reflections my aim is to contribute one possible vision of human rights to come.

Rethinking Objectivity

From the perspective of the humanities and critical social sciences it should seem quite odd that human rights practice has remained so attached to the positivistic tradition, which first emerged out of liberal Enlightenment thought and has historically been much more at home in the exact and natural sciences. After all, there is hardly a subject more critiqued in the social sciences than positivism and the attendant notions of neutral knowledge and objectivity onto which it is grafted. In different ways, the best of feminist science studies, postcolonial thought, and poststructural and critical theory have demonstrated that the possibility of faithfully capturing the real, or of accurately knowing the world from the 'outside' without intervening in it, is misleading (at best).[19] The determination with which mainstream human rights has remained largely blind to these developments perhaps speaks to the degree to which the movement remains invested in the imaginary of information systems and the possibility of transparent communication that coagulates around particular epistemological tropes. From my perspective, however, it also means that these theoretical tools remain a source of a generative critique that lays the foundations for a perspectival approach to human rights information.

An important starting point in this respect is the work of Donna Haraway, whose scholarship I have already gestured to over the course of this book. Haraway's writing on 'situated knowledges' builds on feminist epistemological approaches such as 'standpoint theory' and developments in postcolonial strands of feminist science studies, particularly the work of Sandra Harding.[20] Directed at the kinds of technoscientific knowledge-making that I have traced across this book, it combines a biting critique of objectivity with a robust account of her own feminist epistemological framework. As we shall soon see, what is particularly interesting about Haraway's theoretical approach is her refusal to discard objectivity entirely. Realising that such a move would no doubt reduce the status of what is knowable to the subjective – a term that is scarred by derogatory connotations of bias not only in the natural sciences where she is making her intervention but also in the field of human rights – Haraway instead attempts to retheorise and reformulate objectivity from a feminist perspective which takes 'situatedness' as its starting point. In doing so, Haraway's work helpfully frames what is at stake in the epistemological shift that I aim to develop using theoretical tools that move beyond unhelpful divisions between 'real' objective knowledge and 'biased' subjectivity, which tend to hamstring these debates.

Centring her critique of objectivity around the metaphor of vision, Haraway argues that the traditional notion of objectivity appears to provide a disembodied form of vision, which claims 'the power to see and not be seen, to represent while escaping representation'. For Haraway, the problem with objectivity is its faith in this possibility of leaping 'out of the marked body and into a conquering gaze from nowhere', which she contends is always an illusory promise.[21] What appears as disembodied vision never really marks an escape from the body but instead signifies the power of the seer to leave their own position unmarked and thus to naturalise and then universalise their own perspective. For Haraway, this is significant because so-called objective knowledge has often been made from the unmarked position of white, bourgeois and male and reflects project(s) of heteropatriarchal and racial capitalism that are the often-occluded socio-political and economic preconditions of liberal Enlightenment knowledge. Objectivity is thus an expression of power, a 'god trick' in which particular forms of vision are made to appear as a view of everything from nowhere.

In drawing attention to the obfuscated embodiment that inheres in objective knowledge, Haraway also lays the groundwork for developing her own alternative conception of objectivity. If all knowledge is perspectival, even when it appears not to be, then one cannot ever hope to find a distanced vantage point from which to faithfully produce a total, mirror image of the real. All practices of knowledge-making are, in other words, situated within specific social positions. Haraway thus argues for forms of knowledge-making that are transparent about, and thus accountable to, their 'positionality' – the social 'somewhere' from which they are produced. What emerges then is not a mode of knowledge-making that promises universality or transcendence, but partial knowledges constructed from situated positions.[22] This provides the groundwork for knowledge-making practices no longer organised around the (im)possibility of a safe distance or 'outside' but accountability to, and responsibility for, the viewpoints from which knowledge is constructed.

Importantly, by shifting the locus of what counts as objective vision, Haraway furnishes her epistemology with considerable political potential. In the absence of a 'proper' or privileged site from which knowledge can be legitimately produced, Haraway's perspectival approach opens up the possibility of constructing knowledge from multiple positions, particularly those 'subjugated standpoints' whose value is often denied by traditional conceptions of objective knowledge. In fact, knowledges from subjugated points of view:

> are preferred because in principle they are least likely to allow denial of the critical and interpretive core of all knowledge. They are knowledgeable of modes of denial through repression, forgetting and disappearing acts – ways of being nowhere while claiming to see comprehensively. [. . .] 'Subjugated' standpoints are preferred because they seem to promise more adequate, sustained, objective, transforming accounts of the world.[23]

Haraway thus acknowledges the value of subjugated standpoints and the knowledge that is possible to construct from them, not only because they are most likely to provide much needed critical suspicion and awareness of the god trick but also because they harbour the transformative potential of imagining the world otherwise.

Nevertheless, Haraway's optimism about the capacities of subjugated standpoints should not be confused for a romanticism, idealisation or even a fetishisation of knowledges from below. As she suggests, the positions of subjugated subjects are not innocent and need to be engaged through processes of critical judgement and examination, as well as deconstruction, decoding and interpretation. Such critical activity is not easy and demands the careful work of 'passionate construction' in order to assemble knowledge which neither reintroduces the god trick by totalising a single vision nor descends into a nebulous relativism. On the one hand, Haraway suggests that not just any standpoint will do. Instead, 'we are bound to seek perspective from those points of view, which can never be known in advance, that promise something quite extraordinary, that is, knowledge potent for constructing worlds less organized by axes of domination'.[24] On the other hand, the purpose of these constructions is not universalisation but 'partial, locatable, critical knowledges sustaining the possibility of webs of connections called solidarity in politics and shared conversations in epistemology'.[25] The work of passionate construction is thus an explicitly political act of knowledge-making that involves 'the joining of partial views and halting voices into a collective subject position [. . .] of views from somewhere'.[26]

The concept of objectivity that emerges from this process is one of accountability, of knowing the limits and affordances of particular standpoints, of understanding where different positions imbricate in the web(s) of partial connections, and, perhaps most of all, leaving the positionality of one's knowledge marked. This latter point, as Haraway contends, takes into account the fact that 'vision is always a question of the power to see – and perhaps of the violence implicit in our visualizing practices'.[27] An objectivity worthy of that title does not hide its violence in totalising claims but is transparent about, and takes responsibility for, the lines of inclusion and exclusion that necessarily mark all knowledge-making practices.[28] Perhaps most of all, accountability means taking responsibility for the violence of translation, deconstruction and critical inquiry that is part and parcel of assembling knowledge from the perspectives of the subjugated. Objective knowledge is positionality *and* accountability or, as Haraway puts it, both 'the fantastic element of hope for transformative knowledge and the severe check and stimulus of sustained critical inquiry'.[29]

For human rights, the feminist epistemology outlined by Haraway provides a provocative intervention. With its surfacing of the relationships between what is considered legitimate knowledge and power and its insistence on the validity of transformative knowledges constructed from within specific socio-political positions, this epistemological framework is diametrically opposed to the informational logic of human rights. Unlike Weizman, who makes an argument for strategic objectivity that leaves politics at the door, Haraway insists on positionality as the foundation for a feminist objectivity and thus sees politics, solidarity and criticality as inextricable from the practice of knowledge-making. There is no question here of attempting to leap, strategically or not, into the disembodied view of global capitalism with its prism of classed, gendered and racial lenses. The pressing question, however, is what might it mean to develop and construct 'positional' human rights information?

In her TWAIL-inflected epistemological investigation of human rights, Pooja Parmar suggests that the positions of Third World peoples provide an important basis for developing alternative conceptions of human rights. As she suggests, the subjugated positions of the Third World represent 'interests, concerns, histories and struggles [that] have been relegated to the margins [. . .] primarily as a consequence of colonialism and imperialism'.[30] The possibility of producing knowledge from these locations, she suggests, thus represents an opportunity for developing potentially transformative knowledge. Like Haraway, however, Parmar is also alert to the dangers of 'uncritically privileging the stories of essentialised Third World Peoples'. Against this tendency, Parmar draws on the work of Harding to argue for Third World perspectives as a vantage point that is neither reified nor fetishised but simply 'starts off thought'.[31] Where human rights are concerned, the socio-economic and political positions of the South are therefore not read as ends in themselves but become the beginning of a process of knowledge formation that requires all of the criticality and passionate construction that Haraway centres in her own epistemology.

What might perspectival knowledge-making mean in practice? As she develops her theory, Parmar suggests that 'starting off thought from a particular "local" [. . .] does not preclude investigation of the constitution of that local itself'.[32] I would suggest even more emphatically that attentiveness to the ways that locatable positions are constituted is absolutely crucial to developing a more transformative vision for human rights and provides a vital frame of reference to the critical question she poses later: 'how does a proposed human rights theory respond to the suffering of *particularly situated* human beings?'[33] As propositions for knowledge-making, the form of critical positionality these quotations imply precludes the tradition of bearing witness to suffering through an assemblage of brute facts that might today be called 'digital' or 'data witnessing'.[34] Instead, critical positioning demands a thoroughgoing investigation of suffering as a socially and economically situated experience, forging connections between experiences of violence and the classed, raced and gendered formations that make some social positions more vulnerable to those experiences than others. Put more forcefully: since cybernetic capitalism's 'abstract operations are too often posited as unconnected to or even incommensurable with material violence', the first task of human rights information is to render these connections visible.[35]

Returning to the issue of racialised policing touched on in Chapter 2 helps to demonstrate what this kind of situated knowledge-making might look like. Against a human rights tradition focused on establishing the 'bare facts' of police brutality, a more radical project that took situatedness as its starting point would aim to forge connections between the violent policing of Black lives and the iniquitous structures of racialised capitalism. Among the many necessary connections, this account would need to connect police violence not only to the ongoing socio-economic inequalities and deprivations inscribed into the geographies of urban spaces like the ghetto or banlieue brought to light by scholars like Loïc Wacquant.[36] It would also need to account for the ways that the over-policing of Black bodies in these geographies has enabled a massive outgrowth of cheap and exploitable prison labour that has, in various ways, served to enrich private corporations.[37]

Importantly, human rights discourses would take a central role in forging these connections, becoming the operative terms that identify, name, and develop a situated critique of domination. This would mean refusing to isolate facts about individual acts of violence from the broader structures of socio-economic violence within which they are situated. It would therefore require taking seriously the apparent interconnectedness and indivisibility of social, economic, civil and political rights, which, while much vaunted in the human rights community, as Manfredi suggests, has not materialised in practice.[38] Hence, in the case of racialised police violence, acts of brutality meted out by police must be seen as rights violations that are intrinsically, and not tangentially, connected to the ongoing violations of the rights to food, housing, education and social security that are a direct consequence of cybernetic capitalism and which form the everyday experiences of many Black lives. In the articulation of situated knowledges, the multifaceted nature of human rights, especially its capacity to straddle civil, political and socio-economic issues, thus becomes a valuable tool insofar as it provides a language of violence that can both span and connect all of these issues.

Battle Truths

The foregoing sketches out an epistemic infrastructure for human rights that does not assume consensus; situated knowledge holds no truck with disembodied objectivity. But this poses important questions about the ways human rights information might function once recognition is no longer a presupposed. What is the relationship of situated knowledge to power and the hegemonic and institutionalised knowledge of the powerful once human rights no longer seeks to operate on the latter's epistemological terrain? To investigate this question, I want to draw on the interrelated concepts of 'counter-expertise' and 'battle truths' developed by Maurizio Lazzarato in his recently translated *Experimental Politics*.[39] These concepts are particularly compelling because Lazzarato's development of them is rooted in his own experiences of being part of the struggles of the *intermittents et précaires d'Île-de-France*, precarious French creative and cultural workers, which erupted in the early noughties in response to deleterious, neoliberal welfare reforms imposed by the French state.[40] Accordingly, Lazzarato's concepts offer important insights into how knowledge production operates within material struggles according to a logic of confrontation rather than of consensus.

At the same time, because Lazzarato's concepts are rooted in an epistemology that has much in common with Haraway's vision of situated knowledges, there is plenty of scope for productive and generative engagement between them. Indeed, Lazzarato's work can fruitfully sharpen some of Haraway's own epistemological insights whilst also introducing a more forceful account of how situated knowledges operate within the context of political struggle. Like Haraway, Lazzarato is sceptical of anything like an 'objective science of society', in which knowledge is a 'copy of reality', of simply 'what is already there'.[41] For Lazzarato, this is a particularly 'reactionary' understanding of what objective knowledge might mean. Instead, Lazzarato suggests that the world is defined by a kind of plasticity; it is 'constituted from a multiplicity of points of view and a multiplicity of heterogeneous relations'.[42] For Lazzarato, each of these viewpoints or locations provides a 'single point of view from which the multiplicity can be partially and provisionally grasped', and, consequently, objective, scientific knowledges emerge from the specific 'choices made possible by these different points of view'.[43] In this sense, Lazzarato shares with Haraway a concern for reshaping objectivity around situated, locatable knowledge that is transparently constructed from a specific standpoint.

But Lazzarato's account of how these perspectives come to be seen and understood also elaborates the concept of situated knowledge. As Lazzarato contends, each perspective needs to be articulated through point-of-view-words that shape both the meaning of the position and the relations of power that it engages. Point-of-view-words are discursive nodes that function by 'defining the problem' in ways that enable the perspective it references to adopt, delimit and fix possibilities for both knowing and acting. As Lazzarato argues of the *intermittents*, different point-of-view-words such as 'wage-earner', 'precarious worker' or 'artist' could each provide different points for 'starting off thought', as Parmar might put it, furnishing different possibilities for knowing. This insight helps to enrich our understanding of what 'situatedness' does and does not mean. Most importantly, Lazzarato avoids the prospect of an essentialised conception of social position by emphasising that positionality also has a certain plasticity; the act of positioning is itself a process of identification, negotiation and construction within any knowledge-making procedure.

For Lazzarato, this plasticity is central to his account of how particular situated knowledges can gain potency as forms of 'counter-expertise' that function by opposing dominant knowledge formations. Between different point-of-view-words, Lazzarato suggests, are 'differences of potential [. . .] [C]ertain among them express the virtualities and potentialities proper to a situation, and are opposed to and enter into conflict with current power relations, where other [perspectives] are restricted to legitimizing and reproducing them.'[44] For instance, the concepts of 'free worker' and 'proletarian' in Marx both refer to the standpoint of labour but hold radically different possibilities for knowing and making the world otherwise. Lazzarato insists that as knowledge-making in struggle, counter-expertise rests on identifying those point-of-view-words that have the most capacity to confront hegemonic power and destabilise its knowledge claims. Hence, Lazzarato's insistence on positionality's discursive plasticity provides more concrete ways to work through the identification of those 'points of view' that Haraway insists 'can never been known in advance', but that 'promise [. . .] knowledge potent for constructing worlds less organised by axes of domination'.[45]

Lazzarato also concurs with Haraway that the knowledge or counter-expertise emerging from these points of view 'tend to form part of the process of the construction and transformation of the collective subject'. But for Lazzarato, this subject is also necessarily one in struggle and, consequently, what he adds to Haraway's work is the sense in which situated knowledge is necessarily a multiplicitous assemblage whose different components work to support and articulate this collectivity in its confrontation with hegemonic power. On the one hand, counter-expertise is connected to modes of what Lazzarato calls *being-against*, 'the intensity and form of opposition to what it contests'.[46] For human rights, this undoubtedly includes the situated critique of domination I outlined in the previous section. But it also includes those forms of knowledge that make it possible to 'structure [. . .] a collective action'.[47] In this sense, knowledges assembled for being-against also incorporate the question of strategy and tactics; the know-how of confrontation that assembles the collective self into political action.

At the same time, counter-expertise also structures what Lazzarato calls the *being-together* of the collective self: 'the form of the links between those who struggle'.[48] In the valence of being-together, then, counter-expertise refers to those processes of critical examination, deconstruction and translation by which Haraway suggests knowledges fabricated from partial perspectives weave into a web of partial connections.[49] This is what, following Deleuze and Guattari, Lazzarato calls the 'disjunctive synthesis', by which situated critiques of domination are assembled. In this process, the position of labour, for instance, would not be universalised so that it subsumes all other relations, but would instead be 'positioned' as 'a specific, partial singular relation that can only function when assembled, and by way of relations of sexual, racial, and cultural domination'.[50] Crucially, however, insofar as counter-expertise also helps to 'structure and bear a demand', this work of disjunctive synthesis also necessarily encompasses that shared speculative work by which those who struggle share in a vision for a world transformed.[51] In a development of Haraway's work, then, the role of situated knowledges in political struggle also includes the processes by which the desire for – and necessity of – socio-political and economic transformation is worked through into concrete proposals for change.

Accordingly, when the epistemology of situated counter-knowledge underpins a more radical conception of human rights, the latter becomes a discourse that not only holds together a situated critique of suffering but that also articulates and crystallises socio-political demands that adequately respond to the causes of that suffering. In such a project human rights work would not hinge, as McNeilly puts it, 'on claiming, applying, or enforcing existing articulations of human rights', but instead operate by radicalising the content of existing rights as well as forming demands for new social, political and economic rights. The alternative epistemology for human rights information I am developing thus underpins a project of reconfiguring the human in novel and emancipatory forms through new and radicalised rights claims whilst simultaneously operating as a process of 'worldmaking' in the sense that Adom Getachew gives to it. That is, as a mode of seeing and doing human rights that connects accountable and locatable critiques of domination to transformative proposals for a 'domination-free and egalitarian [world]', built around more expansive figures of the human.[52]

To return to an earlier example, emerging traces of these kinds of transformative human rights demands are already taking shape within those communities and activist organisations that both suffer under and resist racialised policing. For example, the Movement for Black Lives (M4BL) has already developed a set of legislative demands, termed the BREATHE Act, designed to address the issue of police brutality. What is interesting about these demands is not the radical call for defunding police that makes up the first section of the bill, necessary as this may be, but the ways that abolition is connected to additional demands that respond to a broader set of structural issues. In the third section of the bill, for example, M4BL calls for social and structural changes aimed at 'repairing the harm of decades of community divestment from non-punitive approaches to safety and wellbeing'.[53] Crucially, these are articulated as radical demands for rights, particularly the fundamental rights to education and housing, which M4BL argues have 'for too long been made out-of-reach to Black, Latinx, Indigenous, and other communities of color'.[54] In forging connections between material violence and the abstract forces of racial capitalism, I would suggest, M4BL's approach provides one potential model for a radical human rights project.

My outline of Lazzarato's conception of counter-expertise is already suggestive of the ways it embraces a logic of confrontation which remains implicit in Haraway's work. But precisely how knowledge-making can operate as a confrontational practice is better grasped through his exploration of the relationship between counter-expertise and the question of truth. For Lazzarato, counter-expertise raises the issue of what counts as true once it can no longer be assumed to unproblematically 'belong' to those positivistic facts that appear as the most accurate or faithful copies of the real. Or, put another way, once the tendency to ascribe truth to positive knowledge is understood as an operation that simply valorises those knowledges that are *readily recognised by*, or acceptable to, the classed, raced and gendered perspective of cybernetic capitalism, then how do we separate the true and the false? And furthermore, how does one avoid collapsing into an easy relativism once the social world is understood to be constituted from a 'multiplicity of points of view that all, in different ways, are anchored in "reality"'?[55]

Lazzarato approaches this quandary by drawing on the pragmatic philosophy of William James. For James, truth is not a 'stagnant property inherent in [an idea]'. Instead, it is something that 'happens to an idea. [. . .] Its verity is in fact an event, *a process, the process namely of its verifying itself.*'[56] Lazzarato develops this procedural concept of truth in order to understand how knowledge imposes itself in a situation where recognition cannot be presupposed. The Jamesian notion of truth as process underpins what he calls 'battle truth'. Battle truth is the process through which the veracity of a knowledge emerges as it 'enter[s] into the tournament of public space', as it 'challenge[s] other truths, interpellating them [. . .] in a strategic process at the heart of which it is verified'.[57] The truth of a knowledge is in this way the 'result of a political battle', in which it confronts other points of view, hegemonic knowledges, and is judged by its capacity to interpellate, integrate or overcome them. Battle truths are thus neither monolithic nor are they embraced uncritically. They undergo a process of 'adaptation that imposes and integrates other truths', enabling them to develop a certain agility by providing space for processes of iteration, reworking and modification.[58]

As battle truths, then, counter-knowledges aim to both interpellate and disarticulate the dominant logics of hegemonic knowledge and to impose themselves on the situation. Referencing Foucault's insights regarding the relations between power and knowledge, Lazzarato thus surmises that 'knowledge is radically power, because "to speak the truth" is only possible by the imposition of rules through a fight, a struggle'.[59] Through his concept of battle truths, then, Lazzarato emphasises that the knowledge-making practices of counter-expertise must be leveraged through processes of struggle and imposition. In doing so, he furnishes situated knowledges with a form of political expression that is completely oppositional to the informational logic of human rights. Against the primacy that informational logic gives to recognition, counter-knowledges are aimed at overwriting the epistemologies and knowledges legitimated by the institutions that predominate under cybernetic capital with their own epistemic forms and their own information. In this sense, a commitment to the struggle for, and solidarity with, perspectival human rights knowledges is an epistemic requirement for a human rights movement that embraces, as Wall suggests, the radical potential of rights as 'tools for sedition'.[60]

In(-)formation: A Proposal

The shift towards situated counter-knowledges developed here challenges the conception of information as well as the model of information politics that has hitherto defined human rights. Clearly, the dominant, common-sense meaning of information as a thing-like substance that flows through systems, which rose to prominence alongside cybernetic capitalism in the 1970s, cannot begin to describe this new epistemic terrain. Insofar as this 'thingness' of information tends to reify and valorise those positive, deracinated facts that seem to appear as simply given, its common-sense meaning has no purchase on the perspectival and confrontational knowledge-making practices sketched above. But, as I have already suggested, the solution is not to refuse to engage with information, a move which, in an age where information striates even the most mundane of practices, surely concedes too much ground. Rather, my aim is to develop an adequate alternative concept of information, one that expands what it can and does mean, in order to move beyond the dominant informational imaginary.

The re-envisioning of information I have in mind does not start from scratch but instead draws from existing ideas that can nevertheless afford new possibilities. I thus follow Yoshimi in his contention that while the reified, thing-like understanding of information emerged from the cybernetic sciences and followed its diffusion through military, industrial and, eventually, socio-cultural practices, potent alternatives also loom large within information's etymological history. As Yoshimi reminds us, before cybernetics, information originally denoted 'the process of imparting "form" – of imbuing a spirit – to some entity'. That is, information has also meant "giving form to something"'.[61] For him, this alternative and broader notion of information as 'life "giving form" to things' necessarily opposes the reductive conception of information as substance that is situated within the 'taken-for-granted horizons of military and information society'.[62]

Yoshimi's recovery of information as 'form-giving' provides an important starting point for a rethinking of information. But taking up this definition also requires some care, particularly because the apparent alterity that Yoshimi affords it is not entirely warranted. As Franklin has shown, Yoshimi's 'originary' definition of information is also entangled in the history and theoretical armature of cybernetics, even if this aspect of cybernetic theory has been misunderstood and marginalised as the concept has undergone its socio-cultural diffusion.[63] Retracing Shannon's famous theory of information, Franklin suggests that while Shannon did define it as 'a quantity of *something* that must be transferred along a channel', there are parts of his work where information takes on a different sense. At times, information also appears to mean a 'general mechanism of abstract, indirect form-determination', whereby information '*connects and shapes its material substrates*'; information, in other words, as life giving form.[64] To make matters worse, Franklin contends that this concept of information cleaves to 'capital's linked modes of abstraction and organization'. As he suggests, in signifying 'the capacity of abstractions to inform material systems', information is also a synonym for the 'social function of value' under capital – a prospect that takes on considerable weight in the age of cybernetic capitalism.[65]

Despite Franklin's misgivings, I would still maintain that the idea of information as form-giving does harbour certain possibilities, especially if we remember O'Connell's point about the inadequacy of any tools we might care to choose. These possibilities can be grasped by comparing this version of information with its reified alternative. One could argue that when defined as a 'thing-like' substance, information is analogous to what Marx identified as commodity fetishism in which the social relations of production become veiled 'in the fantastic form of a relation between things'.[66] After all, what is information-as-substance if not the veiling of the social and material processes that constitute information as such (some of which are collated in this book) through its reification as a thing that flows through systems?[67] In contrast, the vision of information as form-giving serves as something of a demystification of this information fetishism insofar as it returns us to the sense of information as a process, more precisely, *as a social process of shaping material into an organised form*. Moreover, while Franklin identifies the ways that this conception of information is synonymous with value, this resonance need not be reduced to the commodity form. It might instead take on the broader meaning of the shaping of social forms that have value; in other words, the assembly of things that serve social and political purposes, that furnish new possibilities for knowing and acting.

This is surely a more workable definition of information. Information not as thing or object but as *in(-)formation*: the process or the movement by which knowledge is in(-)formation, that is, those procedures whereby not only abstractions and concepts but also materials and bodies assemble and are gathered into formation. Such a definition is particularly generative for the epistemology of human rights information that I have already sketched out in this chapter. From this perspective, what might now be called human rights in(-)formation would refer to all the sites of assembly counter-knowledge engenders. It encompasses the construction of a situated critique of domination and the critical and careful thinking that stitches many partial perspectives together. It also necessarily denotes the process by which this critique folds out to form speculative worldmaking practices that then crystallise into radical demands for rights, old and new. And, moreover, as the form-giving process that 'connects and shapes its material substrates', human rights in(-)formation also describes the arrangement of bodies into a collective subject and structures the strategy and tactics, the actions, by which this subject seeks to transform the world.[68]

But what does this mean for the work of human rights as an information politics, particularly the technologies and the practices by which the contemporary movement attempts to both 'see' and 'do' human rights? In other words, what are the more concrete consequences for the ways that human rights groups come to know and intervene in the world? In what follows, I want to reflect on two aspects of this question that have loomed large across this book. On the one hand, there is the problem of how the movement might relate to digital technologies and informational practices in the process of knowledge-making once traditional notions of objectivity are displaced. On the other hand, there is also the issue of what information as form-giving process means for the organisation of the movement itself, particularly the network form that has tended to characterise it. Maintaining my commitment to thinking both within and against information, each of these reflections seeks to grapple with how existing informational practices and relations might be thought otherwise once they are informed by the perspectival approach to human rights outline above. My aim in developing these reflections is not to offer a definitive roadmap for the future but rather to introduce some considerations about what human rights in(-)formation could mean in practice.

The Technologies and Practices of Knowledge-Making

The perspectival, processual approach to information developed above necessitates a careful repositioning of the use and value of information technologies and practices that have so far defined the movement. As I have demonstrated throughout this book, the gradual integration of information technologies and associated practices, from the Events Model and its implementation in databases to the use of advanced machine learning techniques, has largely been directed at a single objective: fact-finding. Information technologies are primarily enrolled in the production of positivistic facts that, deracinated from socio-political context or analytic and theoretical framings, appear as somehow 'noninterpretive' or 'preinterpretive' – objective slices of the real.[69] The crucial question, therefore, is how can information technologies and associated socio-technical practices be realigned or reimagined so that they helpfully support, rather than hinder, a more radical vision of human rights information as a form-giving process?

My own proposal is that the socio-technical practices that scaffold human rights work might be productively thought otherwise by displacing the objective of fact-finding with a computational metaphor that gets at in(-)formation's form-giving qualities: concatenation. In vectorised programming languages like R the concatenation function makes it possible to bring together and connect values from disparate columns of data into a single vector that can then be subjected to further operations. But as a 'material metaphor' (as Hayles might put it) that guides informational practice it emphasises the capacity to make connections between different aspects of the social world whose relations might not seem immediately obvious.[70] Furthermore, because concatenation functions do not only bring together values of the same type but can bridge together number, text and Boolean operators into a vector, concatenation also symbolises that capacity to bring together different knowledge forms in order to better understand the problems that confront human rights. Concatenation does not ask 'how can technologies help us get to the bare facts?' Instead, it poses the question 'how can technologies help us to forge the necessary connections to properly understand, and therefore address, violence, injustice or inequality?'

Given that I have defined human rights in(-)formation as the generative process that assembles knowledges adequate for political struggle, concatenation provides a potentially productive guiding metaphor for socio-technical practices aligned to this form-giving process. The challenge for organisations and activists using information technologies would be to try to understand and develop informational practices that are amenable to, or even embody, concatenation. What might happen if it is not fact-finding but the connective process of concatenation that pervades the technical imaginary of human rights? Unfortunately, a detailed and technical answer to this question is not only beyond the space constraints of this chapter but also sits at the edges of this author's expertise. The material metaphor of concatenation is, in this respect, designed principally as a kind of theoretical provocation intended to incite more critical-technical thinking. With that said, a more detailed picture of what is at stake in this potential can perhaps also be achieved by thinking it through an example.

In the wake of the intensification of 'fortress Europe' over the last decade, the issue of migration has become increasingly pressing within the human rights field. The growing epidemic of border violence has resulted in widespread human rights abuses aimed at migrants, particularly as they attempt to make the treacherous journey across the Mediterranean Sea.[71] Human rights groups have largely responded to this problem through fact-finding investigations designed to shed light on these abuses. Forensic Architecture, for example, now has several projects that use video footage, satellite imaging and 'forensic oceanography' to verify the use of illegal push-backs, where migrants are illegally forced back over a border, by the Italian and Greek states.[72] Undoubtedly, these projects represent careful and skilled acts of fact-finding. But if, as thinkers like the Out of the Woods Collective insist, the issue of migration is all but insepa-rable from the imbricated crises of climate and capital, which make it 'increasingly impossible to live in places largely occupied by the racialized, the colonized and the impoverished', then these projects also appear unable to address these crucial aspects of the problem.[73] What is needed, then, are informational practices that can approach the issue of border violence rather differently.

A perspectival approach to human rights might develop situated knowledges of the border violence faced by migrants that forges the necessary connections between migrants' experiences and the totality of structural conditions that makes that violence not only possible but also desirable. Operating according to a logic of concatenation, the task of information technologies and socio-technical practices might then be to render visible the links between climate, capitalism, migration and border violence. Such a project might ask: how does the economic and ecological ruination of parts of the South result in the movement of particular communities of migrants? And more-over, how do the economic or socio-political benefits of this ruin-ation accrue to the agglomerations of states and capital concentrated in the North where these migrants face border violence? How might these relations be mapped? Of course, an extensive answer to these questions is well beyond the limits of this book. But the crucial point is that their formulation sketches the outlines for an informational practice oriented by concatenation, which necessarily belongs to a human rights movement that is yet to come.

Solidarity in and beyond the Network

The other issue that bears some reflection, here, is the ongoing place of the network as an organisational model for the human rights movement. In Chapter 1, I demonstrated that the imaginary of infor-mation systems and, most of all, the network has been central to the organisation of the contemporary human rights movement since it emerged in the late 1970s. In the forty years that have followed, the network form has been universalised and naturalised as the assump-tive organisational model for the movement. By the rise of the inter-net in the 1990s, the human rights movement was organised into a 'transnational advocacy network'. For human rights organisations, advocacy networks have become the primary vehicle for forging 'new links among actors in civil societies, states and international organizations, [multiplying] the opportunities for dialogue and exchange', as well as making 'international resources available to new actors in domestic political and social struggles'.[74] That is, the network is the model through which human rights groups imagine their connections to others, including states and international actors, and across which their information, here alluded to as 'resources', is exchanged. Consequently, and as intimated throughout this book, the contemporary movement has become entirely synonymous with the network.

As an organisational model for a more radical information politics, however, the position of the network is much less certain. Across this book, I have harboured a suspicion of the network form as a model for the social world, not only because of the ways it limits what can and cannot be represented but also because of the forms of visibility that represented subjects, objects and actors are forced to take once reticulated in network form. I have broadly agreed with Ulises Mejias's argument that the network sets 'parameters for interaction [. . .] by prescribing, or obstructing, certain kinds of social relations', such that the deleterious 'effect of superimposing this technological template and episteme onto social structures is the rendering illegible of everything that is not a node'.[75] Hence, I also share his concern that the figure of the network can pose serious limits for a progressive politics because of its relationship to issues of recognition and difference. For human rights, then, perhaps the time has come to 'unmap the network, to transcend its determinism through whatever strategies we might devise'.[76]

But dismantling the network form is easier said than done; there is also a bind here. Because a central feature of cybernetic capitalism has been totalisation of the network such that there is nowhere 'outside' of its logic, it is also difficult to imagine a movement that does not work 'within the spaces of resistance that digital networks have already made available'.[77] That is, for strategic reasons, any movement would likely need to 'look and act just like a network'.[78] The difficulty, then, is working through the problem of how to move beyond the network whilst also being part of it. Of course, accepting that the network form might continue to be necessary for the human rights movement does not mean adopting it uncritically. A more radical information politics might understand that it is, for the time being, bound to the logic of the network, whilst also critically asking what other organisational forms might come after it. In other words, those interested in human rights might organise themselves through the network whilst also imagining new ways of being-together that are qualitatively 'different from the template-based communities of the digital network'.[79]

How to navigate this tension? Perhaps one path ahead is to both appreciate the value of the network as an imperfect but *ready-made* model for the kinds of horizontal social organisation required to weave together a web of situated knowledges whilst also recognising that weaving this web would simultaneously necessitate rethinking the network form in both its organisation and its operations. Above all, this means moving beyond the notion of the network as a mere 'channel' for resources, dialogue and exchange, especially if these are taken simply to mean the circulation of deracinated, positivist facts, or, on the other hand, updates regarding the latest developments in informational law. To think the network in this way would not only reinscribe the information politics this book has critiqued. It would also harbour the danger of reducing all parts of the network to identical nodes, simply transmitting information across the system.

Against *this network*, a radical information politics would more carefully consider the polyvalency of the situated perspectives that it webs together. Above all, this means being attentive – and accountable – to what is lost when the assembly of perspectives is premised on their adherence to the nodal form while also thinking through what might be productively recovered when connection can take more varied and expansive forms. Critically engaging with the network form in this way can provide a productive starting point for imagining new ways of being-together that might eventually crystallise within a human rights movement that is yet to come.

After Informational Logic

As I indicated in the Introduction to this book, the proposals outlined above may well prove grating to many of those who cluster in the institutions and legal forums that most conspicuously represent the human rights movement as it stands today. The open embrace of political confrontation is likely to worry organisations and activists concerned about spending the 'moral capital' their practices have enabled them to accrue over the last forty years. But at the present juncture, human rights appear to have largely failed to halt the mutually imbricated crises of capital and climate and their promise of a near future defined by more violence, more immiseration, and fewer rights. For the racialised, colonised and impoverished who already stand at the sharpest edges of these crises, it is increasingly clear that the informational project of human rights has so far been inadequate to these challenges. As I have suggested throughout this book, the inadequacies of human rights today are rooted in an informational logic that has attenuated their capacity to either resist or move beyond cybernetic capitalism. There is, therefore, little reason to think that the movement, in its current form, will present meaningful pathways away from this bleak horizon.

The times ahead call for heeding Slaughter's reminder that human rights have always been 'an uncertain and unstable discourse',[80] with an openness towards the discursive instability that emerges when these 'inadequate tools' are appropriated and refashioned to investigate the speculative possibilities of a world made otherwise. My hope is that the perspectival in(-)formation politics outlined above has charted one pathway to a more radical, transformative vision of human rights that is equal to this task. This is not to argue that the ideas sketched above should be read as a definitive roadmap for a radical information politics. The concretisation of a human rights politics, as I hope this chapter makes clear, could only ever emerge from within the form-giving process of human rights in(-)formation. Instead, my aim has been to sketch a point from which it might be possible to 'start off thought' about alternative future(s) for human rights that escape from the informational logic of human rights. If, as Jessica Whyte has recently argued, 'the inequalities of our time call for the reinvigoration of political contestation over ends', then departing from the imaginaries of information developed under cybernetic capitalism provides a crucial first step in articulating not only alternative ends but the forms of political contestation necessary to realise them.[81] The human rights movement(s) to come begins with a leap from the distant heights of disembodied objectivity to the situated perspectives of an in(-)formation politics.

Notes

1. Eyal Weizman, *Forensic Architecture: Violence at the Threshold of Detectability* (Cambridge, MA: Zone Books, 2017).
2. Weizman, *Forensic Architecture*, 74
3. Weizman, *Forensic Architecture*, 74.
4. Weizman, *Forensic Architecture*, 75.
5. Shunya Yoshimi, 'Information', *Theory, Culture & Society* 23, no. 2–3 (2006): 277.
6. Obiora Chinedu Okafor has recently given an important overview of what is meant by TWAIL, which as he suggests is a movement specifically organised around 'opposition to all the international norms and institutions that facilitate and maintain the domination, impoverishment and immiseration of Third World peoples'. For more on the praxis of TWAIL,

see Obiora Chinedu Okafor, 'Praxis and the International (Human Rights) Law Scholar: Toward the Intensification of TWAILian Dramaturg', *Windsor Yearbook of Access to Justice* 33, no. 3 (2016): 1–36.

7. Joseph R. Slaughter, 'Hijacking Human Rights: Neoliberalism, the New Historiography, and the End of the Third World', *Human Rights Quarterly* 40, no. 4 (2018): 755.

8. Illan Rua Wall, 'On a Radical Politics for Human Rights', in *The Meanings of Rights: The Philosophy and Social Theory of Human Rights*, ed. Conor Gearty and Costas Douzinas (Cambridge: Cambridge University Press, 2014), 106–20.

9. Norbert Wiener, *The Human Use of Human Beings* (London: Free Association Books, 1989), 105, 110.

10. Wall, 'On a Radical Politics for Human Rights', 108.

11. Balakrishnan Rajagopal, 'The International Human Rights Movement Today', *Maryland Journal of International Law* 24, no. 1 (2009): 56.

12. Paul O'Connell, 'On the Human Rights Question', *Human Rights Quarterly* 40 (2018): 982.

13. Alexander G. Weheliye, *Habeas Viscus: Racializing Assemblages, Biopolitics, and Black Feminist Theories of the Human* (Durham, NC and London: Duke University Press, 2014); Sylvia Wynter, 'Unsettling the Coloniality of Being/Power/Truth/Freedom: Towards the Human, after Man, Its Overrepresentation – An Argument', *CR: The New Centennial Review* 3, no. 3 (2003): 257–337.

14. Alexander G. Weheliye, '"Feenin": Posthuman Voices in Contemporary Black Popular Music', *Social Text* 71, no. 2 (2002): 26.

15. Kathryn McNeilly, *Human Rights and Radical Social Transformation: Future, Alterity, Power* (Abingdon and New York: Routledge, 2018).

16. O'Connell, 'On the Human Rights Question'; Zachary Manfredi, 'Against "Ideological Neutrality": On the Limits of Liberal and Neoliberal Economic and Social Human Rights', *London Review of International Law* 8, no. 2 (2020): 287–315.

17. McNeilly, *Human Rights and Radical Social Transformation*, 81.

18. Karin Knorr Cetina, *Epistemic Cultures: How the Sciences Make Knowledge* (Cambridge, MA: Harvard University Press, 1999), 5.

19. The critique of Karl Popper's positivism performed by members of the Frankfurt School is perhaps the most famous example, but it is also central to feminist theory and science studies such as through the work of Sylvia Walby and Sandra Harding. See Theodor W. Adorno, Hans Albert, Ralf Dahrendorf, Jürgen Habermas, Harald Pilot and Karl R. Popper, *The Positivist Dispute in German Sociology* (London: Heinemann, 1977); Sandra Harding (ed.), *The Feminist Standpoint Theory Reader: Intellectual and Political Controversies* (London and New York: Routledge, 2004).

20. As well as the pathbreaking work on standpoint theory by sociologists such as Dorothy Smith and Patricia Hill Collins, Haraway's work is clearly indebted to the postcolonial tradition of feminist science studies and its commitments to destabilising Western epistemologies.

See Dorothy E. Smith, 'Women's Perspective as a Radical Critique of Sociology', *Sociological Inquiry* 44, no. 1 (1974): 7–13; Sandra Harding, *The Science Question in Feminism* (Ithaca, NY: Cornell University Press, 1986); Harding, *The Feminist Standpoint Theory Reader*. Haraway's position in this tradition and her relationship to scholars like Sandra Harding has also been recently discussed in an article by Angela Willey. See Angela Willey, 'A World of Materialisms: Postcolonial Feminist Science Studies and the New Natural', *Science Technology and Human Values* 41, no. 6 (2016): 991–1014.

21. Donna Haraway, 'Situated Knowledges: The Science Question in Feminism and the Privilege of Partial Perspective', *Feminist Studies* 14, no. 3 (1988): 581.

22. Haraway, 'Situated Knowledges', 582–3.

23. Haraway, 'Situated Knowledges', 584.

24. Haraway, 'Situated Knowledges', 585.

25. Haraway, 'Situated Knowledges', 584.

26. Haraway, 'Situated Knowledges', 590.

27. Haraway, 'Situated Knowledges', 585.

28. Consequently, I would agree with Eva Haifa Giraud's recent argument that 'exclusion is not just a negation of something but plays a necessary and creative role in the fabric of the world', whilst also reiterating her emphasis on the importance of 'find[ing] ways of taking responsibility for the exclusions that are fostered in specific entanglements'. See Eva Haifa Giraud, *What Comes after Entanglement? Activism, Anthropocentrism, and an Ethics of Exclusion* (Durham, NC and London: Duke University Press, 2019), 171–2.

29. Haraway, 'Situated Knowledges', 585.

30. Pooja Parmar, 'TWAIL: An Epistemological Inquiry', *International Community Law Review* 10, no. 4 (2008): 365.

31. Parmar, 'TWAIL', 365.

32. Parmar, 'TWAIL', 365.

33. Parmar, 'TWAIL', 370.

34. Lilie Chouliaraki, 'Digital Witnessing in Conflict Zones: The Politics of Remediation', *Information Communication and Society* 18, no. 11 (2015): 1362–77; Lilie Chouliaraki, 'Digital Witnessing in War Journalism: The Case of Post-Arab Spring Conflicts', *Popular Communication* 13, no. 2 (2015): 105–19; Jonathan Gray, 'Data Witnessing: Attending to Injustice with Data in Amnesty International's Decoders Project', *Information Communication and Society* 22, no. 7 (2019): 971–91.

35. Seb Franklin, *The Digitally Disposed: Racial Capitalism and the Informatics of Value* (Minneapolis and London: University of Minnesota Press, 2021), 10.

36. Loïc Wacquant, *Urban Outcasts: A Comparative Sociology of Advanced Marginality* (Chichester: Wiley, 2008).

37. For an overview of the relationships between racialised policing, capitalism and prison labour, see Anil Shah and Christoph Scherrer, 'The Political Economy of Prison Labour: From Penal Welfarism to the Penal

State', *Global Labour Journal* 8, no. 1 (2017): 32–48; Julia Sudbury, 'Celling Black Bodies: Black Women in the Global Prison Industrial Complex', *Feminist Review* 80 (2005): 162–79.
38. As Manfredi suggests, 'While mainstream human rights advocates have read the texts of human rights instruments to indicate that different categories of rights are "indivisible" and deserving of "equal" recognition, a socialist theory should interrogate the assumptions of this framework. In practice, the liberal approach to indivisibility has not led to the equal valorisation of social and economic rights, but rather their subordination and marginalisation in relation to civil and political rights – indeed, it is a curious form of "equality" that treats one set of rights as imperative and immediate and another as primarily aspirational.' See Manfredi, 'Against "Ideological Neutrality"', 313.
39. Maurizio Lazzarato, *Experimental Politics: Work, Welfare, and Creativity in the Neoliberal Age* (Cambridge, MA: MIT Press, 2017).
40. For more on these struggles, I highly recommend Jeremy Gilbert's introduction to the English translation of *Experimental Politics*. It provides a good overview of the politics of the *intermittents* as well as Lazzarato's place as an activist and researcher.
41. Lazzarato, *Experimental Politics*, 120–1.
42. Lazzarato, *Experimental Politics*, 121.
43. Lazzarato, *Experimental Politics*, 121.
44. Lazzarato, *Experimental Politics*, 121–2.
45. Haraway, 'Situated Knowledges', 585.
46. Lazzarato, *Experimental Politics*, 125–6.
47. Lazzarato, *Experimental Politics*, 120.
48. Lazzarato, *Experimental Politics*, 126.
49. Lazzarato, *Experimental Politics*, 140.
50. Lazzarato, *Experimental Politics*, 138.
51. Lazzarato, *Experimental Politics*, 120.
52. Adom Getachew, *Worldmaking after Empire: The Rise and Fall of Self-Determination* (Princeton, NJ: Princeton University Press, 2019), 2.
53. Movement for Black Lives, *The BREATHE Act Federal Bill Proposal* (2020), <https://breatheact.org/learn-more/> (last accessed 25 February 2022).
54. Movement for Black Lives, *The BREATHE Act Federal Bill Proposal*.
55. Lazzarato, *Experimental Politics*, 122.
56. William James, *Pragmatism and the Meaning of Truth* (Cambridge, MA: Harvard University Press, 1978), x, emphasis added.
57. Lazzarato, *Experimental Politics*, 123.
58. Lazzarato, *Experimental Politics*, 124.
59. Lazzarato, *Experimental Politics*, 125.
60. Wall, 'On a Radical Politics for Human Rights', 113.
61. Yoshimi, 'Information', 271.
62. Yoshimi, 'Information', 277.
63. Franklin, *The Digitally Disposed*.
64. Franklin, *The Digitally Disposed*, 46, original emphasis.

65. Franklin, *The Digitally Disposed*, 46.
66. Karl Marx, *Capital*, vol. 1 (Ware: Wordsworth Editions, 2013), 47.
67. A similar idea can be found in John Roberts and Jonathan Joseph's critique of popular conceptions of the information economy as a kind of fetishism. They make the important argument that theorising the economy as a network of fluids and flows veils the relations of production that constitute these flows. See John Roberts and Jonathan Joseph, 'Beyond Flows, Fluids and Networks: Social Theory and the Fetishism of the Global Informational Economy', *New Political Economy* 20, no. 1 (2015): 12–13.
68. Franklin, *The Digitally Disposed*, 46.
69. Mary Poovey, *A History of the Modern Fact* (Chicago: University of Chicago Press, 1998).
70. N. Katherine Hayles, *Writing Machines* (Cambridge, MA: MIT Press, 2002).
71. For background on the recent intensification of the policies and commitments that uphold 'Fortress Europe', see Caterina Molinari, 'Digging a Moat around Fortress Europe: EU Funding as an Instrument of Exclusion', in Tesseltje de Lange, Willem Maas and Annette Schrauwen (eds), *Money Matters in Migration: Policy, Participation, and Citizenship* (Cambridge: Cambridge University Press, 2021), 38–54.
72. Forensic Architecture's work on border violence using Forensic Oceanography is detailed in Forensic Oceanography, *The Nivin Case: Migrants' Resistance to Italy's Strategy of Privatized Push-Back* (London: Forensic Architecture, 2019), <https://content.forensic-architecture.org/wp-content/uploads/2019/12/2019-12-18-FO-Nivin-Report.pdf> (last accessed 25 February 2022). Their project using video footage is detailed on the Forensic Architecture website: Forensic Architecture, *Pushbacks across the Evros/Meriç River: Analysis of Video Evidence* (2019), <https://forensic-architecture.org/investigation/pushbacks-across-the-evros-meric-river-analysis-of-video-evidence> (last accessed 25 February 2022).
73. Out of the Woods Collective, *Hope against Hope: Writings on Ecological Crisis* (Brooklyn, NY and Philadelphia, PA: Common Notions, 2020), 22.
74. Margaret E. Keck and Kathryn Sikkink, 'Transnational Advocacy Networks in International and Regional Politics', *International Social Sciences Journal* 51, no. 159 (1999): 89.
75. Ulises Ali Mejias, *Off the Network: Disrupting the Digital World* (Minneapolis and London: University of Minnesota Press, 2013), 10.
76. Mejias, *Off the Network*, 8–9.
77. Mejias, *Off the Network*, 15.
78. Mejias, *Off the Network*, 15.
79. Mejias, *Off the Network*, 15.
80. Slaughter, 'Hijacking Human Rights', 755.
81. Jessica Whyte, *The Morals of the Market: Human Rights and the Rise of Neoliberalism* (London and New York: Verso, 2019), 242.

Index

200